D0149101

Three Eastern Traditions

AN INTRODUCTION TO ASIAN PHILOSOPHY

3RD EDITION

DAVID GRIESEDIECK

UNIVERSITY OF MISSOURI—ST. LOUIS

Pearson
Custom
Publishing

Cover Art: "Clairvoyance," by Kathryn Fanelli.

Copyright © 1992 by Ginn Press.
Copyright © 2000 by Pearson Custom Publishing.
All rights reserved.

This copyright covers material written expressly for this volume by the editor/s as well as the compilation itself. It does not cover the individual selections herein that first appeared elsewhere. Permission to reprint these has been obtained by Pearson Custom Publishing for this edition only. Further reproduction by any means, electronic or mechanical, including photocopying and recording, or by any information storage or retrieval system, must be arranged with the individual copyright holders noted.

Printed in the United States of America

10 9 8 7

Please visit our website at www.pearsoncustom.com

ISBN 0–536–60241–7

BA 990629

PEARSON CUSTOM PUBLISHING
75 Arlington Street, Boston, MA 02116
A Pearson Education Company

This book is dedicated to all of my students, who, during the past thirty years, have constantly sustained my belief in the importance of this subject.

CONTENTS

I. ISLAM

I. MUHAMMAD

Few, if any, have had a greater impact on the course of human history than Muhammad, the Messenger of God. He was born in either 569 or 570 A.D. in what was then an obscure place, unknown to the wider world. This was Mecca, in the heart of Arabia. Muhammad's early years were marked by tragedy. By the time he was born, his father had already died. In a few more years, his mother was dead as well. As a six-year old orphan, he passed into the care of his aged grandfather. At this man's death two years later, Muhammad's uncle Abu Talib took him in. If you would like to understand why Muhammad came to believe so passionately in a loving and ever-present God, you may as well begin by contemplating these facts of his childhood.

Growing toward manhood in his uncle's far from lavish household, Muhammad was naturally drawn to the profession of caravan trading. Mecca was an important center for this; it was a livelihood that would have attracted any energetic and ambitious Meccan boy. Muhammad was about fifteen when he began to go with the caravans. Soon he worked his way up to a position of responsibility. It was exacting work, calling for a knowledge of men as well as of camels and commodities. Muhammad had continually to negotiate, not just with buyers and sellers, but the desert tribes through whose lands he passed. He acquired the nickname *al-amin*, "the trustworthy", from his dealings.

A turning point in Muhammad's life came when, at the age of twenty-five, he was hired by a wealthy widow named Khadija to manage one of her caravans. She was very favorably impressed by his handling of the assignment—so much so that she proposed marriage to him. (Her wealth and status, along with the fact that she was somewhat older than her intended husband, made this action socially acceptable.) Muhammad eagerly accepted, and it is quite clear that this was not based merely on the economic security that his wife could provide. Khadija was very much a kindred spirit for Muhammad: strong, practical, supportive. She shared his religious leanings and encouraged him in developing them. While Khadija lived, Muhammad never took another wife. Later, when he had many wives, he used to say, much to their annoyance, that he would dwell with Khadija in Paradise.

To understand the development of Muhammad's religious ideas, we must understand the beliefs and practices of ancient Arabia. These involved a great multitude of gods and goddesses who were depicted with idols and worshipped for the various blessings they could provide. There was a also certain Allah who stood apart from the other deities. He was a remote and austere figure, too exalted to be portrayed with any material representation. He was spoken of with great reverence but largely ignored in the Arabs' everyday worship.

Mecca, as it happened, enjoyed a unique place in this system of worship, based on its possession of the Kaaba. This was a shrine centering around a black stone—a meteorite, apparently. The stone was venerated as a symbol of divine power, and in its vicinity an entire religious complex soon grew up, with idols and altars dedicated to the various deities. At specified times of the year, pilgrims from everywhere in Arabia would throng to the Kaaba. Vendors would set up stalls to sell animals for sacrifice. The holy precincts became a scene of distinctly unedifying activities—gambling, drunkenness, prostitution. In revulsion at this, Muslims would later call this ancient time the *jahilliya*, the era of ignorance.

The Meccans of Muhammad's day were far from feeling any such revulsion. Their city's religious importance was precisely what had made it such a great center of trade. The comings and goings of pilgrims had built a network of relations throughout Arabia, which could be turned to a secular purpose. Thus, Mecca had become a major staging point for caravans, and so it is that Muhammad came to take up his livelihood.

The caravans took Muhammad even beyond Arabia, and this was what set him on a course of religious change. His visits to Syria were especially frequent, and there he encountered Christian monks. (The whole country was overwhelmingly Christian at that time.) Muhammad was deeply impressed by the piety and serious demeanor of these monks. What impressed him still more was the nature of their religious belief. As Christians they abhorred the polytheistic gods. They believed fervently in a single, all-powerful God from whom all creation had come.

From time to time, Muhammad also met members of the various Jewish communities that were scattered through the ancient world. They too affirmed the principle of monotheism (belief in one God), and they spoke of a long *prophetic* tradition, by which this God had sent messengers to mankind. The chief mission of these prophets had been calling people to worship the one God and to reject false gods.

Muhammad began to think that his own people's gods were false. Certainly, they were crude and paltry, compared with the exalted deity that Jews and Christians worshipped. And yet there was something in the Arabian belief that still inspired him: Allah. That deity alone, of all the beings worshipped by the Arabs, possessed the majesty and the uniqueness appropriate to God. Thus, Muhammad concluded that Allah was the very same God of whom the Jews and Christians had told him. They, of course, did not know Him by the Arabic name of *Allah*, but the concept was identical.

Therefore, Muhammad became a convinced monotheist, but there was still much he was uncertain of. He could not yet see just what Allah wanted of him. Though Muhammad respected the Jews and Christians, he would not convert to either of their religions, for they presented such a spectacle of bitter disagreement with each other. The Christians, moreover, were divided into many ferociously contending sects. Now in his late thirties, Muhammad took less and less interest in business. Encouraged by Khadija, he would often seclude himself in a cave near Mecca to meditate on religion.

On such an occasion, in the year 610, Muhammad underwent the experience that transformed his life. It was three or four in the morning. He was standing there in the pitch darkness of the cave after having spent all day and all night wrestling with the question of what he must do. Suddenly, a shining being stood before him, holding out a book. "Recite!" was its command. Muhammad was terrified, for he was illiterate. But somehow he managed to read out the written words which had been thrust before him: "In the name of your Lord, who created man from a tiny clot of blood." Again, he was ordered to recite, and now he read the words "And your Lord is most generous, who teaches by the Pen, teaches man that which he is ignorant of."

The words of this encounter form the beginning of Sura (Chapter) 96 of the Koran. They are the first in a long series of revelations which were given to Muhammad to be recited. *Koran* in fact means "recitation" in Arabic, and this book, the "Bible" of Islam, is the compilation of the many revelations which Muhammad received. For the remainder of his life he would periodically be spoken to by that same being who first appeared in the cave, a being who eventually identified himself as the angel Gabriel (in Arabic: Jibril). Gabriel made clear that he spoke, not on his own behalf, but as the conveyer of God's word.

The confident knowledge of these matters was yet in the future that morning as Muhammad made his way home, still trembling from his encounter. The words he had read out most certainly referred to Allah, but Muhammad could not say for sure whether they came from Allah. It might have been a hallucination, he reasoned, knowing full well his distraught state of mind. It might even have been some demon, seeking to make a fool of him.

To Khadija he excitedly related what had taken place and his confusion over what it meant. She comforted and calmed her husband, assuring him that the message could be no delusion. Gradually, Muhammad was convinced that he had received the word of God. In the light of what he knew of Jewish and Christian traditions, this fact assumed an awesome significance. It meant that he had been *called* to be a prophet, that he now stood in the company of Abraham, Moses, Jesus and all the other messengers of God.

Initially, few besides Khadija knew anything of this—just members of the household. This included his youthful cousin, Ali, the son of Abu Talib. The latter had fallen on hard times financially, and so Muhammad had taken Ali under his care. This was his way of showing gratitude to Abu Talib for the care that he himself had received years before. So Khadija, Ali and others in the household embraced *Islam*. This word signifies "submission" in Arabic. Related to it is the word *Muslim*, "one who submits." These are most appropriate terms for the religion and its believers. To be a Muslim is to give oneself unconditionally to Allah, rejecting the worship of any other god. It also entails that one accept the authority of God's prophet, Muhammad.

Outside the household, Muhammad found hardly any support. Even Abu Talib, though he remained on good terms with his nephew, could not bring himself to break with the old polytheistic religion. Another uncle, Abu Lahab, was infuriated with Muhammad's new ideas and became one of Islam's most implacable enemies. Thus, there were practically no converts beyond Muhammad's immediate family. A significant exception was Abu Bakr, an old friend of Muhammad's and his eventual successor as leader of the Muslim community.

Indeed, Muhammad, well aware of the controversial nature of his ideas, hesitated to discuss them with any but family and close friends. This state of affairs continued for some three years. Then, about 613, Muhammad received his second message from God, delivered again by Gabriel. It is recorded in Sura 74 of the Koran and is summed up in the command "Arise and warn!" The meaning of this was that Muhammad must bestir himself from the security of his home and proclaim Islam to all the people of Mecca. They had to be warned of the terrible fate that lay in store for them if they persisted in their pagan ways.

Accordingly, Muhammad began to call upon the Meccans to submit to Allah and to give up their old religion. The results were exactly as he had feared. The overwhelming reaction was one of anger and scorn. Overnight, Muhammad went from being a highly esteemed member of the community to being regarded as a crackpot or a charlatan.

Any challenge to traditional religious belief would be bound to meet a hostile reception; but, what was worse for Muhammad, his ideas seemed to threaten Mecca's commercial importance. That importance was founded, as we have seen, on the Kaaba and its veneration throughout Arabia. For the Meccans any threat to the Kaaba was a threat to their livelihood as well as to their religion. Muhammad certainly posed such a threat, for he regarded the various activities at the Kaaba as an outrageous insult to Allah. At the very core of his preaching was the demand that the Kaaba be purified.

Note that I say "purified" rather than "destroyed." Muhammad believed the Kaaba to have been, originally, a holy place. Long ago Abraham and Ishmael had first built a shrine around that black stone. These two (known to Muslims as Ibrahim and Ismail) were prophets, like Muhammad himself, charged with the task of spreading the true religion. They had built the Kaaba in homage to Allah, but later generations had contaminated it with the worship of false gods. Thus, Muhammad insisted that the Kaaba be purged of every vestige of polytheistic religion. And so it was in due course, and it stands today as the holiest place in Islam, the destination of millions of pilgrims each year.

Of the few who who did answer Muhammad's call to Islam in the early years, some were slaves and other humble folk. The Prophet was deeply aggrieved to see them persecuted for their religious convictions. He even sent a group of Muslim converts to Ethiopia, hoping that the Christians of that land, as monotheists, would

ILLUMINATED KORAN PAGE

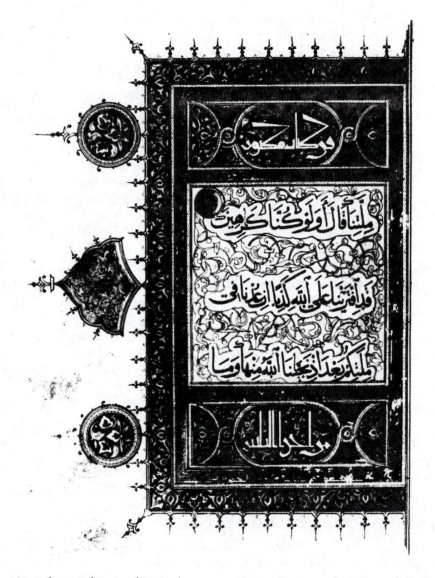

An illuminated page from a thirteenth-century Koran. Because depiction of the human form was frowned on as suggestive of idolatry, Islamic artistry found its highest expression in non-representational forms, such as architecture, embroidery and calligraphy. This resulted in the production of exquisitely beautiful Koran manuscripts. [Corbis-Bettmann]

give his followers refuge. The Muslims did find refuge there, but after a while, perhaps from homesickness, they returned to Mecca. Thus, the question of how their faith might be practiced freely and securely was raised again.

Muhammad's own status was such that he did not yet have to worry about his personal safety. Still, life at Mecca became harder and harder to bear. An especially devastating blow was Khadija's death in 619. The frequent comings of Gabriel with new revelations for the Koran sustained Muhammad at this time. The revelations assured Muhammad of his ultimate vindication.

One revelation around this time was particularly significant, involving far more than the usual words of comfort and exhortation. This was the miraculous night-journey, briefly alluded to in the first verse of Sura 17:

> Glory to Allah, Who did take His servant for a journey by night from the Sacred Mosque
> to the Farthest Mosque, in order that We might show him some of Our signs.

In this journey Muhammad was somehow transported from the precincts of the Kaaba to the site of the old Jewish Temple in Jerusalem. From there he was carried up through the various heavens, so that he might see God's splendor. An unbeliever would naturally think of all this as a dream or hallucination, but Muslims have taken this episode very seriously and found it a major source of inspiration. This is especially true of the Sufis—see later on.

Meanwhile, the situation at Mecca grew worse, and Muhammad began to fear for his own safety. It became clear to him that he and all his followers must remove themselves from Mecca. Soon, an opportunity to accomplish this presented itself. Muhammad, as was his custom, happened to start a religious discussion with some pilgrims at the Kaaba. These pilgrims were from the town of Medina (then called Yathrib), some 200 miles to the north. They were moved by his message. Their town had been wracked by tribal strife, and they hoped to find in Islam a basis for living in harmony.

Plans began to be made for what is known as the Hegira, the emigration of the Muslims to Medina. This took place in the year 622. In small groups, the Muslims abandoned their homes and made their way to Medina. Muhammad himself (accompanied by Abu Bakr) was nearly the last to leave, going by a secret, circuitous route so as to elude his enemies.

The Hegira proved decisive for the development of Islam. Muslims number their years from this event, as Christians do from the birth of Jesus. From this time onward Islam steadily grew in strength. The Medinans gave not just their religious adherence but their political loyalty to Muhammad. They undertook to support him in the struggle with pagan Mecca, a struggle which now entered a new phase. Muhammad, without necessarily wishing it, had thrust upon him the role of a military commander.

Indeed, conflict between Mecca and Medina was inevitable, and the first skirmishes were soon taking place. Mecca, on the face of it, had the advantage. It was a far larger and wealthier town, and it could draw on alliances with the desert tribes. But Mecca was also vulnerable by virtue of its caravan trade. The Muslims could and did strike at their adversaries' lifeline by raiding the caravans.

These raids continued, with varying success, for several years. The leaders of Mecca saw that their only effective reply was to lay siege to Medina and crush Islam once and for all. To defend the city, Muhammad ordered a long, deep trench dug around it. With ample supplies of food and water within, the Muslims fended off every attempt by the enemy to pass over the trench. Meanwhile, the besiegers, out in the desert, found their own supplies dwindling. Finally, a fierce sandstorm completed their discomfiture. It was clear that the siege must be given up.

The Battle of the Trench (as Muslim tradition names it) was a clear victory for Islam. The leaders of Mecca now saw that they could not defeat Muhammad, and protracted negotiations began. Muhammad was surprisingly conciliatory. While tenaciously holding to his religious principles, he sought no vengeance against his old enemies. The Meccans were welcomed into the ranks of the believers. Now they stood aside as Muhammad, with his most trusted followers, returned to Mecca and carried out the long-sought purification of the Kaaba. This triumphal return took place in 630, just eight years after Muhammad had fled in fear of his life.

The people of Medina were somewhat distressed at Muhammad's reconciliation with his native town, but he took great pains to reassure them. He stayed only briefly at Mecca and made it clear that Medina, which had sheltered him, was to be his permanent residence. As such, Medina was the capital of a vigorous and growing domain. After the Battle of the Trench, nearly all of the Arabian tribes had hastened to acknowledge Muhammad's authority. Islam stood on the verge of a spectacular expansion. But Muhammad himself did not live to see this, dying suddenly in 632.

II. AFTER MUHAMMAD

The death of Muhammad was a profound shock for the Muslim community. He was, in the most literal and absolute sense, irreplaceable, for Allah had proclaimed him the Seal of Prophecy, that is, the last in the long line of prophets which had begun with Adam (Sura XXXIII, v. 40). But the community was strong and confident in the wake of its decisive victory over the paganism of Mecca, and it was soon agreed that Muhammad's trusted friend and supporter, Abu Bakr, would be *khalif* (Arabic for "successor"—the word is usually given in English as *caliph*). Note that the title of khalif was not taken to mean that Abu Bakr assumed the role of God's chosen messenger. That position was, for all time, concluded with Muhammad, as we have just seen. But Muhammad had also, from the time of his arrival at Medina, functioned as the political leader of the community, skillfully guiding his converts in the struggle against Mecca. It was that role of "Commander of the Faithful" which Abu Bakr now assumed.

He was immediately put to the test in the exercise of this responsibility. Many of the desert tribes, who had eagerly given their adherence to Muhammad when they saw him victorious over Mecca, now reverted to their pagan ways. They had no real appreciation of this new religion to which they had nominally converted. The Khalif firmly opposed this, and, by threat of force, required the would-be defectors to return to the fold. In taking this action (for which he duly cited Muhammad's own authority) Abu Bakr established a principle of the utmost importance: there must not be apostasy from Islam. The rationale of this should be clearly understood. Adherence to Islam is a matter of freely given consent. By Muslim law, no one must be compelled to convert. (Recall that Muhammad had not forced the Meccans to become Muslims; he had only demanded that they surrender the overlordship of the Kaaba.) It follows that the act of conversion, as the free and deliberate submission to Allah, cannot be retracted. It is a promise, from which only the promisee, God himself, can give release.

This principle has had significant reverberations in the history of Islamic thought, down to the present day. Some of the most eminent philosophers, among others, have been held by some authorities to be liable to the charge of apostasy by reason of their writings which contradicted Islam. In theory, the charge carries a penalty of death. A recent case, which has captured the attention of the world, is Iran's condemnation of author Salman Rushdie.

To return to Abu Bakr and the newly reunited Muslim community. Most of the vast Arabian peninsula now stood firm in its commitment to Islam. But to the north of Arabia lay far more populated and civilized lands which knew and cared little about Islam. In these regions two great empires held sway. First, the Byzantine, successor to the old Roman Empire. From his capital at Constantinople, the Byzantine emperor ruled Greece, Turkey, Italy, Syria, Palestine, Egypt and all of North Africa. And he ruled in the name of the orthodox Christian faith, upholding it against other religions and against what were considered heretical forms of Christianity flourishing in Syria and Egypt. East of the Byzantine Empire stood the Sasanid, centered in Iran and Iraq, ruling a vast domain stretching into central Asia. This empire also had its official religion, Zoroastrianism, an ancient Iranian faith which saw the world as the scene of relentless struggle between two divine powers embodying good and evil.

These two empires had long been bitter rivals, battling for supremacy throughout the lands of the Near East. Sometimes, their conflict had spilled over into Arabia, but for the most part the Arabs were little involved. Now, under Islam, Arabia was united and energized as never before. Abu Bakr and the Muslim community saw these empires as enemies of Islam and lost no time in launching assaults against them.

To an impartial observer, it would have seemed preposterous. The Byzantines and the Sasanids, though depleted by their long mutual struggle, had military and economic resources that dwarfed anything that Islam might muster. The Arabs would have seemed no more than turbulent barbarians who could create annoyance with their raiding but who could not pose a serious threat. That the Muslims would simultaneously take on these two empires represented the height of foolhardiness.

Such appraisals were soon proven wrong, as there now ensued one of the most remarkable epochs in all of military history. Abu Bakr saw only the opening skirmishes, dying after a reign of just two years. But his successor Umar (khalif from 634 to 644) vigorously carried on the campaign, and Umar's successors were equally determined and successful. Within twenty-five years of Muhammad's death, the Byzantine Empire was humbled and shorn of the bulk of its territory, including Syria, Palestine and Egypt. The Sasanid Empire, for its part, was not merely humbled but destroyed. Its last ruler was hunted down like a criminal and all its lands passed into the domain of Islam. By the early 700s the khalif from his capital (now removed from Medina to Damascus) governed in the name of Allah an empire as large as any that had ever existed, stretching from Spain in the West across North Africa through the Middle East to the borders of India.

It is vitally important to understand precisely what these amazing conquests involved from a religious standpoint. The new empire contained an extraordinary range of religious belief: Christianity (Orthodox, Nestorian, Monophysite), Judaism, Zoroastrianism, Manicheism, even lingering pockets of ancient paganism. These deeply entrenched faiths were not swept away in the conquest, their cowering adherents converting to Islam at the point of a sword. It is one of the silliest of the many misconceptions about Islam that prevail in Western culture to suppose that such a thing did happen or could have happened. These various faiths, each with its own cultivated and well organized clergy, sustained by centuries of tradition, could never have been so easily disposed of. And it was not the policy of Islam to do such a thing, had it even been possible. We have already seen that Muslim law requires that one's conversion to Islam be freely made. In the Koran, Sura 50, verse 45 clearly states this. Sura 10, verse 99 adds the point that God could himself have compelled all mankind to believe, if He had wished, so then "Thou must not presume to convert them against their will."

In the particular case of Christians and Jews, tolerance is explicitly enjoined by the Koran. They are "People of the Book", that is, followers of the earlier prophets. They are in grave error on account of their failure to accept the prophetic status of Muhammad. They may be subdued and made to pay tribute (jizya, the so-called poll-tax), but they must be allowed to continue in their traditional belief. In practice this same tolerance was extended to other non-Muslims. So it is that conversion to Islam took place very slowly. In the first Muslim centuries, the khalif's domain consisted in a military-political elite of Muslims (mainly Arabs) ruling over a great mass of "infidels." Over the centuries, most of these non-Muslims gradually, as a result of individual and freely-made choices, gave their adherence to Islam. Even today, in some Muslim countries, there are sizable groups who have never done this (for example, the Christian Copts in Egypt).

These matters are of profound importance for an understanding of the development of Muslim civilization. That civilization emerged in the midst of an overwhelmingly non-Muslim society. An enormous array of cultural influences came to bear upon the Islamic world. Many, if not all, of the Muslims were more than willing to profit from these ancient traditions. We will see this, time and again, in the study of Muslim philosophy, theology and spirituality.

This cultural diversity was magnified by the growing political complexity which manifested itself in the domain of Islam. In the time of the first khalifs, there was a unity of purpose which has never since been regained. The year 661 is pivotal. It saw the assassination of the fourth khalif, Ali (Muhammad's cousin). In the ensuing disorder, a man named Muawiya, military governor of the province of the province of Syria, seized the khalifate for himself. This action had no warrant in Muslim custom or law, which saw the office of khalif as having profound religious significance, not to be usurped by anyone whose military position might enable him to do so. Muawiya compounded his offense by moving the capital from the holy city of Medina to Damascus, and , still more, by enforcing the principle that his son and other descendants should follow him as khalif. Thus a dynasty was born, the Umayyad.

Though the military advances of Islam were not stayed by these controversial developments, serious dissension now existed. In 680 Husayn, Ali's only surviving son, attempted to lead a rebellion against the Umayyads. This was crushed at the Battle of Kerbala (in Iraq), in which Husayn perished. Out of this tragedy evolved the religious and political movement of the Shiites. Their name derives from the Arabic *shia*, "party", for they are the party of Ali and his descendants. Shiism uses the term *imam* rather than *khalif* for Muhammad's successor and holds that Ali rather than Abu Bakr ought to have been the first successor. The imamate ought then to have passed to Ali's sons and later descendants. On this basis the Umayyads and most later dynasties could have no rightful political authority.

Shiites form only a small minority in the Islamic world, approximately 10-15%. Practically all other Muslims are Sunnites. They too disapprove of the Umayyads, considering that just the first four khalifs (through Ali) were "rightly guided." From the Sunnite standpoint, the khalifate should be held by the most worthy man among all the believers, regardless of family lineage. Any dynasty, even of the Prophet's own family, would violate this principle. Abu Bakr was properly chosen in 632 by the general consensus of the community. Likewise Ali, when he became khalif in 656.

The dispute between Shiites and Sunnites remains unresolved. It involves far more than the obvious issue of how the succession to Muhammad should have been handled. There are fundamental issues about the very nature of religious authority. The controversy shows itself in various aspects of Islamic religious and intellectual life. The Shiites have made contributions to Muslim civilization well out of proportion to their rather small numbers. For many centuries Iran has been the chief center of Shiite Islam.

Meanwhile the Umayyad dynasty fell in due course, to be replaced by the Abbasid (750). The new dynasty moved the capital to Baghdad, where a lavish program of construction was undertaken. Baghdad soon became the most splendid city in the entire world. At a time when Athens and Rome were ruined shells of their former selves and when London and Paris were still humble villages, Baghdad was the center of a vibrant culture, as Islam drew on the resources of earlier civilizations to build its own.

The Abbasid dynasty was truly the golden age of Islamic civilization. The bulk of what we are now to consider falls within this period, a good deal transpiring in the confines of Baghdad itself. But the political fragmentation of Islam continued. A surviving member of the Umayyad royal family set up an independent regime in Muslim Spain. The Fatimids, espousing a form of Shiism, set up their own regime in Egypt in the tenth century. Many parts of the Abbasid empire, while still giving nominal allegiance to the khalif, became de facto independent. The khalif himself eventually became a mere figurehead, manipulated by various powers behind the throne. Mongol invaders dealt the final blow. Their destruction of Baghdad in 1258 extinguished the feeble remnants of Abbasid power. Islam eventually recovered from this (and even converted many of the Mongols), but the golden age was over.

Before beginning to discuss the varied forms of Muslim thought that arose in the historical context just described, it is well to pause and review the fundamental beliefs of Islam as enunciated by the Koran and solidified in centuries just after Muhammad's time.

III. BASIC IDEAS OF ISLAM

GOD. It is easy to state the most fundamental of all the ideas which Muhammad taught: the oneness of God, His uniqueness and absolute superiority over any other being. There is one recurring phrase in the Koran which most vividly expresses the sovereignty of God: "His way to say to a thing 'Be' and then it is." (Sura 2, v. 117, Sura 16, v. 40 and many other places). The utter dependence of every creature on God is thus made clear.

The gravest possible sin and error is *association* (Arabic: *shirk*), the placing of any creature on a level with Allah. From the Muslim standpoint, this divine transcendence is compromised by any attempt to represent God in pictorial form. To Muhammad, as to the prophets of ancient Israel, this was one of the most revolting features of ancient paganism: its setting up of idols of the gods to be worshipped. These idols, so much like ourselves in appearance, could not possibly represent the supreme, transcendent God.

However, the transcendence of Allah does not make Him utterly mysterious and unknowable. There are in Him personal, moral characteristics akin to what (in vastly inferior degree) are possessed by humans. First and foremost, there is His loving kindness. Every chapter of the Koran begins with the invocation *bismullah ar-rahman ar-rahim*, "In the name of God, the compassionate, the merciful." In its beauty, order and adaptation to our purposes, the world everywhere displays Allah's love for his creatures.

Allah is also a God of justice who demands what is His due from us creatures and holds us to a standard of moral dealings with one another. So that He may do this, He possesses a knowledge extending to all things and a limitless power. Even the deepest secrets are not hidden from Him.

> He knows what is in the heavens and on earth. And He knows what you conceal and what you reveal. Verily, Allah knows well the secrets of all hearts. (Sura 64, v. 4)

LAW. In view of all this, the proper acknowledgement of Allah's sovereignty is the most important of all human responsibilities. Conformity to divine law (Arabic: *sharia*) is the means of expressing this. By adhering to the rigid and precise laws given by God, Muslim believers place themselves under God's authority. The laws may be quite arbitrary. Why must Muslims fast during Ramadhan? Why must they pray facing Mecca? There is no essential reason other than that God, through Muhammad, has commanded it. The requirements are, in general, what God has chosen to make them; and they could well have been different. Indeed, the qibla (direction of prayer) was originally Jerusalem before being switched to Mecca.

The subject of law brings us to the Ulama (literally the "learned ones"), who play the essential role of interpreting this law for believers and applying it to the varied circumstances of life. Law is provided , of course, by the Koran, but it can also gleaned from Muhammad's own life. As God's prophet, he was protected from sin and error, so that in reliable accounts (hadith) of his words and deeds, we may be confident of having guidance for ourselves. The compilation of these hadith is known as Sunna ("regulation").

Koran and Sunna are what the Ulama make themselves "learned" in. These two are, by the general reckoning, the only sources of religious truth. It is a consuming study through which the Ulama have achieved a position of enormous respect and authority in the Muslim world. The Ulama have consistently stood as the rigorous guardians of orthodoxy, opposing alien intrusion and innovation of every kind. This attitude has brought them into conflict with many of the currents of thought we will be considering.

PROPHECY. The extraordinarily important role played by prophets in Islam is already evident. It remains now only to give a more detailed idea of just who these prophets are and what is Muhammad's special position among them.

A prophet is essentially a messenger, and God had sent many, many prophets before Muhammad. In fact, the first prophet was the first man, Adam. God did not merely create him; He gave him a message to convey to his descendants. Following Adam there are, among others, Nuh (Noah), Ibrahim (Abraham), Musa (Moses), Salman (Solomon) and Yunus (Jonah). Most of the holy figures of the Old Testament have been accorded prophetic status by Islam, though the Koran also names as prophets certain non-Biblical figures known to the ancient Arab tradition (Hud, Salih, Shuaib).

From the New Testament there are Yahya ibn-Zakariya (John the Baptist) and Isa ibn-Maryam (Jesus the son of Mary). Muslims revere these two, and, in particular, Jesus.

PILGRIMS AT THE KAABA, MECCA

Pilgrims worshipping at the Kaaba. Having spent a lifetime praying in the direction of this shrine, they now have it right in front of them. It is a simple cubical building, surrounded by a large square. No doubt, it presented a far more cluttered aspect in pre-Islamic times, when polytheistic worship still flourished there. [Hulton Getty]

The miracles associated with Jesus' life, beginning with his birth of the virgin Mary are accepted. Sura 19 of the Koran relates Jesus' miraculous birth. Sura 3 quotes Jesus as follows:

> By the power of God I heal blind men and lepers, and I raise the dead to life. Surely, this is a sign for you, if you would believe. I have come to reaffirm the Law, but also to make lawful part of what before was forbidden you. (verses 49–50)

What Muslims absolutely refuse to accept is the idea that Jesus could be the son of God. Allah is absolutely unique. He cannot have a son, for then this offspring would be of the same kind as He. In this spirit the Koran insists on the humanity of all the prophets:

> Of those We sent before you [Muhammad], they were all mere mortals—question the people of the Remembrance [the Jews], if you do not believe this. These messengers were not supernatural beings with bodies immune to hunger and illness. (Sura 21, v. 7–8)

What is the position of Muhammad among all these prophets? As a worker of miracles, he is inferior to Jesus and others. Muslims believe that Muhammad's only miracle consists in the beauty and power of the Koran that was revealed through him. The special status of Muhammad consists in what has already been mentioned. He is the Seal of Prophecy, the conclusion of the long line of divine messengers. Various prophets have given out various versions of God's law, though they do not differ on basic theology. The laws given out through Muhammad supersede all previous versions. In this way Muhammad's prophetic authority transcends that of all others.

LAST JUDGMENT. There is perhaps no theme which is more persistent in the Koran than the final judgment of mankind, in which all wrongs will be righted. At some future date (known only to God) there will be a destruction of every living thing. After this, God will resurrect the bodies of all who have ever lived, and in their vast throngs they will be gathered to face the judgment of God.

The Koran is very explicit and emphatic about the physical nature of the existence into which we will be resurrected by God:

> They say, "When we are reduced to bones and scattered particles, shall we really be raised up and made anew?" Do they not see that God, who made heaven and earth, has the power to create the likes of them? (Sura 17, v. 98–99)

The torments of hell and the delights of paradise are also described in graphic detail:

> Behold, hell will be an ambush, an abode where the insolent will languish for ages. Therein they will not taste any refreshing drink, only boiling water and pus. They expected no reckoning. They cried "Lies!" to Our signs. All this We have set down in a book. Therefore, it is said to them, "Taste! We shall do nothing but increase your torment."

> But for the godfearing there awaits a place of repose, gardens and vineyards and maidens with swelling breasts. They shall no longer hear banter or taunting. Such is their reward from your Lord, a gift measured out for them. (Sura 78, v. 21-36)

These promises were a great comfort to Muhammad and his followers in those early days at Mecca when Islam was persecuted.

JIHAD. This is an Islamic concept that has come into general use but without an understanding of its full meaning. Jihad is Arabic for "exertion." It refers to any kind of struggle for the true faith and, as such, is a duty for every Muslim. The exertion may consist in exhorting others to practice Islam; it may even consist in the struggle with one's own recalcitrant nature to fulfill the will of God.

Jihad may also take a military form, as "holy war." It is in this aspect that it is best known. In fact, the Koran clearly expounds the duty to wage war in certain circumstances. There is this statement with particular reference to Christians and Jews:

> Fight against those to whom the Scriptures were given [by earlier prophets], if they do not forbid what Allah and his messenger have forbidden and do not embrace the true faith. They must be subdued and made to pay tribute. (Sura 9, v. 29)

Muhammad, in his conflict with Mecca, and the first khalifs, in their wars of conquest, zealously carried out the duty of jihad. For them the Muslims constituted a small, tightly-organized community, the Abode of Islam. Ranged against this was the Abode of Unbelief, with which no true peace was possible. As already explained, this holy war definitely did not involve forced conversion. But it did seek the political subordination of unbelievers.

In this, Islam was no different from Christianity, Judaism and most other faiths. Holy war is a pervasive concept. One need only think of the Crusades or of Joshua's conquest of the Holy Land. There are very few pacifist religions. Buddhism might be considered an example of such; Islam most certainly is not.

Today's world is very different from that of Muhammad and the first khalifs, and the great majority of Muslims would maintain that holy war cannot now be practiced as it was then. Muslims are scattered among practically all the countries of the world, so that there is no longer a single Abode of Islam. Above all, the modern world is characterized by the prevalence of the secular state in which no religion has a privileged status. In Muhammad's day practically every state was established on some religion. This religion would sanction the state even as it received material support from it. The state might well contain adherents of other faiths, but they would invariably be of lower political status. By special taxes, exclusion from certain professions or other restrictions, those of the other faiths would clearly be marked as second-class citizens.

The secular state is a relatively recent innovation, the United States of America being one of its first manifestations. It should be no surprise that in earlier times religion was often the motivation, or at least the pretext, for waging war. This is no more characteristic of Islam than of other religions such as Christianity, and it is a grave error to believe that there is anything uniquely aggressive about the Muslim religion.

PLACE OF WOMEN. No aspect of Islamic society has been more criticized in the modern world than its treatment of women. It is of the utmost importance here to reach a balanced judgment based on what is actually taught in the Koran. The following passage is a good starting point:

> Men are the protectors and maintainers of women, because Allah has given the one more strength than the other, and because they support them from their means. Therefore, righteous women are devoutly obedient and guard in the husband's absence what Allah would have them guard. (Sura 4, verse 34)

The subordination of women to men is clearly ordained here, and so it must be recognized right away that there can be no agreement between traditional Islam and modern feminism.

The practice of polygamy has, through the ages, seemed to the Western world to epitomize the degraded status of Muslim women. In fact, the Koran allows a man as many as four wives—but only on condition that he treat them all equally. The wives are not mere concubines, serving their husband as slaves. Muslim marriage is (in our quaint old phrase) an "honorable estate" in which the wife has clearly specified rights, including the right of divorce.

Of the greatest importance is the fact that that the Koran teaches the spiritual equality of woman. She is, like any man, answerable directly to God for the fulfillment of religious duty. She will be judged in her own right, not as an appendage to her husband. In Sura 33, verse 35, there is an entire litany of injunctions making this clear:

> For Muslim men and women, for believing men and women, for men and women who are devout, true and patient, for men and women who humble themselves, give charity and fast, for men and women who guard their chastity, for men and women who engage much in Allah's praise—for them has Allah prepared forgiveness and a great reward.

This is underscored by repeated condemnations of female infanticide. In ancient Arabia, as in some other places, it was all too common that baby girls, seen as a burden on the family, would be left to die. The Koran teaches that all who do this will answer for it on the Day of Judgment. The souls of their murdered daughters will confront them that day: "By what right have you taken our lives?" (See Sura 81, v. 8–9.)

Every human soul, therefore, is precious in the eyes of God, a female's no less than a male's. Still, the significance of this spiritual equality is debatable in the context of the clear inequality prevailing within the social and political domain.

IV. MOVEMENTS AND FIGURES IN ISLAMIC THOUGHT

1. Mutazilites and Asharites: The Talkers

The word *kalam* means "talk" in Arabic. It acquired a special new meaning in reference to a movement that emerged in the early days of the Abbasid khalifate (that is, in the late 700s). This was a time of great intellectual ferment, as Islam confronted the many religions in its newly conquered lands. Some Muslims were eager to engage these adversaries in debate, confident that the teachings of Islam possessed a clear intellectual superiority. There were even public forums, sponsored by the khalifs, in which representatives of the various religions, including Islam, might present their cases.

Thus, there came to be a class of Muslim specialists in rational religious discourse. They were known as the Talkers (Mutakallim), and their discipline was simply called *Kalam*. In English, the best word to express this is probably Theology.

There were eventually two distinct schools of theology, which opposed one another quite vigorously: the Mutazilites and the Asharites. The Mutazilites were the earlier of the two schools and the real founders of Kalam. The name means "those who have withdrawn" and evidently refers to the fact that these thinkers (or *talkers*) had by their rationalistic approach set themselves apart from the more conservative thinkers of the Ulama. The Mutazilites called themselves "the People of Unity and Justice" which very neatly sums up their theological standpoint.

"Unity" refers to divine unity, a principle which the Mutazilites felt necessary to articulate against their Christian opponents. Christianity, like Islam, emphatically affirms the existence of just one God. But this monotheism was, in Muslim eyes, tainted by the Christian doctrine of the Trinity. According to that doctrine the one God contains three distinct persons, representing different facets of His being: Father, Son (i.e., Jesus) and Holy Spirit. This is utterly wrong, according to Muslims, especially as it claims a divine status for the prophet Jesus.

The Mutazilites felt that the Christian error must be confronted by denying any kind of diversity or multiplicity in God. This has profound consequences for the way in which God will be understood. Believers in God affirm numerous divine *attributes*: love, wisdom, power, mercy, etc. The Mutazilites certainly do not wish to deny these, but they insist that these cannot be different attributes. Accordingly, God's love is the same as His wisdom, which is the same as His power, and so forth. In a human, of course, the (imperfect) qualities represent different aspects of a personality. In the perfection of God they are completely the same. This, say the Mutazilites, is the absolute unity of God which monotheists must affirm.

The justice in the Mutazilite credo is also divine justice, and this involves quite another issue. Some earlier Muslim thinkers had affirmed a doctrine of predestination. That is, they held that God exercises a total control over all human action (and everything else). What we do is not the result of a free choice. God has planned in advance the course that every human life will take, so that each one is predestined to merit paradise or hell. These predestinarians could easily find Koranic passages which supported their view: For example,

> Those whom God wishes to guide, He opens their hearts to Islam. Those whom He wishes to lead astray, He closes up their Hearts, so that punishment is heaped up for them. (Sura 6, v. 125)

This verse certainly does appear to say that people's religious commitments and choices are determined by God rather than themselves.

To the Mutazilites, predestination was a misguided doctrine which made Islam look cruel and arbitrary. They could cite their own Koranic passages which seemed to assert the reality of human choice:

> The truth is from your Lord. Let him who so chooses believe it, and let him who chooses otherwise reject it. (Sura 18, v. 29)

They saw the matter as an issue of divine justice, an attribute of God acknowledged by all. In the Mutazilite view, predestination was refuted by an elementary argument. God is just, and (as the Koran so vividly depicts) God does punish sinners—therefore, predestination is false. A just God would not punish sinners for what He himself has made to happen.

For a time the Mutazilites enjoyed great influence. Under the Khalif al-Mamun (reigned 813-833) and his immediate successors, their doctrines received official sanction, and dissenters were subject to persecution. The focal issue at this time was the status of the Koran: whether created or eternal. Many of the Ulama, notably ibn-Hanbal (died 855), believed that the sanctity and authority of the Koran were diminished if it was produced by God "on the spur of the moment," so to speak. They believed that it must exist eternally in the mind of God.

The Mutazilites rejected this notion, as it led to a diversity within God, a compromise of His perfect unity. Convinced of their arguments, al-Mamun decreed that all Muslims must abjure the teaching of the eternal Koran. Ibn-Hanbal refused to do this, as a result of which he was beaten and jailed. In due course, a khalif of different views came to power, and ibn-Hanbal was set free. He was vindicated, and the Mutazilites never again enjoyed such influence (except in Shiite countries, where even now theirs is the preferred theology).

The Mutazilites' decline coincided with the rise of the second major school of theologians, the Asharites. Named after their founder, Al-Ashari (died 935), the Asharites vigorously disputed the positions just explained. As to the attributes of God, they held that love, wisdom, etc. would become meaningless if all rolled into one. How can such a thing as divine love still have emotional impact for the believer if it is merged with such non-emotional qualities as wisdom and power? Needless to say, the Asharites still believed that God is one, but this did not have to be the absolute oneness which the Mutazilites (and later the Philosophers) insisted on.

Justice with respect to the Mutalizites (handwritten)

Predestination posed a far more complex question for the Asharites. They shrank from the extreme predestinarian view that human beings have nothing to do with their own actions and that it is a misnomer to speak of them acting at all. But the Asharites were still more opposed to the Mutazilite position that we freely choose our actions. They evolved their own doctrine which, in the end, is just a modified form of predestination.

The Asharite position featured the concept of acquisition. They held that God is the author of all actions. However, by the process of acquisition, these actions become the property of human beings, who are then responsible for them. It is a most peculiar concept, for if God has caused the actions, how can anyone other than He ever be responsible? To say that this happens "by virtue of acquisition" seems little more than a verbal trick. It is like saying, "God creates something white in such a way that it is black"—if it is white, then it cannot be black!

A more interesting defense of predestination is expressed in a famous story of Al-Ashari's:

> There were three brothers who came before God to be judged. One brother had led a virtuous life, another had been a great sinner and the third had died in infancy. The third brother inquired of God, "Why did you cause me to die so young?" "Ah," replied God, "I saw that you would lead a bad life. If allowed to grow up, you would have merited hell." Upon this, the second brother cried, "Alas! Why then did you not cut off my life?"

" Just because it doesn't make sense to you, doesn't mean it's wrong" (handwritten)

Here the story ends, for Ashari's point is that we humans are completely unable to understand the ways of God and have no business putting such questions to Him. It is never our place to pass judgment on God. The great error of the Mutazilites, he believes, is that they have presumed to hold God to their standard of justice. They say, "Predestination is not just and, therefore, God cannot do it." Rather say this, according to Ashari: "Whatever God does is just. Therefore, predestination, as taught in the Koran, is just *whether we can understand it or not.*"

Al-Ashari's successors developed an interesting theory which gave a metaphysical basis for their predestinarian views. The theory's starting point was the notion that all material objects were composed of *atoms*: tiny, indivisible bits of matter. The Mutazilites had actually introduced this idea into Muslim thought, borrowing it from certain Greek philosophers. The Asharites ingeniously adapted the theory to their own doctrines.

They described the atoms as existing independently of one another. Though many atoms might be collected together to form some larger object, they would have no inherent link among themselves. The quintessential characteristic of these atoms was their perishability. Each atom, along with every one of its properties (place, movement, color, etc.), had no power or tendency to maintain itself in existence. The atom would continue to exist only if God chose to sustain it. Whatever properties it possessed would be present only because God chose to confer them at that particular moment.

The theory gave vivid expression to the Asharite belief in the absolute power of God and the corresponding impotence of the material world (including ourselves). This world was presented as a fragmentary, incoherent domain, ever at risk of disintegrating or disappearing.

2. The Beginnings of Muslim Philosophy

The Arabic word for philosophy, *falsafa*, was simply taken over from the Greek. By its clearly foreign origin, the word suggested that philosophy was an "intruder", something that did not belong in the Muslim world. Indeed, the Muslim philosophers almost unanimously revered the Greeks as their mentors. As a result, *falsafa* did not have the broad meaning which the English word *philosophy* has come to have. We might say, for example, "She has a hands-on philosophy of management" or "He was philosophical about losing his job." By contrast, philosophy in the Muslim world comprised a very specific intellectual endeavor, following models provided by the ancient Greeks.

The treasures of ancient Greek philosophy—especially the works of Aristotle (379–322 BC)—had begun to be translated into Arabic in the 800s and 900s. Considerable resources were expended on this task, much of it taking place at Baghdad under the sponsorship of the khalifs. The enormous range of Aristotle's intellectual and scientific attainments gave him a pre-eminent place, but Plato (420-347 BC) and many others also became well known to those Muslim scholars who chose to take an interest.

There certainly were some, notably the Ulama, who frowned on such an interest and saw it as subverting the truth of Islam. For them, the ancient Greeks were mere pagans who could not possibly have anything to teach a good Muslim—at least, not anything beyond practical matters like mathematics and medicine. Nevertheless, there were a rather sizable group of intellectuals who did not consider themselves compromised as Muslims by delving into the Greeks.

In the Muslim world, then, a philosopher was not just a "deep thinker." Philosophy involved a specific commitment to the life of reason as led by Plato, Aristotle and others. The nature of this commitment can be understood from a famous story told by the Spanish philosopher ibn-Tufayl (c. 1100-85). It is the story of Hayy ibn-Yaqzan, a purely allegorical tale which was never supposed to have any basis in fact.

As a newborn infant, Hayy was packed into a basket by his mother and launched to sea. The basket came up on the shore of a deserted island, and Hayy would soon have perished but for the fact that a deer adopted him. She nursed and sheltered the helpless baby, and in due course he grew to manhood. Hayy was endowed with a keen intellect and an insatiable curiosity. Even though he had no one to teach him, he soon learned much of the world around him. He observed the stars in their regular course through the heavens. He carefully studied the animals, plants and minerals of the island. All that he came to know pointed unmistakably to the existence of a supremely wise and benevolent creator.

Thus, Hayy had acquired a firm belief in God, without depending on a prophet or any kind of formal religion. Along with this belief came a knowledge of the human soul and its unique status. All this was through the exercise of his own reasoning power.

His story took a new twist with the arrival on his island of Absal, a young man of similar age. Absal soon taught Hayy to speak, and they became fast friends. Absal, raised as a Muslim, was amazed that his friend could have understood such religious truths on his own. He prevailed upon Hayy to return to civilization. Absal was anxious to show off to his fellow Muslims this extraordinary example of spiritual insight.

However, the sojourn in Absal's land proved a bitter disappointment for the two friends. The people there were absorbed in the dogmatic and legalistic details of their religion. They resented Hayy because he did not agree exactly with what they had been taught. Hayy and Absal resolved that they would return to the island and seek truth in that isolated setting, free from the narrow-mindedness of formal religion.

The story expresses the philosophers' passionate belief in the power of human reason, a power to gain a purer and clearer grasp of the truth that can come by merely believing the words of the prophets. Only a few persons have the gift for this kind of thinking, and, as the conclusion to the story shows, this gift is likely to excite the fear and resentment of others.

Certainly, both the Ulama and the Theologians rejected the implications of this story. For either of these, prophecy was the indispensable core of religious belief. The notion that anyone might find religious truth on his own was dangerous and repugnant. The history of much controversy in the Muslim world can be read between the lines of ibn-Tufayl's little story.

The first actual person in Islam to embody this philosophical ideal was al-Kindi (about 800-870). He flourished during the khalifate of al-Mamun, that same ruler who so avidly sponsored the Mutazilites. There is, indeed, a considerable agreement between al-Kindi and these theologians, but he, as a philosopher, carried their rationalism much further. Though himself of the purest Arab descent, he eagerly welcomed the multitude of foreign influences which had come to bear on the Muslim world. At the beginning of his book *On First Philosophy*, he clearly enunciates his intellectual commitment:

> We ought not to be ashamed of appreciating the truth and acquiring it, wherever it comes from, even if it comes from races distant and nations different from us. For the seeker of truth, nothing takes precedence over the truth. (quoted from Ivry, *Al-Kindi's Metaphysics*, p. 58)

For Kindi, as for other philosophers, Aristotle stood highest among those non-Muslim figures whose wisdom was welcomed. By a strange accident of history, another philosopher's thought received a nearly equal prominence. This was Plotinus (204–270 AD). A synopsis of his teachings, translated into Arabic, had somehow been confused with the genuine work of Aristotle and given the title *Theology of Aristotle*. So, for his Muslim readers, Plotinus' ideas acquired the immense weight of Aristotle's authority. This despite the fact that there were marked differences between the two philosophers. Plotinus thought of himself as a Platonist rather than an Aristotelian.

What particularly impressed al-Kindi about the (so-called) *Theology of Aristotle* was its presentation of God as an absolute unity from which all creation flowed. The Mutazilites had already placed great stress on this unity, and now Kindi was able to give it a deeper philosophical meaning. Every created thing, he says, is a mixture of unity and complexity. That is, it is *one* thing, but it consists in a diversity of properties and activities. The creature exists only insofar as this diversity is held together somehow, that is, unified. It is the oneness of God, transmitted to things, which enables them to exist as individual beings.

In this way of thinking, God himself must be an absolute unity, without any differentiation of qualities. Were He not, then some higher principle would be required by which His diversity could be united in a single entity. Thus, God is the ultimate and perfect unity from which all other things derive their own relative and incomplete unities.

3. Al-Farabi: The Second Teacher

Abu Nasr al-Farabi (870–950) was from the district of Farab in modern Kazakhstan. No one was more important than he in determining the course of Islamic philosophy. He was able to take the ideas of the Greek philosophers and creatively adapt them to the new religious context. Muslim teachings such as Prophecy and Angels, which would have been meaningless to Aristotle himself, were given an interpretation in terms of the Aristotelian philosophy. Thus, Farabi was acclaimed as the Second Teacher (after Aristotle).

Inspired by the *Theology of Aristotle*, al-Farabi devised an extraordinary account of how the entire hierarchy of existing things derived ultimately from the perfect oneness of God. The key concept, which is straight out of Plotinus, is *emanation*. This must be distinguished from *creation*, which is a deliberate act taking place at a specific time. By contrast, emanation is a natural, continuous flowing. It is by emanation that the entire universe, directly or indirectly, comes from God.

Because of God's perfect unity, only one being can directly emanate from Him, for God's activity cannot have any diversity in it. This entity is an angel, or in al-Farabi's philosophical terminology, an *intellect*. It is a pure mind, having no dependence upon any physical organism. It is an active power of thinking, and its thought is perpetually directed onto two objects, God and itself.

From this Intellect's two contemplations there emanate two further beings. A Second Intellect-Angel arises from the thought about God, and from the self-contemplation comes what ancient astronomers called the First Heaven. This is a pure, crystalline sphere enclosing all the rest of the physical universe. This First Heaven is a living body, possessing a soul which endows it with thought and movement. The soul's thought of God's perfection leads it to move its spherical body in an eternal circular motion, the circle being the closest to perfection that a moving body can attain.

The Second Intellect carries on a twofold thinking (on God and itself) which exactly parallels that of the First, so that from it emanate a Third Intellect and a second living sphere, which contains all the stars and has its own circular motion. In this way a total of ten intellects come into being. With each, except the last, there is associated a living heavenly sphere, with some astronomical object embedded in it. In order of their emanation, these are: Saturn, Jupiter, Mars, the Sun, Venus, Mercury and the Moon. So there are nine spheres altogether, each the emanation of a certain one of the first nine intellects. The Tenth Intellect, emanating from the Ninth, has a different kind of role and status, as we will see.

In the midst of all this is our earth, remaining stationary as the spheres orbit it. Indeed the earth is produced by material effluences coming from the surrounding spheres. This picture of unmoving earth encircled by heavenly spheres was, in fact, the prevailing scientific view in Farabi's time. It had been established, almost without dissent, in Greek astronomy, and thus it possessed a formidable authority. Our modern view of the structure of the physical universe would have been inconceivable in the light of the science then existing.

Al-Farabi's great contribution lies in having systematically linked this physical structure to a metaphysical hierarchy of spiritual realities, culminating in God himself. By the principle of emanation, all these realities are accounted for and given a distinctive place in what has been called the "Great Chain of Being." His view had serious religious implications, however. He saw the world as only *indirectly* originating from God. More importantly, he saw the emanation process as *eternal*. Without beginning the First Intellect had been flowing out of God, and likewise the emanation of all the other Intellects and their spheres had been proceeding. The eternity of the world had been Aristotle's explicit view, and al-Farabi felt compelled by the logic of his own emanation theory to agree with him.

This notion of the world existing forever alongside God seems to contradict Koranic teaching, which presents God as summoning things into being by His word of command. The Koran's concept is what philosophers call *ex nihilo* (from nothing): things attain existence (by God's will) after a preceding non-existence. It is important to understand just why Farabi rejected this view. He believed that the perfection of God entailed that His activity be sustained and unchanging. God would not and could not suddenly begin to create after a time of inactivity. Whatever God does, He must do eternally, and so the entire sequence of emanation proceeds without beginning.

We have still to consider that mysterious Tenth Intellect, the last of Farabi's emanations. He identified this with what Aristotle called the Active Intellect, and nowhere is Farabi's philosophic ingenuity more evident than in the extraordinary range of functions which he gave to this entity.

EARTH SURROUNDED BY 9 SPHERES

A diagram of the earth, surrounded by the nine spheres. Long after al-Farabi's time, this conception of the universe continued to be dominant, in Europe as well as in the Muslim world. This particular diagram is from Peter Apian's Cosmographia, printed in 1539. Four years later, Copernicus published his new astronomical theory, which was destined to change forever the way we view the universe. [Peter Apian]

First, it is essential to survey what can be understood of Aristotle's theory of the Active Intellect. Aristotle believed that the human soul was inherently adapted to function in coordination with the human body. In the gathering of knowledge the soul must work with the specific sensory images which the body's perceiving faculties provide. But there can be no true knowledge until the mind is able to see the general concepts which these images embody. For example, the mind receives images of Peter, Paul, John, etc., but it must somehow extract from them the idea of humanity. The Active Intellect performs this vital task. Aristotle compares it to a light revealing colors which have only a potential reality in the darkness.

In a tantalizingly brief discussion (*On the Soul*, Book III, Chapter 5), Aristotle suggests that the Active Intellect alone, of all the aspects of the human soul, will enjoy immortality. He further hints this entity is not actually a component of the individual soul. Rather, it is a kind of supermind, existing apart from human souls but shining into them. These suggestions are taken up by Farabi and developed into a complex theory of how the Active Intellect operates in our lives.

Basically, there are three functions that it performs, in addition to the one originally specified by Aristotle: it is the giver of forms for all life on earth, it is the source of prophetic inspiration, and it provides for the possibility of an individualized life after death. As giver of forms, the Active Intellect solves a problem which baffled Aristotle himself: how are the souls of living things created. Aristotle understood perfectly well how parents, in the biological process of reproduction, provide the physical materials for life. But how can a soul enter into this, since neither parent can give up or replicate his/her own? Farabi put forward the idea that the Active Intellect is continually radiating forms (that is, souls) of every living species. Like electronic signals these bombard the whole surface of the earth. Wherever some reproductive activity provides the appropriate body for a given soul, that soul will then be lodged and a new life will begin.

As the inspiration for prophets, Active Intellect clarified a matter of acute importance for all Muslims. Prophecy was the fundamental link between Allah and humanity. For all Muslim philosophers, it was essential to have some theoretical account of what prophecy involved. Farabi's view was that the Active Intellect could affect imagination as well as reason. As it gave clear concepts to reason (sufficiently gifted), it could give powerful images to a mind endowed with the appropriate receptivity. The special character of the prophet's mind, then, was the capacity to receive images, which in a vivid, symbolic way would express the religious truths which philosophers could grasp in a more purely logical way.

Let me try to clarify this by an example. Muhammad's prophecy contained detailed and gripping descriptions of the torments of hell awaiting sinners. As we will see in the next few paragraphs, such a conception was not at all what Farabi believed to be the precise truth about afterlife. Nonetheless, the prophetic vision of afterlife did express a profound truth about the retribution that would befall those who led wicked and materialistic lives. That truth, essential to religion, is simply that our actions do have just and appropriate consequences. We must live with this thought constantly in mind. Muhammad's prophetic gift, so vital for the guidance of humanity, was to express this basic truth in such a way that anyone could appreciate it.

Now to the details of Farabi's account of life after death, in which Active Intellect was so vitally involved. Recall that Aristotle seemingly held that there was no immortality for individual souls but only for the "Supermind", i.e., Active Intellect, which transcended those souls. Aristotle saw the individual human soul as uniquely adapted to the human body, so that the existence of the two must coincide in time. It would make no sense for the soul to linger on when the body, which (through the senses) was the essential provider of material for thinking, had perished.

Understanding all this, Farabi still tried to find *some* basis for the soul to live on. His means of doing this was the concept of *Acquired* Intellect. This mental capacity comes to exist for those who make use of their rational powers so as to comprehend the existence of God and the entire hierarchy of spiritual realities. With this deep knowledge, there exists within the soul an array of concepts which will nourish and sustain the mind when the body no longer exists. The soul *acquires* this basis for immortality by its own intellectual exertions.

The immortalized soul experiences either a blissful or a tormented afterlife depending on the use it has made of its spiritual knowledge in this earthly life. The virtuous soul chooses a life which continually affirms and deepens its spiritual values—a religious life in the fullest sense of the word. After death, this soul will eternally enjoy its pure spiritual condition in the company of like-minded souls. But there are also wicked souls which, knowing their spiritual destiny, nonetheless reject it and live only for the gratifications of the material world. Their afterlife is an endless affliction, as the contradiction between spiritual knowledge and materialistic commitments festers within.

Those prophetic statements about hellfire are just the figurative expression of the acute suffering of these wicked souls. They serve to teach anyone who will reflect at all of the awesome choice that faces us: to submit to God or to turn away from Him.

In addition to the virtuous and the wicked, there is a third and very sizable segment of humanity who do not attain immortality at all. They are, in Farabi's terminology, the ignorant, and they are completely lacking in acquired intellect. They have no conception of any purpose in life other than money, power, fame and sensual gratification. Unlike the wicked, they do not see two ways and choose the worse. They simply follow the only way their minds comprehend. Their souls, being entirely conditioned to life in this material world, cannot survive the death of the body.

Thus, for al-Farabi, the question of the human soul's immortality has quite a complex answer. Unlike other philosophers, he does not see life after death as existing either for all persons or for none. It is an extraordinary view, far from what Aristotle had ever taught on the subject. And it is even farther from orthodox

Muslim teaching. Al-Farabi understood perfectly well the extent of his departure from standard belief in this matter and in many others, such as the denial of creation ex nihilo. He saw this as the inevitable result of following the dictates of pure reason. In this he differs considerably from his predecessor, al-Kindi. The latter's generous spirit glossed over discrepancies between Islam and philosophy. He adhered quite closely to orthodox Islamic belief, using philosophy where he could and not fretting overmuch when it seemed in conflict with his religion.

Farabi, on the other hand, saw the fundamental nature of the conflict. He most certainly did *not* think that this entailed his abandonment of Islam. For him, the essential truths were the same, whether enunciated by reason or by prophecy. But he saw that controversy, such as the story of Hayy had portrayed, was inevitable as the different versions of these truths confronted each other. The negative reaction to philosophy is a major part of our story, and we will find it articulated with particular effectiveness by al-Ghazali (1058-1111). First, however, it is necessary to consider the career of Farabi's illustrious successor.

4. Ibn-Sina: The Culmination of Muslim Philosophy

Known in the West as Avicenna, ibn-Sina (980–1037) is recognized, by friends and foes alike, as the pre-eminent Muslim philosopher. Indeed, his accomplishments ranged far beyond that. He was a skilled physician, and for a long time he reigned as the supreme authority on medicine in the Islamic world. As personal physician to a number of rulers, he acquired considerable political influence. In contrast to al-Farabi's quiet and rather reclusive life, ibn-Sina's days were filled with demanding responsibilities, so that he struggled to find time for his philosophy.

Ibn-Sina carried on the development of philosophy from just that point where al-Farabi had left it off. He frankly acknowledged his debt to Farabi, recounting how he had read the *Metaphysics* of Aristotle forty times without being able to comprehend it. Then, quite by chance, he came upon a book of Farabi's on the subject at a bookseller's stall in the marketplace. With this assistance he felt that he finally understood Aristotle and could proceed to the development of a systematic philosophy that was both Muslim and Aristotelian.

He kept closely to the general scheme of Farabi's thought, especially to the emanationist account of how all creatures derive ultimately from God. But he made many refinements and adjustments. Above all, he articulated and contrasted the concepts of *essence* and *existence*, in which the whole theory could be grounded. This is ibn-Sina's great contribution to philosophy. The distinction between essence and existence proved to be of the utmost importance for the subsequent history of Muslim thought.

Simply put, essence is *what* a thing is, and existence is *that* it is. Aristotle understood essence to consist of form and matter. A knife, for example, has the form of sharpness embodied in the matter of metal. Form, for Aristotle, is a dynamic principle, a power that is characteristic of a certain kind of thing. Matter is the passive recipient of form.

contingent things are unnecessary if not having their dependant.

Ibn-Sina, by contrast, saw essence in its entirety as passive. Until "activated" by existence, it was a lifeless, abstract possibility, a definition of what might exist. His revealing phrase, in reference to the essences of all created things, is that they do not *deserve* to exist. Thus, in every creature, we see this fundamental duality: the essence, which is its nature, and the existence, which is the realization of that nature. Ibn-Sina, departing completely from Aristotle, treats existence as a kind of separate, indefinable reality which is added to essence

The ultimate inspiration for this new way of thinking came from those Koranic passages which portrayed God as summoning things into existence with the command "Be!". Clearly visualized in these passages was a vast shadow world of possible beings, waiting to receive God's command. This became, in ibn-Sina's philosophical rendering, the domain of essence. From God, existence somehow flowed into selected parts of this domain.

With these concepts of essence and existence, ibn-Sina was able to give a deeper meaning to the concept of divine unity and to formulate a new proof of God's existence that was extraordinarily simple and cogent. Consider first his proof of God. In every being of this world, we see essence conjoined with existence, that is, possibility which has been actualized. But there is nothing in the essence which requires or "deserves" existence. It is perfectly conceivable that this essence might not be actualized. There must be some explanation for the fact that this essence is joined to existence.

Ibn-Sina's point here is simply that it is reasonable to ask of anything: why does this entity remain in existence? Why does it not vanish before our eyes? The question is *not* about origins, not about how something came into being. It is a question about the continuing existence of something right now. It is a question stemming from the fundamental *contingency* of every existence in our world.

The answer to the question must be some external power, which is able to confer existence upon a given essence. But what of this power? If it is a combination of essence and existence, then it too relies on some other power for a continuation of its existence. There can be no real explanation unless we suppose that there is some reality in which essence and existence are not distinct, a reality whose essence *is* existence. This is God, whom ibn-Sina refers to as the Necessary Being. God is necessary because it is in His very nature to exist. Existence is not something added to His essence.

Notice how ibn-Sina's proof differs from that which is commonly given in religious discussion. In this more usual proof, the world is seen as something which cannot have existed forever. It must go back to a beginning, and God is the author of that beginning. This may be called a *horizontal* proof, since it sees the world as existing on a horizontal time-line which must extend back to a point of origin. Such a way of proving God was completely useless in ibn-Sina's view, since he followed al-Farabi (and Aristotle) in holding the world to be eternal. So the time-line would go back and back into the past without ever reaching a beginning.

Ibn-Sina's proof may be characterized as *vertical*, since it involves a relation-ship between creatures below and their God above *in the present moment*. The present existence of any creature must be sustained. That is, its essence must be actualized. Only the Necessary Being, whose own essence does not need to be actualized, can accomplish this. This has nothing to do with any beginning of the universe. It is based solely on the urgency of that question already considered: why does anything remain in existence, given that by its essence there is no reason why it should?

In his conception of God as Necessary Being, ibn-Sina also gave new meaning to the principle of divine unity. God is unique in having no distinction between essence and eixtence. His being is devoid of that differentiation which is in every contingent being. These contingent beings, from the angelic intellects on down, have their natures defined in terms of specific characteristics. But the nature (essence) of God is existence itself: not to be this or to be that but simply *to be*. This is an extraordinary idea, given that God is generally thought of in terms of specific forms of being: power, love, knowledge, etc. In a way that went beyond the Mutazilites, ibn-Sina was denying the reality of these various divine attributes.

To say that God is existence itself also entails a new conception of the relation between God and ourselves. Wherever we encounter existence, we encounter God. He is not something apart from us; He is the very being of every existing thing. We shall see that it was ultimately the Sufis rather than the Philosophers who plumbed the depths of this amazing idea.

5. Al-Ghazali: The Defense of Orthodoxy

In the whole history of Islamic thought after Muhammad, there is probably no figure more respected than abu-Hamid al-Ghazali (1058-1111). He made contribu-tions of many kinds, but what most concerns us now is his response to the impos-ing philosophers we have just studied—especially ibn-Sina. Ghazali saw these Philosophers as an intolerable danger to the purity of the Muslim faith. Certainly he was not the first to be provoked by their controversial ideas. From its beginnings with the very orthodox al-Kindi, philosophy had incurred hostility. But Ghazali differed from earlier critics. Rather than merely venting his outrage, he meticu-lously studied the writings of ibn-Sina and the others. He mastered their theories and arguments. Thus, his criticism, when finally published, was born of a profound understanding of what he was dealing with.

That criticism was presented in a work entitled the *Tahafut al-Falasifah* ("The Incoherence of the Philosophers"). In this book Ghazali laid against the Philoso-phers two fundamental but very different charges. (Note that when Ghazali speaks of "the Philosophers", it is almost always ibn-Sina—sometimes al-Farabi as well—whom he has in mind.) The first charge was that they had committed apostasy, that is, they had ceased to be Muslims on account of their unorthodox beliefs. The second was that their views were flawed from a purely rational standpoint. The first charge was far more important, practically speaking. As the incident at the beginning of abu-Bakr's khalifate had shown, the abandonment of the Muslim faith was a crime which could not be tolerated.

The charge of apostasy involved three issues: the duration of the world, the nature of the afterlife and the extent of God's knowledge. Ghazali had many objections to the Philosophers' teachings, but on these three points the disagreement was irreconcilable.

On the duration of the world, the Philosophers (that is, al-Farabi and ibn-Sina) were quite clear. The world, consisting of the earth and all the surrounding spheres with their souls and Intellects, has existed forever. It was *co-eternal* with God. Ghazali considered this view to be incompatible with the uniqueness and majesty of God. The Creator must have existed prior to His creation as various Koranic passages indicate. Before the beginning of the world there was nothing but God, and out of this nothing (ex nihilo) God created.

We have already examined the extraordinary view of al-Farabi on the subject of afterlife. Ibn-Sina's position was somewhat less radical, but what they held in common was a rejection of any survival of the physical body. There was absolutely no reason for the body to survive this worldly life when the soul represented what was most noble and essential in human existence. For Ghazali, such a view stood refuted by the clear statement of the Koran that God would resurrect our bodies for the Last Judgment. The Koran is very emphatic on this point, insisting on the literal truth of bodily resurrection in the face of various objections. While Ghazali was not averse to understanding some Koranic passages in a symbolic sense, there was no mistaking here that the literal meaning was intended.

The third issue in dispute is really the most significant. It goes to the very heart of religion in that it concerns God's relationship with us. The question is: how does God know His creatures? The Philosophers' understanding of this matter was premised on the belief that God, as a perfect being, cannot change in any way. Therefore, says Ghazali, they are driven to the conclusion that God cannot know us in any direct, individualized way. God could not know what I am now doing, for then His knowledge would have to change, as my activity changed.

This is an intolerable notion, according to Ghazali. The Koran continually emphasizes God's perfect knowledge of every detail of this world, including our most secret thoughts. How can religious acts, such as prayer, retain their significance if they are not immediately and directly known to God? The whole basis for religion is destroyed if the Philosophers' abstract, impersonal notion of God is accepted.

We should pause to take stock of this controversy. Why did such irreconcilable religious views come to be held in the same Islamic context? It is clear that the Philosophers and Ghazali were operating with utterly different motivations. Philosophy is a quest for understanding, and the great Muslim philosophers believed that the concept of God was the indispensable tool that would provide them this understanding. Only with God as the ultimate principle, the Necessary Being, could the rest of reality be understood. God was a theoretical concept, then. The Philosophers needed Him much as a physicist needs the electron or a biologist needs the gene.

This is far from what motivates most people to believe in God. The usual motivation, most certainly shared by al-Ghazali, is an emotional need, not an intellectual one. God exists as the provider of security, consolation and hope. In order for Him to do this, it is absolutely essential that He know us personally. That is why Ghazali was so outraged by the Philosophers' view of God's knowledge.

If we reconsider the issue of world's duration, we can see further illustration of how these different motivations conditioned thought. To the Philosophers, it was inconceivable that the world could have had a beginning, created ex nihilo by God. There would, in the vastness of eternity, be no reason for God to prefer one time rather than another for the commencement of His creative activity. But whatever God does, He does with good reason. Rather than arbitrarily choose one time of creation over another, God will then create (or rather *emanate*) eternally.

To Ghazali, on the other hand, the incomprehensibility of God's creative decision was no obstacle at all. It only *enhanced* the status of God as our supreme Lord that, for us, there was no rhyme or reason to His having chosen a particular time to create. It served to reaffirm our humble condition beneath Him.

Remember that there was a second basic criticism which al-Ghazali had of the Philosophers. That line of attack was founded on pure reason rather than religious dogma. Ghazali thought he saw a way of bringing down the entire edifice of philosophy by focusing on one central but vulnerable concept: *causality*. The Philosophers had put forward an elaborate array of causation, culminating in the Necessary Being. The whole enterprise depended on the assumption that we can know the causes of things, but that is precisely what Ghazali now challenged.

Take the simplest sort of case, he says, such as a flame burning a piece of cotton. What do we really know about this event? We see the cotton in contact with the flame, and, simultaneously, changes in its qualities begin to manifest themselves. But there is nothing but the *association* of the fire with these developments to justify a claim of causation. It is entirely conceivable that some hidden cause was operating to make the cotton blacken and disintegrate into ashes. If the causation of this ordinary event cannot be indubitably proven, how much more doubtful are the cosmic causal links which were so important for the Philosophers?

The gist of the argument is that only the association or sequence of events is observed, never the causation itself. Therefore, whatever is believed about the cause of something is always in the nature of an assumption. What should we assume, then? The Philosophers (along with most of us) assume that created things do indeed cause the events that are seen to be conjoined to them. Ghazali thinks that it is more in tune with the tenets of the Muslim faith to assume that *God* is the cause of every event. The burning of the cotton, for example, takes place because God contemplates that particular situation and decides that incineration, rather than some other effect, shall occur.

This extraordinary position was, in fact, quite natural for Ghazali to hold, for as a Theologian, he adhered to the Asharite school. The belief that God controls all was a plausible extension of the doctrine that He predestines humans. Moreover, we have seen that Ghazali insists on God's total and present knowledge of the world. To Ghazali, then, there is nothing strange in the idea that God, as He observes the tiniest happenings in the universe, is also choosing their outcomes.

The patterns that we observe, such as the repeated association of fire with burning, are no proof of any power in created things. They are only tokens of God's mercy to provide us a secure and predictable world, and these patterns can be violated at any time. Ghazali liked to cite a story of Abraham from the Koran (Sura 21: 51–69). Here, in the typical prophetic manner, Abraham had stirred up the wrath of his community by his attacks on idolatry. For this he was cast into a fire, but God commanded the fire to be cool and safe, and Abraham emerged unscathed. To Ghazali this showed that any effects associated with fire are simply the will of God. He chooses what shall result from fire on any given occasion.

The basis for Ghazali's position should be carefully noted. He does not claim to *prove* that God is the cause of every event, any more than his opponents can prove that created beings are causes. Nothing is provable here; that is the weakness of our reasoning power, which the Philosophers failed to recognize. Once it is understood that we cannot *know* the cause, it is time to choose where we will place our faith. Ghazali puts his faith in the power of God rather than natural objects.

6. Ibn-Rushd: The Defense of Philosophy Rushd thinks Ghazali is wrong.

For approximately five centuries, Islam was dominant in Spain, and many eminent philosophers arose in this far western corner of the Muslim world. The greatest of them was ibn-Rushd (1126–98), who became known in Christian Europe as Averroes. He was the last of the great Muslim philosophers to share the deep commitment to Aristotelianism which had imbued al-Farabi and ibn-Sina. Indeed, he carried it farther than they had done on the basis of a more accurate understanding of what Aristotle had actually taught. The largest component of his work is a series of commentaries on the various works of Aristotle. In all the two thousand years that Aristotle reigned as the "master of those that know" there was probably no one who studied Aristotle more devotedly or with more discernment.

Ibn-Rushd set himself the task of purifying Aristotelianism of the contamination and misinterpretation which had affected it. In particular, he saw, as his predecessors had not, that the *Theology of Aristotle* was not Aristotle's work at all. This entailed the abandonment of the emanation theory which the philosophies of al-Farabi and ibn-Sina had featured. Ibn-Rushd still believed in a series of spheres around the earth and in a hierarchy of Intellects to preside over them. But he saw God as simply the first in this series of Intellects, inspiring all the others but not emanating or creating them in any way. This was indeed a view far closer to Aristotle's own teaching.

On the subject of life after death, ibn-Rushd's view evolved over many years, as he pondered Aristotle's complex teachings on the human soul. His final conclusion (against al-Farabi and ibn-Sina) was that these teachings did not allow for immortality of any individual human soul. Only a collective "supermind" lived on forever. Particular souls with their distinctive moral and intellectual attainments must perish with the body. Here too ibn-Rushd showed himself a more authentic student of Aristotle. (The extent to which he himself believed this doctrine he attributed to Aristotle is a matter of dispute. It is a most urgent—though unresolvable—dispute, given ibn-Rushd's insistence on the religious duty of belief in afterlife, as explained below.)

Ibn-Rushd's differences from his philosophical colleagues were minor compared with his objections to al-Ghazali. To answer the latter's *Tahafut al-Falasifa*, he produced his own *Tahafut al-Tahafut* ("The Incoherence of the Incoherence") in which he sought, point by point, to respond to the many criticisms which Ghazali had made. Another work, in which he makes his defense of philosophy much more succinctly, is the *Decisive Treatise on the Agreement of Philosophy and Religion*. In these books he had to justify philosophy's right to its very existence in the Muslim world. He had to show that the Philosophers were not apostates who had betrayed the faith.

Responding to Ghazali's charge of apostasy, ibn-Rushd appealed to a distinction between the core principles of religion and the varied interpretations which these principles may receive. God's power, justice and benevolence are prime examples of these core principles. Any religious person must believe in them. Whoever does not is worthy of severe censure, or worse.

But how are they to be interpreted? That is, in what ways do these divine characteristics express themselves? Most people need to understand them in a very simple and direct way, a way that involves imagination more than intellect. So the power of God is understood as His creating things by direct command. What could be more vivid and compelling than the image of things materializing out of nowhere in response to the divine decree? Likewise, justice is expressed most dramatically in the image of a divine judgment sending each person either to excruciating physical torment or to endless sensual delight; and benevolence is seen in images of God's direct awareness of and tender care for individual beings.

Unfortunately, these inspiring images conflict with what can be logically demonstrated of God, according to ibn-Rushd. A philosopher must have a different interpretation of the divine power, justice and benevolence. This interpretation will deal in very abstract notions, hardly intelligible to most people.

We can take the case of justice as the clearest example to expound for ibn-Rushd's theory. The essential religious idea is that each person be accountable for his life. In some form, one must survive this life, so as to receive the merited reward or punishment. Philosophers saw this survival in terms of the soul, while ordinary Muslims perceived just the bodily aspect. Such was only to be expected, given that *soul* is a deep concept barely understood by most. The supremely important fact (to ibn-Rushd) is that both groups retain the crucial principle that divine justice will be done. If the essential principle is preserved, then no charge of apostasy can be sustained.

Now we can better understand how the Philosophers dared to contradict the Koran's explicit teaching on the future life. They saw the Koran as revealed for the benefit of the great masses of humanity—ones for whom the soul would be a difficult notion. These people had to be taught afterlife with the vivid images of bodily resurrection, paradise and hell. Abstract accounts of the soul would never have moved them. Thus has God taught afterlife in the Koran, so that all of mankind might comprehend. On this understanding, the Koran is still absolutely the word of God, but we must appreciate exactly what purpose it serves.

Ibn-Rushd insists that, even as we see the Koran as God's gift for the common folk, we must also see that He has bestowed reason on a select few. That gift must also be cherished and used. That is, the Philosophers must be allowed to pursue the truth in their own way—assuming, as always, that those core religious principles are respected. There is another condition which the Philosophers must also be acutely mindful of. They must pursue the truth in a discreet manner so that the common people will not be disturbed in their simplistic belief. Philosophers may freely think and discuss and write, but they must be very careful to disseminate their ideas only among the like-minded. In public they must show the utmost respect for those teachings which God has given for the faith of ordinary people.

Ibn-Rushd considered that it was al-Ghazali who had disturbed the people's faith. *He* had publicized the teachings of the Philosophers for the purpose of condemning them. As a consequence, the Muslim public were left confused as to what they must believe. In his *Decisive Treatise* (end of Chapter Two), ibn-Rushd tells us that he himself would never have taken up these issues but for the fact that Ghazali had broadcast them far and wide.

It remains to see how ibn-Rushd dealt with that other aspect of al-Ghazali's attack on philosophy, namely, his critique of the concept of causation. Ghazali's ultimate view, as we saw, is that God is the only doer. No created thing has the power to cause an effect. Ibn-Rushd argues that this is untenable. To exist, a creature must be endowed with some degree of power. Any quality that we perceive in a thing is an expression of such power.

Take the black color of a piece of coal, for example. The coal's having this color is a matter of its being able to *cause* certain perceptions in those who see it. Now suppose we deny it this power and hold that God is the cause of our seeing the blackness. Then it no longer makes sense to say that the coal is black.

The same argument applies to any quality that any object might possess. To have a quality is to have a certain causal power. If we say that creatures are devoid of causal power, we are saying that they are devoid of all qualities, that they do not exist at all. If God is the only doer, then He is also the only being; and that is an absurdity which defies both religion and common sense.

Thus, with determination and skill, ibn-Rushd contended against Ghazali's attacks. But one senses a certain feeling of resignation in the last lines of his *Tahafut al-Tahafut*:

> I have decided to break off my inquiry about these things here, and I ask pardon for their discussion, and if it were not an obligation to seek the truth for those who are entitled to it—and they are, as Galen says, one in a thousand—and to prevent from discussion those who have no claim to it, I would not have treated all this. And God knows every single letter [indirectly, he means], and perhaps God will accept my excuse and forgive my stumbling in His bounty, generosity, munificence and excellence—there is no God but He!

Indeed, ibn-Rushd's success, if it is to be measured by public approbation, was very limited. Ghazali's view prevailed, and his adversary was largely forgotten in the Muslim world. He was more widely read and revered (though still controversial) in Christian Europe. After ibn-Rushd, pure Aristotelianism no longer had a Muslim following. Where Aristotle's ideas survived at all, they did so in conjunction with another stream of thought, to which we now turn.

_ascetics of Islam (giving up stuff for the religion)

7. The Sufis: A Way Transcending Both Logic and Dogma

Even as the Theologians and Philosophers were following their intellectual paths, there took root in Islam a very different kind of movement, founded on pure religious devotion. The Sufis took their name from the Arabic *suf*, "wool." The literal meaning of *sufi* was "one clothed in wool." The significance of this lies in the fact that wool clothing was very cheap at this time. Only the poorest wore it. The Sufis wore wool to give expression to their belief in the need for poverty. The wealth, fame and power that the world has to offer are serious obstacles to closeness with God. One cannot love these things without diminishing the love that must be given to God.

The most famous of the early Sufis is Rabia of Basra (713–801). Her long life was a model for later Sufis in its simplicity and single-minded devotion. She disapproved of those whose religion was motivated by the fear of hell or the yearning for paradise. God's own adorable beauty was the most compelling reason to love Him. (It is a noteworthy fact that Sufism, of all the Islamic movements we are discussing, is the only one in which women ever came to prominence.)

Gradually, from the example of Rabia and others, the Sufis developed a fairly clear concept of their goal and of the discipline needed to achieve it. The goal was a special kind of intimacy with God which is called *mystical experience*. This is a most important concept with applications to many religions. It must be carefully defined, for it is not just any kind of experience which is strange or inexplicable. Mystical experience is an experience of God in His true nature. In this experience there cannot be anything which is distorted or merely symbolic. When God appeared to Moses in the burning bush, for example, this was not a mystical experience, because God was manifesting Himself in a physical way. God is spiritual, not physical, so a true experience of Him must involve pure thought rather than the senses.

Even more importantly, the mystical experience must somehow encompass the *infinity* of God. It must grasp Him as infinitely good, wise, powerful, etc. This poses what may seem to be an insurmountable difficulty: how can the finite human mind take in this divine infinity?

The Sufis, nevertheless, set their sights on this daunting goal, and they worked out methods that could lead them in its direction. One essential part of the methodology is reliance on a spiritual master, the *shaikh*. The Sufi way is difficult and dangerous. One's mind and spirit are pushed to the limit. This path cannot be trodden alone. The shaikh with his (or her) experience is an indispensable guide and must be accorded the utmost respect and obedience. In many other Eastern religious traditions we find a similar emphasis on the role of the spiritual master.

The shaikh will guide the Sufi novice in a variety of particular techniques. The best known of them is dhikr, which involves the constant repetition of the name of God. This may be mental rather than verbal. In either case, it is a way of focusing the mind entirely on God.

There are, in fact, many distinct stages in the path to mystical experience, and one of the shaikh's most important roles is to clarify these for the novices and make each one understand what state has presently been reached. A very significant aspect of Sufi teaching is that each of these stages is classified as either *attainment* or *gift*. Attainments are those stages which a Sufi can reach by his own efforts (aided by the shaikh). Gifts are not attainable by any amount of human effort. They must be bestowed by God, and there is no telling whether He will choose to do so. One of the famous Sufi mottoes is that we must never *expect* these gifts.

Above all, mystical experience itself, the culminating stage, is a gift. By their emphasis on the bestowed nature of this and many other spiritual states, the Sufis express a characteristically Muslim attitude. We are completely subordinate to God. Whatever condition we reach depends on Him, not ourselves.

Now we are in a position to confront the most difficult and amazing part of Sufism: the actual onset of mystical experience through the gift of God. There is deep paradox here, as already noted, since the human mind is somehow grasping the true, infinite nature of God. This can happen only insofar as the mind is absorbed into God, losing its own individual being. The Sufis call it *fana*, "annihilation." The situation may be compared to an intense light and its effect upon the eyes. If the light is too strong, one will be blinded temporarily or even permanently. Likewise, the true experience of God will overwhelm the mind. If the experience is brief enough, the mind may recover and return to normal functioning; but a mystical experience of any significant duration will truly be fana: the permanent destruction of the mind and, with it, one's personal existence.

Surprisingly, this result is desired rather than dreaded by the Sufis. They feel that the persistence of our individual being is a burden and an obstacle to the complete realization of our love for God. As long as a person still exists, there is a separation from God. Al-Hallaj (857–922) made this prayer to God:

> Between me and Thee there lingers an "It is I" that torments me. Ah, with Thy grace, take this I from between us.

For some Sufis fana was understood in a way that seemed blasphemous. It was presented as the assuming of God's identity in place of one's own. Abu Yazid al-Bistami (?–874) expressed it as follows:

> I plunged on into the angelic sea and the veils of divinity until I reached the throne, and, lo, it was vacant. Therefore, I threw myself upon it and said, "Lord, where will I find you?" And behold, I was I, yes I was I. Then I returned to what I was seeking, and it was no other than I. (from Fakhry, *Short Introduction to Islamic Philosophy, Theology and Mysticism*, 76)

Thus al-Bistami seemed to negate the subordination of creature to God which Islam stresses so fundamentally. Al-Hallaj gave voice to equally bold statements of this sort, which were used as a pretext for putting him to death. Al-Bistami escaped such a fate by pretending to be insane.

As a result of such statements, Sufism became a very controversial movement in the Muslim world, exciting the fear and anger of many. But this did not really weaken its influence. The fact is that most of the Sufis led lives of exemplary piety, and this ultimately earned them the respect of most Muslims. Al-Ghazali is a particularly important example. Though he enjoyed an immensely successful career as a Theologian and a Jurist, he felt, in his later years, a spiritual emptiness. This led him to give up wealth and position, donning the woolen Sufi garb. He was very cautious, to be sure, and orthodox in treating of fana; but he made very clear his conviction that the Sufi way was superior to every other religious endeavor.

Ibn-Sina is another who turned to Sufism in his later years, sensing a deficiency in the pure rationalism of his philosophy. It is a great irony that, while al-Ghazali the Theologian and ibn-Sina the Philosopher were so irreconcilably opposed, the two could find common ground as Sufis. Al-Farabi and Ibn-Rushd did not share their colleague's attraction to Sufism, but virtually all of the later Muslim philosophers did. We will now see, in particular cases, how philosophy and Sufism were blended.

8. Al-Suhrawardi and Ibn-Arabi: The Convergence of Sufism and Philosophy

Al-Suhrawardi ("he of the town of Suhraward"—in Iran) usually has the word *Maqtul* ("he who was put to death") added to his name, to distinguish him from a similarly-named thinker. It is a sad fact that for him philosophy and Sufism were a potent and dangerous mix. He incurred the wrath of the conservative Ulama; and in 1191, at the age of thirty-eight, he was executed by order of Saladin, the famous adversary of the Crusaders.

The core of Suhrawardi's philosophy is a passionate belief in the unity of wisdom through all the ages and all the nations of mankind. Against all sectarianism, he avers that the wise everywhere have found and cherished the same truth. From the ancient Greeks, he names Pythagoras, Empedocles and Plato as the embodiments of this perennial wisdom. (He conspicuously does not name Aristotle.) From his native Iran, he cites various ancient figures.

Suhrawardi criticized those Muslim philosophers like ibn-Sina, who had placed so much reliance on Aristotle. In particular, he criticized ibn-Sina's evaluation of the concepts of essence and existence. The latter had clearly regarded existence as the vital, dynamic principle. Indeed, existence was identified with God himself in ibn-Sina's philosophy, while essence was mere passive possibility "undeserving of existence."

Taking Plato as his guide, Suhrawardi reversed this judgment of essence and existence. In order to comprehend Suhrawardi's thought, it is necessary to give a very brief account of the Platonic philosophy.

Plato believed in a realm of ideal objects (Forms) which were far superior to anything in the material world. Physical things could never attain anything better than weak imitation of these Forms. A physical circle, for example, could never be more than a rough approximation of the perfect circularity in the ideal domain. The Forms themselves were arranged in a vast hierarchy, at the pinnacle of which stood Goodness. This was the Master Form, from which every other was derived. Every other Form was simply a particular kind or manner of Goodness.

Now these Forms were in fact the essences of things. Both Plato and Suhrawardi saw the essences as constituting a grand hierarchy; and Suhrawardi, at least, was prepared to name the highest principle in the hierarchy God, Allah. This, in contrast to the hierarchy of *existences* which ibn-Sina's philosophy featured.

The great error in ibn-Sina's way of thinking was to see essences as abstract, *uncreated* possibilities, waiting to receive existence. But essences are not, cannot be uncreated. They come from God, as the lesser Forms come from Goodness. Moreover, ibn-Sina's view is not even coherent. On the one hand, he defines essences as distinct from existence, as thus non-existent. But, on the other, he must acknowledge that essences are somehow present in order to be joined to existence— so in some way they do exist.

The Forms have, in Suhrawardi's philosophy, a concreteness that goes beyond what Plato envisioned. The Iranian here invokes his own national heritage and sees the Forms as living spiritual beings, as *angels*. Every kind of life has its guardian angel, presiding over it. This notion is straight out of Zoroastrianism, and Suhrawardi even uses some of the Zoroastrian names for these angels.

We have still not quite come to the very heart of Suhrawardi's philosophy. We must understand the real character of all these essences, from the Supreme Essence, God, down through the angelic Forms. Essence is basically the *illumination* of an entity, that which shows its true nature. Physical light reveals something and enables us to see it, and essence accomplishes the same purpose on a more profound level. It reveals the spiritual reality of an object rather than its physical appearance.

It is vital to understand that Suhrawardi does not intend to use light as a metaphor. He means to say that essences are *literally* lights, and that God himself is the Light of Lights, from which all other illumination is reflected. What *we* call light, here in the physical world, is just the pale reflection of the pure illumination of God's being. In fact, the physical world is the meeting place of light and darkness. Each material object is an "isthmus" (as Suhrawardi puts it) where light and darkness mingle. The Aristotelians had analyzed material objects into matter and form; and Suhrawardi explicitly rejects this view in favor of his own duality of light and darkness.

However, darkness is not a positive reality. It is just the absence of light. The only true reality is God, the Supreme Light. The inevitable yearning of each creature, each isthmus, is to be purified of darkness and to return, through the angelic Forms, to the originating Light of Lights. Like many Sufis, Suhrawardi cited the story of Muhammad's miraculous journey (See p. 8) to show that the Prophet himself had reached such spiritual heights. The whole theory was Suhrawardi's way of making sense of the Sufi principle of fana (annihilation). To see ourselves as mere contaminated reflections of the Divine Light gave more credibility to the idea that our true being is in God. Fana is just the dispelling of that false separation from God which darkness creates.

Suhrawardi thus made the concept of illumination (Arabic: *ishraq*) his central principle. In spite of his tragic demise, he acquired a considerable following, who were known as the *Ishraqis*. Many of the later Sufis embraced his idea that light, of all the entities in the physical world, could best tell us something about the nature of God and about the nature of their own religious experiences.

Even more important in the history of Sufism is the extraordinary figure of ibn-Arabi (1165–1240). His ideas were every bit as controversial as Suhrawardi's, though he managed to avoid the latter's fate. Throughout his life he experienced strange apparitions and bizarre episodes. Reading his biography, one might even suppose that he lived on the brink of insanity. Nevertheless, he managed, in both his life and writings, to give a more powerful expression to the values of Sufism than anyone else before or since. He is certainly one of the most controversial figures in the entire history of Islam, and even today there is still debate about whether his views were allowable for a Muslim to hold.

Ibn-Arabi was born in southern Spain, which then was still the center of a flourishing Muslim culture. Sufism was especially vigorous there, and ibn-Arabi began to take a keen interest in it while still an adolescent. As fate would have it, his father was a close friend of the great philosopher, ibn-Rushd. The two met once, at the philosopher's request. He politely asked the young man (about twenty at the time) whether what he had learned though the Sufi path coincided with what philosophers understood by their rational speculation. Ibn-Arabi evasively replied, "Yes and No," and went on to invoke some rather vague images. It would appear that there was no meeting of the minds between these two thinkers, representing such different approaches to the truth.

Some years later, there was another meeting, of a sort, between the philosopher and the Sufi. Ibn-Rushd had died while in Morocco; and as ibn-Arabi happened to be there too, he accompanied the body back to Spain for burial. The casket was placed on one side of a donkey's back, and, to provide balance, a large bulk of the philosopher's writings were placed on the other. As he walked along, ibn-Arabi reflected on the irony that this great intellectual labor had come to such a final purpose. It is clear that he respected the philosopher but nevertheless found his purely rationalistic way inadequate. Ibn-Arabi was not one to hurl charges of apostasy at the philosophers. His concern was only whether their way really led our hearts to God.

In his thirties, ibn-Arabi left Spain for good, drawn to the Islamic heartland in the Middle East and, especially, to Mecca. He was deeply moved by the Kaaba and performed the rituals of the pilgrimage many times. In Mecca he stayed with a learned Iranian shaikh and fell in love with the shaikh's daughter, Nizam, a young woman of extraordinary beauty and intelligence. The love poems he wrote in her honor stirred much criticism, as some accused him of abandoning the Sufi way for sensual love. Ibn-Arabi vehemently denied this charge, and we will shortly examine just what he said in his own defense. In any case, it is quite certain that his relationship with Nizam was never other than what we call "Platonic."

Ibn-Arabi was somewhat less inclined than Suhrawardi to develop his thought in a philosophical framework, and so the bulk of his work consists in ecstatic, visionary statements rather than clear formulations. Nonetheless, he did attempt to give some logical account of his ideas. The paramount principle is *unity of being*, meaning that there is just a single being, God. There is no creation existing apart from God. The entire universe, including ourselves, is just God's self-manifestation.

The term *pantheism* is often applied to ibn-Arabi's philosophy. Pantheism is, literally, the teaching that God is everything, i.e., that God is simply identical with the world in its entirety. Is ibn-Arabi a pantheist, then? Yes and No, as he would say. God certainly is infinitely more than this world we see around us, and yet this world is an integral part of His being. Here is what this means with regard to the phenomenon of prophecy:

> None sees Him other than He. His prophet is He, and His sending is He, and His word is
> He. He sent Himself with Himself to Himself. (quoted from Nasr, *Three Muslim Sages*,
> p. 107)

Thus, what the uninitiated see as God's relation to His creatures is really just the manifestation of successive phases of God's own being. Above all, this is true of love. In every act of love, God is the lover, the beloved and the loving itself. This is precisely what ibn-Arabi wanted to be understood about his relationship with Nizam. He loved her because he saw God in her, and it was God in him that felt and expressed this love.

The underlying purpose of all this, as in Suhrawardi's case, was to make some sense of the experience of fana. Ibn-Arabi philosophized about the unity of being because that is what his Sufic experiences presented to him. He readily acknowledged that his words fell far short of expressing those experiences. Accordingly, he entreated his readers to bear this in mind when confronted with apparently contradictory or unorthodox statements. The luminous sincerity of his life and writing has been a powerful factor in attracting followers to his philosophy, though, as mentioned, he has also had many severe critics.

9. Ibn-Khaldun: The Reflective Historian

Ibn-Khaldun of Tunis (1332–1406) stands apart from all the thinkers we have previously considered. He was most certainly not a philosopher in the sense of the word that he and his fellow Muslims employed. Nor was he a Theologian or a Sufi, though he held these endeavors in much more esteem than philosophy. His great achievement lies in theorizing about the basic patterns and forces in history. In this respect, he stands comparison to the most eminent Western philosophers of history, such as Saint Augustine and Hegel.

He spent most of his adult life in the service of various petty rulers in North Africa. All pretense of unity in the Muslim world was long since departed by his time, and ibn-Khaldun's own career gave him abundant evidence of how chaotic the political life of Islam had become. These experiences provided the motivation to reflect on history so as to understand how things had come to such a sorry state. Amid his official duties, he struggled to find time for his scholarly activities. His most famous work is *al-Muqaddimah*, the "Introduction" to world history. It is an extremely broad-ranging work, as ibn-Khaldun's interests extend far beyond the usual details of dynasties and wars. He is concerned with all the cultural phenomena which emerge in the course of history, including philosophy.

Ibn-Khaldun had an extremely negative opinion of philosophy. It had no usefulness, in his view, other than a certain capacity to sharpen one's power of logical reasoning. In seeing philosophy as a menace to religious faith, he closely followed the views of al-Ghazali, a thinker for whom he had unreserved admiration. And yet there is another aspect to his criticism of the philosophers which is more interesting. The criticism has a distinctly modern character to it in condemning speculative philosophy for going beyond the limits of experience. This is precisely how "positivist" philosophers in the West have been chastising metaphysics for well over a century.

Here is his explicit assessment of philosophy's attempt to transcend the material world into the domain of spirit:

We cannot perceive the spiritual essences, and abstract further essences from them, because the senses constitute a veil between us and them. We have, thus, no logical arguments for them...Competent philosophers have clearly said so, because it is a condition of logical arguments that their premises must involve essences. [Here ibn Khaldun boldly—and dubiously—cites the great Plato as his authority.] ...If after all the philosophers' toil and troubles, we find only conjectures, then what use does their discipline have? For one can always make conjectures. (al-Muqaddimah, Chapter VI, Section 30)

The empiricist tenor of ibn-Khaldun's thought is confirmed in the very next section of this work when he proceeds to criticize astrology in much the same manner. This was an era when that particular study still enjoyed enormous prestige among the learned. It is quite remarkable to find ibn-Khaldun directing against the astrologers many of the same charges that modern science has made. He sees the whole theory of astral influences as unverifiable conjecture.

On the other hand, ibn-Khaldun is far more indulgent toward the Sufis. He does not condemn *their* bold speculation. Nor does he dwell on harm they might do to religious belief, as he does with both the philosophers and the astrologers. He benevolently notes that Sufism has to do with things that are beyond human expression. Therefore, we must not be too upset at strange things they may say. (See Chapter VI, Sect. 16.) Ibn-Khaldun's attitude is clearly a tribute to the honored position that Sufism had won for itself in the Muslim world, in spite of unorthodox appearances.

As indicated, the subject which truly interested ibn-Khaldun was history. He brooded over the rise and fall of empires, like ancient Rome and like the mighty regimes which had emerged earlier in the history of Islam. Each empire began with vigor and confidence; but eventually it perished, mocking the pride of its founders. There was a pattern to all this, a cycle of flourishing and decline, which was beyond human control.

While ibn-Khaldun certainly believed that God was the ultimate ordainer of this pattern, he identified more observable factors as the immediate causes. The great empire builders, like the early Romans and the Arabs of Muhammad's time were simple, uncultured peoples. Often, like the Arabs, they came out of a harsh desert environment. This gave them a strength and a unity of purpose by which they could conquer established civilizations. But with this conquest came luxury and leisure. The conquerors no longer cherished martial valor above all else, and they turned to more refined pursuits. In this manner they gradually weakened themselves. Their unity was shattered as they divided their energies and loyalties among competing cultural movements. Thus, the way was prepared for the next great wave of conquest.

The entire process had almost a tragic character. Ibn-Khaldun valued the achievements of civilization. But in his view they came at the price of political weakness. The noblest cultural attainments of humanity were, at the same time, symptoms of decay. He saw no way to reverse or prevent this process, for it was founded in the very nature of man.

The empiricist nature of ibn-Khaldun's thought is again evident here. His theory was based, not on speculative flights, but on detailed knowledge of dozens of regimes, especially in the Muslim world, which had undergone this cycle. The governing principle of this cycle was simply human inability to combine the virtues of action and thought, that is, to simultaneously be strong and wise.

It is quite a different way of looking at history than what we find in St. Augustine (354-430), Tunisia's other great gift to philosophy. In his masterwork, the *City of God*, Augustine too contemplated the fall of empires; but he saw it as the consequence of sinful human pride. For him the religious perspective completely dominated the interpretation of history: God's judgment throwing down those towers which man's selfishness and arrogance had built. By contrast, ibn-Khaldun saw the course of history with melancholy resignation rather than righteous anger. He scrutinized the past with patient observation rather than theological deduction. His approach might even be considered *scientific*, and that accounts for the fact that he, of all the thinkers considered in this section, has attracted the most interest and admiration in the modern West.

REVIEW QUESTIONS ON ISLAMIC PHILOSOPHY

1. Describe the religious environment in which Muhammad was brought up. Why did he rebel against this?

2. Describe Muhammad's calling to be a prophet. How did he initially react? What happened when he began to preach his new ideas to the people of Mecca?

3. What is the Kaaba, and what was Muhammad's attitude toward it?

4. What does the word *Koran* actually mean, and how did the book known by that name come into being?

5. What was the Hegira, and how did this fundamentally change the situation for the Muslim community?

6. Explain the controversy that arose in Islam about who should be the "successor" of Muhammad. Why could no one truly be his successor?

7. Describe the conquests of the early khalifs. How were they justified? What policy was adopted toward the religions of the conquered peoples?

8. Discuss the concept of God (Allah) presented in the Koran.

9. Who were the Ulama, and what has been their role in the history of Islam?

10. What is the Islamic concept of prophecy? What makes Muhammad so special in relation to all the other prophets?

11. What do Muslims believe about Jesus?

12. How does the Koran depict the Last Judgment and the events preceding it?

13. What is the meaning of the term *jihad*? How does today's world differ from that in earlier times when Muslims practiced jihad in the form of holy war?

14. Discuss the place of women which is ordained by Islamic law.

15. What is the Mutazilite view on the unity of God? Why did the Asharites object to this?

16. What is predestination? Explain the conflicting positions which the Mutazilites and Asharites took on this matter.

17. What was the role of the ancient Greek philosophers in shaping Muslim philosophy? What did the first Muslim philosopher, al-Kindi, say about making use of foreign sources?

18. Give the main events of the story of Hayy. What lessons did the Muslim philosophers draw from it?

19. Explain al-Farabi's account of the physical universe and the intellects which rule over it. What is God's involvement in all this?

20. What is the Active Intellect in Aristotle's thought? Explain the various special roles it plays in al-Farabi's philosophy.

21. How did ibn-Sina use the concepts of essence and existence to prove the existence of God and to define the special nature of God? Explain how ibn-Sina's "vertical" proof differs from the "horizontal" proof of God. Why does ibn-Sina reject the latter?

22. Explain the three doctrines which, in al-Ghazali's view, made the Muslim philosophers guilty of apostasy. Which one raises the most serious issue, and why?

23. Why was there such an irreconcilable difference between Ghazali and the Philosophers in their views of God?

24. How does Ghazali argue that there is a fundamental problem with the concept of causality? What is his own final view about the causation of events in this world?

25. How did ibn-Rushd "purify" the Aristotelianism in the work of his philosophic predecessors?

26. How did ibn-Rushd defend the Philosophers against Ghazali's charge of apostasy?

27. How did ibn-Rushd respond to Ghazali's critique of the concept of causality?

28. What was the basic motivation of the Sufis? How was this expressed in their way of life, their methods and their ultimate goal?

29. What is mystical experience? Why is it so difficult for the human mind to grasp? Why is it thought to lead to fana (annihilation), and why do the Sufis welcome this?

30. Explain how al-Suhrawardi made use of Plato's thought. What was the role of *light* in his philosophy?

31. Discuss the issue of whether ibn-Arabi can be considered a pantheist.

32. What common faults does ibn-Khaldun find in philosophy and astrology? Contrast his appraisal of these with his attitude toward the Sufis.

33. What is ibn-Khaldun's theory about the rise and fall of empires? Contrast his view with the one advanced a thousand years earlier by his fellow Tunisian, St. Augustine.

II. INDIA

I. GAUTAMA THE BUDDHA

The man who is known to the world as "the Buddha" was born in what is presently Nepal about 560 BC. More so than in the case of Muhammad, his life-story has become encrusted with pious exaggerations and fantasies, so it not easy to discern Buddha the man. The name *Buddha* is actually a title meaning "enlightened one." His given name was *Siddhartha*, while *Gautama* is a clan name. In the Buddhist literature one often sees Buddha referred to as *Shakyamuni* (sage of the Shakyas, his tribe).

It is known that Gautama was born into the powerful caste of the kshatriyas, the hereditary holders of political authority. His mother died in childbirth. His father, Suddhodana, was a man of considerable wealth and influence in the tribal republic of the Shakyas. These tribal republics are a significant feature of early Indian history. While some parts of India had become kingdoms, Gautama's own Shakyas had formed a republic. This is not to be taken in the modern sense of the word. It means only that the Shakyas did not accord power to a single ruler. The entire ruling caste of kshatriyas would decide matters in periodic assemblies.

Gautama was thus brought up in circumstances of luxury and privilege. There was not much in these early years to indicate his religious nature. As a kshatriya, he was not *supposed* to have any special involvement with religion. That was the responsibility of the brahmins, the priestly caste who knew the complex rituals around which Indian religion then centered.

Until he was about twenty-five, Gautama's life unfolded in a predictable way. A marriage was arranged for him, and he lived happily with his beautiful bride in his father's sumptuous household. They had a son, and Gautama busied himself learning those things which were required of a leader in society.

Then, unexpectedly, he was plunged into spiritual crisis. It was all the more surprising because there was no extraordinary occurrence which brought it on. Buddhist legend tells of a series of simple experiences which induced the crisis. First, Gautama saw a man afflicted with severe disease, his body covered with ugly sores. Another day he saw an aged man, withered and feeble. Finally, he saw a funeral procession carrying a corpse to the cremation ground. Such things he must have seen many times before, but now they struck him with a new impact.

Powerful, disturbing emotions welled up in the young aristocrat's soul. He was moved to pity for the plight of those he saw. But it was not only pity. Gautama understood that he himself was subject to these forms of suffering which he had observed. He had many privileges as a kshatriya, but he did not have immunity from illness, old age or grief at the loss of a loved one. Above all, he had no immunity from death itself.

His mind had already fastened onto what would be the central problem in the Buddhist religion: suffering. Many would say that Gautama was unduly sensitive, showing the effects of his sheltered upbringing. To Gautama himself, his present plight was just the result of seriously reflecting on matters which he had previously ignored. He was, in any case, filled with a deep depression. All his zest for life was gone. Neither his father, nor his wife, nor his baby son could shake him out of it. He could not put out of mind the thought that, as we have our enjoyments, so much suffering is taking place in the rest of the world. And there was the further realization that these very enjoyments will eventually taken away from us by the vicissitudes of life.

For weeks Gautama continued in his depressed, listless state. Then he had another experience which shook him out if it. Like the others, it was nothing out of the ordinary; even today it may still be commonly seen in India. What Gautama saw was a wandering ascetic, a holy man who had given up home and possessions to go about as a beggar. This man embodied the solution to the problem which had been obsessing Gautama. Sickness, old age and death could not harm the ascetic. In a physical sense, of course, he was as subject to them as the next person. But through his renunciation of the world, he had trained himself not to care about them. For the ascetic, it no longer mattered whether he was healthy or sick, young or old, alive or dead. He had *liberated* himself from those concerns and was at peace.

Gautama was now convinced that the path of renunciation was the only solution. He returned home and prepared to set out on an ascetic's life, giving up all the wealth and privilege of his position. When his father, Suddhodana, learned what was afoot, he was shocked and enraged. To this point, he had been a very indulgent father, proud of his son and eager to fulfill his every desire. Now his expectation that Gautama would follow him in the illustrious way of a kshatriya was shattered.

The basis for Suddhodana's strong feelings must be clearly appreciated. To him it was not the life of an ascetic as such that was abhorrent. Such individuals were already common in India at that time and were treated with much respect by the populace. What disturbed him was that his son wished to take up this life at so young an age. The traditional Indian conception holds that this is appropriate in the final stage of life. More precisely, this traditional view distinguishes four stages (or *ashrams*) in life: learner, householder, forest-dweller, ascetic. One *must* pass through the first three before proceeding to the fourth.

The stage of learner is simply childhood. In this stage all the responsibilities of one's place in society must be mastered. Then, in the householder's ashram, one carries out these responsibilities. This, naturally, is also the time for marrying and raising a family. When the children are grown, a man may retire (with his wife) into some secluded forest dwelling to concentrate on the spiritual development that has been neglected amid the many duties of a householder. The end of the forest-dweller stage is not marked off so clearly as with the first two, but there is a strong sense that a least a few years must be spent in that ashram.

The ascetic differs from all the others in having completely cut family ties. He sends home his wife and thenceforth has no contact with her or other relatives. He no longer has even his humble forest-dwelling to call home. Family and home are the sources of attachment. They are an inducement to clinging which will only bring sorrow in the end. Thus, the ascetic wanders about, free of those fetters which bind the rest of us.

Suddhodana was distressed at his son's refusal to follow tradition. Abandonment of the householder stage (which Gautama had really just begun) was the main problem. The householder is the basis of society. In one way or another, he provides the support of the other three ashrams. How could society continue, Suddhodana asked, if young men left their families and positions to become ascetics?

His son's answer was very simple. The continuation of society does not *matter*. Life in this world brings no real happiness or security, so nothing is gained by preserving human society. The only hope lies in going forth from one's home, renouncing all that we cling to.

In this confrontation of father and son, a basic feature of Buddha's religion was being articulated. The prevailing Hindu religion gave its sanction to the whole system of distinct castes by which people were divided and defined. In addition to Gautama's own caste of the ruling kshatriyas, there were also the priestly brahmins, whose honor was even greater. And beneath the kshatriyas were the vaishyas, who filled the various crafts and professions, and the shudras, who were peasant farmers. In Hinduism, these four castes (or *varnas*) were the essential components of a divinely ordained social order. Each person must faithfully carry out the duties of the caste in which he has been born. Foremost among these duties is raising a family so that the caste can be continued into the next generation.

Gautama was quite prepared to turn his back on all this. Sustaining the social order was not, in his view, a goal of commanding importance. The duties of a kshatriya were just another source of bondage and clinging. Along with other human ties, they must be set aside by the one who is truly determined to make an end of his suffering in this world. In the remainder of his career, Gautama never departed from his opposition to the restrictions of the caste system.

He was quite settled, then, in his decision to go forth. He eagerly put aside the privileges of a kshatriya and took to the road as a beggar. As already indicated, Gautama was not unique in this quest. The roads of India were clogged with holy men, preachers and eccentrics of every description. We must pause now to consider some of these and to describe the society which had spawned them.

Indian civilization had first arisen some 2000 years before Gautama's time in the valley of the Indus river. This ancient Indus civilization achieved a very high level of material culture, with splendidly constructed cities joined in a vast empire (comprising most of modern Pakistan, and beyond). The religion of the Indus civilization is hard to make out from its material remains, but one crucial truth can be known with certainty. The physical and mental disciplines of yoga were practiced. This can be seen from depictions of the god Shiva in the standard yogic posture of the lotus. Nothing has had greater effect than yoga in shaping Indian philosophy and religion, and we will consider it in detail later on.

Around 1500 B.C. the Indus civilization was overwhelmed by invaders from the northwest. These invaders, the Aryans, were a nomadic people who had no use for cities. The Indus civilization was buried and forgotten (though somehow yoga was preserved). Gautama's life, a thousand years later, came at a time when civilization had again taken root in India. This time its center was Ganges River valley. Here, vast tracts of forest were cleared to yield land of extraordinary fertility. Intensive agriculture supported the growth of cities, and these cities fostered the growth of complex political institutions. Tribal republics, such as that of the Shakyas which had nurtured Gautama, were one example. Kingdoms, featuring the authoritarian rule of one man, were another.

It was not a time of political stability. Wars continually raged as the various republics and kingdoms jockeyed for advantage. One political theorist called it the *matsyayana* (the way of the fishes): the bigger gobbling up the smaller with no principle of justice governing. The republics steadily lost ground, and eventually one of the kingdoms managed to establish itself as an empire over most of India— this was the Maurya Empire, about 300 B.C.

This outcome was not yet apparent in Gautama's time, and the political situation seemed to promise nothing but continued instability. In a period when so many were displaced and dispossessed, the ascetics' message of renunciation naturally had great appeal. These ascetics, as mentioned, showed quite a diversity of beliefs and practices. There were the Jains, who went about naked and practiced harsh austerities to free the soul from the body. There were the Ajivakas, who believed that all souls were moving toward the same predetermined fate, without any capacity to change or hasten it. There were a group whom Gautama referred to as the "Eel-wrigglers." They were notable for their refusal to take any position, wriggling out of any view one might try to attribute to them. These, and many others, crossed paths with Gautama in his long years of wandering.

Standing in contrast to these ascetics were the brahmin priesthood. They were and are the representatives of the dominant religion, Hinduism. They primarily devoted themselves to mastering and performing a vast body of rituals. These rituals, which were steeped in mystery, had supposedly the power to bring beneficial effects in this life and the next. At the same time, the brahmins were closely associated with the holders of political power everywhere. They placed their religious authority behind the existing social order and political institutions.

By and large, there was little love between the ascetics and the brahmins. The latter thought of the former as heretics, and the former thought the brahmins nothing but blind, greedy pillars of conventional religion. But, remarkably enough, the call to renunciation was sometimes felt even among the brahmins. In Gautama's time brahmin ascetics were still rare, but, partly from his influence, they were destined to become ever more important.

What practically all the ascetics had in common—whether brahmin or non-brahmin—was a yearning for the liberation of the soul. They believed that each soul was caught up in an endless process of reincarnation called *samsara*. A soul's reincarnation would be determined by the degree of moral merit and spiritual purity it had reached in the previous life. Depending on these, it might reincarnate in any caste and as either sex. It might even sink to the level of an animal or rise to that of a god. But whatever reincarnation was attained, it lasted for only the duration of one life. Much like the political state of Indian society, samsara offered no stability. Souls rose and fell in the scale of life as their present merits dictated.

To the ascetics samsara was futility. They wished to make their souls free of it. They wished to be able to die and *not* to come back to this universe in any form. How, if at all, this might be accomplished was a matter of intense debate, as was the question of precisely what mode of existence was to be enjoyed by those who *had* liberated their souls.

Gautama thus faced quite a range of possibilities as he embarked on the quest for his own liberation. In keeping with the usual practice, he desired to find a spiritual master, a guru. But none of the ascetics he sought out satisfied him, so he remained largely on his own. He did find the Jain disciplines appealing and applied himself to them with vigor. Recall that the Jain way was one of severe physical deprivation. It was necessary to withhold from oneself food, sleep and physical comfort. One would push the body to the limit of its endurance, so that the soul would no longer be beholden to the body's needs.

Over many months, Gautama practiced these disciplines, bringing himself to the brink of starvation. Ultimately, he found them ineffective for the peace that he was seeking. Later, after his enlightenment, he formulated his experience with Jainism in the doctrine of the Middle Way. The correct path, he said, lies between the extremes of self-indulgence and self-torture. The latter is indeed more noble than the former, but it does not lead to liberation. The discipline is too much focused on the body, failing to see that the mind is the key to tranquillity and happiness.

From the day that he gave up the Jain practices, Gautama saw much more clearly the path that he must follow. Constantly, he sought to purge his mind of the delusions that govern everyday life. He vigilantly observed his own mental processes in order to understand and get control of the emotions and lusts that would still well up in him. At last he reached the verge of enlightenment.

He was now about thirty-five years old. Determined to clear away the last vestiges of ignorance and bondage, he sat down under a tree late one evening and resolved that he would not sleep until he saw the full truth. Thus Gautama's enlightenment came to him late that night (at just about the time that Gabriel first came to Muhammad). From that moment he was indeed the Buddha, the enlightened one. He had gained his *nirvana*, which is literally *extinction:* that is, the extinction of all feeling and desire which could bind him to this world. For Gautama the Buddha it was now guaranteed that when he died, his soul would not come back to this world.

In the peace and illumination of nirvana, one matter still was not entirely clear to Buddha. What was he to do with this enlightenment? Could he teach it to others?

BUDDHA FROM SARNATH, INDIA

An image of Buddha, from Sarnath, in East Central India. Though produced a thousand years after his lifetime, it surely is a more authentic depiction than the more familiar images of Buddha which originate from outside India. Buddha's hands are in a gesture of teaching, but what the image most clearly expresses is the perfect repose of nirvana. [Air India Library]

Or would he continue to live a solitary existence, enjoying his own release from suffering? After some hesitation, he concluded that it was his destiny to be a guide and an inspiration for others. He could not express in words the profundity of enlightenment, but he could direct others so that they might see it for themselves.

Gautama made his way to Banaras, then as now the holiest of Indian cities. There he began, as Buddhists phrase it, to put the wheel of Dharma (Truth) in motion. To all who would listen, he preached the lessons that had been won in his own spiritual struggle. He proclaimed the teaching of the Middle Way, which we have already discussed. Then he enunciated the famous Four Noble Truths:

> This is the noble truth of suffering. Birth is suffering, sickness is suffering, old age is suffering, death is suffering, sorrow, lamentation dejection and despair are suffering. Contact with painful things is suffering, not getting what one desires is suffering.
>
> This is the noble truth of the cause of suffering: that craving which leads to rebirth, combined with pleasure and lust, finding pleasure here and there, the craving for passion, the craving for existence, the craving for non-existence.
>
> The is the noble truth of the cessation of suffering: the cessation without a remainder of that craving, abandonment, forsaking, release, non-attachment.
>
> This is the noble truth of the way that leads to the cessation of suffering: the noble Eightfold Path, namely, right views, right intention, right speech, right action, right livelihood, right effort, right mindfulness, right concentration. (*Samyutta-nikaya*, v. 420, quoted from Radhakrishnan, *Sourcebook*, pp.274–75)

These truths are not difficult to understand. They were meant by Buddha to be intelligible to a wide audience. First, there is the truth of suffering, which had been Gautama's focus since the beginning of his spiritual life. The truth of suffering expresses the conviction, not merely that suffering is a part of life, but that it is pervasive and overwhelming. It is foolish to hope for better fortune, or even to hope that one may have a happy life in a future reincarnation. Only the most radical approach can address this consuming problem.

Buddha proceeds in the Second Truth to take up the issue of cause. He very much sees himself as a physician of the soul. Having diagnosed the malady of suffering, he now must identify its origin. Craving—our passionate, desperate craving—is the cause. If we did not have such yearning for things, they would not be able make us suffer.

From this the cure of suffering is evident, as the Third Truth states: we must abandon our cravings and then suffering will be no more. There is then the question of how we can be released from our cravings. The Fourth Truth states that the Eightfold Path will accomplish that purpose. This Truth is not so lucid as the first three, for it enumerates the various categories of "right" without explaining what they consist in.

It would, indeed, require quite a lengthy discussion to explain them, and Buddha surely knew what he was doing in deferring this to later sermons. For us it must suffice to note that the final two—right mindfulness and right concentration— are the most important. By the first of these Buddha meant the process of controlling and directing the mind in order to be aware of the world's true nature and of our own mental life. By the second he meant the deep and illuminating trance that one would attain with sufficient mastery of the mind.

In this way Buddha began a highly successful career as a religious preacher. Eventually, he made tens of thousands of converts to his own distinctive path, which came to be called Buddhism. Though he continued to lead the life of a wandering ascetic, he acquired an entourage of devoted followers. To be sure, he also encountered hostility, from rival ascetics and from brahmin priests.

It is very important to comprehend Buddha's own attitude to his evangelizing activities. Having already reached nirvana, there was absolutely nothing he needed for his own happiness. He therefore had no emotional involvement in his preaching. To say it quite bluntly, he did not care whether anyone followed him or not. He looked upon the rest of mankind with a detached compassion. He clearly saw their plight and was willing to aid them; but he also saw, plainly and calmly, that his guidance would not be heeded by many. It is a profound contrast to Muhammad. The Koran makes it very clear (through Allah's words of comfort to him) how heartsick he was when the people of Mecca rejected his call. He desperately wanted his listeners to heed him and give up their pagan ways.

There is another remarkable feature of Buddha's religious career. That is the very public nature of his teaching. The normal way of a religious teacher (a guru) in India is to impart teachings in private to a few carefully selected students. Buddha, on the other hand, went into the marketplaces and proclaimed his ideas to all. As we will discuss more fully, many of his ideas were not new. They were already part of the spiritual environment. What *was* new was Buddha's willingness to disseminate these ideas to the whole populace.

The caste system had already taken a strong hold in India, and this led to a widespread belief that the lower groups must keep their places. They were expected to carry out their own menial functions and leave higher matters— especially spiritual ones—to their betters. This particularly applied to the outcastes, commonly known as *untouchables*. There were deemed to be inherently unclean and stood far below the four regular, "official" varnas (brahmins, kshatiryas, vaishyas, shudras). Buddha, who had gladly set aside his own caste duty, showed no respect for the distinctions of caste. He preached to all and welcomed all into his religion.

He displayed a similar liberality in regard to gender distinction. Traditional Indian thought held that a woman's highest religious calling was to be a good wife. Even women in the brahmin caste had no religious standing, and female ascetics were almost unknown. Buddha asserted that both sexes had the capacity to reach the goal of nirvana in this present life. When he founded his monastic order, he made provision for both women and men. His essential idea is quite simple: all human beings, regardless of caste or sex, can and should seek liberation now.

Buddha meant his religious message to be accessible to all. We have already seen how he used the Four Noble Truths as a simple introduction to his teaching. Buddhism called, in the first place, for a sound moral life, free of greed and deception. *Ahimsa,* the principle of respect for all living things, was also central. Buddha wanted his followers to be strict vegetarians and to refrain from any activity which involved the taking of life, human or animal.

Beyond morality, what Buddha required was insight into the nature of the world and into our own being. Through careful training of the mind, we can understand and thus reverse harmful processes that normally take place without even being noticed. This is most clearly expressed in the teaching known as the Wheel of Becoming. In its complete version, the Wheel has twelve elements, but we may for simplicity's sake condense them to four.

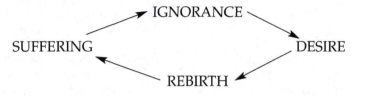

Ignorance is the most fundamental component of the Wheel. From it all other problems stem. Above all, the presence of desire in the soul is founded on our lack of knowledge. If we knew better the nature of what is desired, then desire would be dissipated. But we are in ignorance, and so desire thrives in the soul. This desire propels the soul to seek new reincarnation, and upon such rebirth, all the various forms of worldly suffering surge up. As a result of suffering, the mind is filled with consternation, and its ignorance is reinforced.

Thus, it is a vicious circle but not an altogether hopeless one. By a proper discipline of the mind, ignorance can be rooted out. Then it becomes a wheel of liberation rather than bondage, as desire, rebirth and suffering are done away with. The wheel is the most powerful image in Buddhism, every bit as significant as the cross in Christianity. As mentioned, the beginning of Buddha's teaching career is described as the turning of the wheel of Dharma.

In all his years of teaching, Buddha never proclaimed himself to be God or the messenger of God. Indeed, he denied the existence of God (in the sense of a Supreme Being). This is a very surprising feature of his teaching, since many are accustomed to think that religion necessarily involves belief in a Deity. To Buddha such belief is not merely wrong but quite harmful. It focuses on a higher being to the detriment of our own self-realization. The nature of nirvana is such that it cannot be bestowed on us by any external power. It is only to be attained through the exertion and spiritual capacities of each individual person.

Buddha saw himself solely as a teacher. He could not actually save others; he could only show them how to save themselves. There is a profound contrast here between him and Jesus Christ. For Christians, Jesus is essentially the *Savior*. Christians attain salvation *through him*, not through any merit or ability of their own. A pair of episodes illustrate this contrast very clearly. First, from the Gospel of Luke:

Jesus went to the town of Nain. His disciples and a large crowd were accompanying him. As he reached the town gate, there was a funeral procession coming out. The dead man was the only son of a widow, and many people from the city were with her. When the Lord saw her, his heart was filled with pity and he said to her, "Do not cry." Then he walked over and touched the coffin, and the men carrying it stopped. Jesus said, "Young man! Get up, I tell you!" The dead man sat up and began to talk, and Jesus gave him back to his mother. (Chapter 7, verses 11–15)

Now from the Buddhist Scriptures:

A woman named Gotami had lost her baby son, and she was overwhelmed by her grief. She could not accept the reality of the boy's death and was carrying him about, crying "Give me medicine for my baby!" Some tried reasoning with her, but no one could convince her of the hopelessness of the situation. Finally, someone suggested that she go see the Buddha who was in a nearby town.

On seeing him, Gotami repeated her plea for medicine. To the onlookers' surprise. He seemed to agree to her request. "I will prepare the medicine you seek," he said, "but you must get an ingredient which I need. Bring me a single mustard seed which comes from a household which has never experienced death."

Without pausing to consider the nature of this request, Gotami rushed forth to get the seed. She went from one door to another, asking whether there had been a death in that house. Each time she was told there had been, and she soon realized the truth of the matter. Death is universal and inescapable; we are wrong to become emotionally dependent on that which can die.

She returned to the Buddha and told him, "The mustard seed has done its work." Then she entered the Buddhist monastic order and soon afterward attained her enlightenment. (adapted from *The Teachings of the Compassionate Buddha*, pp. 43–6)

Each story portrays how a mother's bereavement is overcome, but there the resemblance ends. Jesus performs a miracle. It is simultaneously a manifestation of *His* divine power and our helplessness. The nameless mother can do nothing but weep. Jesus alone, with his loving kindness and divine power, can save the situation. Buddha, by contrast, displays no supernatural power. Nor does he even undertake to tell Gotami what she needs to know. Rather he causes her to proceed in such a way that she sees it *for herself.*

The Buddha spent some forty-five years in his career as a preacher of this new religion. He was clearly a charismatic figure who inspired many, like Gotami, to follow his path. But there is something more, in addition to doctrine and personal magnetism, which enabled Buddhism to become a thriving religion, both within India and beyond. This was the institution of the *sangha*, the monastic order. By virtue of the sangha, Buddha's teachings acquired a strong and enduring organization which would preserve them.

The origins of the sangha were in the prosaic fact of weather. For several months each year, the rainy season comes to India. In ancient times this made travel nearly impossible. Ascetics had to bring a temporary halt to their wanderings. Buddha and his entourage would need a place to stay for the duration of the rains. Through the kindness of certain wealthy Buddhist devotees, such places—

monasteries— were provided. They became centers of a vigorous communal life of spirituality.

Buddha understood perfectly well that large numbers of people residing together would need an elaborate body of regulations so that they might function productively and harmoniously. Thus he introduced rules (known as *vinaya*) for the monastic order. There were separate establishments for the male and female monks (*bhikkus* and *bhikkunis*). Eventually (after Buddha's death) monasteries became year-round residences. The monks would still go out daily to beg for their food, but they were no longer homeless as in the days of old.

The occasion of Buddha's death is one on which the Buddhist scriptures particularly dwell. This is known to Buddhists as his *parinirvana*, the completion of nirvana. Buddha had already assured his final escape from this world at the time of his enlightenment, but now, with his demise, came the consummation of that achievement. It can be said that, in the manner of his death, Buddha was able to reaffirm the meaning of his entire life. The following is an especially famous and moving account:

> When the Blessed One had taken up his abode for the rainy season, there fell upon him a severe and painful sickness such that death was near. But, calmly and with full awareness, he bore it without complaint. Then this thought occurred to him: "It would not be right for me to pass away from life without speaking one more time to the members of the monastic order. Let me now, by a strong effort of the will, bend this sickness down again and keep hold of life until the allotted time has come."
>
> And so the Blessed One did this, and the sickness abated. And then he went outside and sat on a mat which had been spread out. The venerable Ananda [who had been his disciple from the earliest days] approached and greeted him and took a seat nearby.
>
> Ananda said, "I have beheld, master, your illness and suffering. I could hardly stand up and my sight was dimmed and my mind clouded. Nevertheless, I took some comfort from the thought that you would not depart without leaving some final instructions for us."
>
> The Blessed One then replied, "What is expected of me then, Ananda? I have preached the truth without making any distinction of public teaching and secret teaching. For in respect of the truth, I have no such thing as the closed fist of a teacher who keeps some things back . . ."
>
> He continued, "I am now grown old, Ananda, and full of years. My journey is drawing to its close, as I reach eighty years of age. Just as a worn-out cart can only with much difficulty be made to move along, so my body can only be kept going with much additional care. Only when, ceasing to attend to any outward thing, I am absorbed in that deep meditation which has no bodily object—only then is my body at ease. Therefore, Ananda, you must all be lamps to yourselves. Rely on yourselves, and do not rely on external help. Hold fast to the truth as a lamp. Seek salvation only in the truth. Do not look for assistance to anyone besides yourselves." (quoted from *The Teachings of the Compassionate Buddha*, pp. 48–9)

Clearly, these last words were something of a rebuke to Ananda and to all those who would give Buddha a superhuman status. The entire account serves to emphasize his humanity, showing him with the frailties that any other eighty-year-old would face. Most importantly, the story reaffirms the call for diligent effort and self-reliance which we saw in the story of Gotami.

In death, Buddha left his followers with one nagging question. It was a question which they had pressed on him many times previously, long before the parinirvana. What precisely became of Buddha, what would become of any liberated person at death? By definition nirvana meant the cessation of life in this world. Would Buddha be in some kind of heaven, then? Clearly not, for heaven, in the Buddhist view, was only an improved version of earthly existence—improved, but far from perfect.

The real question became: would Buddha exist at all after his parinirvana? Never did Buddha answer this question, though it was ever so often asked of him. He maintained a resolute silence on all inquiries about the nature of parinirvana. He used to give this analogy to explain his silence:

> Suppose a man to be wounded with a poisoned arrow. A doctor is brought to him, but the man will not let the arrow be removed. "I must first know the identity of the man who shot me," he demands. "What caste does he belong to? What village is he from? How old is he?" In such a way, the man would die, as the poison was absorbed into his body while he pursued these idle matters. (adapted from Sutta 63 of the *Majjhima Nikaya)*

One can appreciate his point: the need to focus on the cure for suffering and to avoid the distraction of incidental matters. Still, the question seemed an urgent and legitimate one. In any case, the question has never gone away, and Buddhists still debate the meaning of Buddha's silence in this matter.

II. AFTER THE BUDDHA

Buddha most certainly did succeed in setting the wheel of dharma in motion. The dedicated core of followers whom he had assembled in the sangha provided the impetus for further growth, and Buddhism flourished for many centuries in India. Before long, missionaries began to carry Buddha's gospel to other lands. The island of Sri Lanka became a Buddhist stronghold (as it still is). What is now Afghanistan acquired a flourishing Buddhist community. China was ardently evangelized, and later, many other Asian countries.

In India itself the greatest time for Buddhism came, perhaps, with the reign of the emperor Ashoka, about 250 B.C. He was the third ruler in the Maurya dynasty, the first true Indian empire. By a series of vigorously-waged wars, his grandfather and father had created a domain that encompassed the whole heartland of India. Ashoka carried on in this tradition. Then suddenly, in the wake of a massive victory by which the empire was further enlarged, he experienced a change of heart. He was now consumed by the Buddhist principle of ahimsa and gave up the ways of war. He dedicated the rest of his long reign to governance with justice and tolerance. Throughout India there still stand the stone monuments which he caused to be erected. They are inscribed, not with his portrait, but with the moral and religious principles that he came to hold.

Inevitably, divisions arose within the Buddhist fold. Buddha had tried mightily to design rules for the sangha which would prevent bickering and dissension, but it is hardly a surprise that they could not enduringly achieve that purpose. Even in Ashoka's time, conflicts were already evident; and by about 200 B.C. Buddhism had separated into two sharply opposed wings, the Hinayana and the Mahayana. The Hinayana were dedicated to preserving Buddha's recorded doctrines and articulating them within a complete philosophical framework. The Mahayana had radically new teachings, which they believed to have been Buddha's real intent.

All the while this was happening, Buddhism's greatest adversary, Hinduism, retained its dominant position in Indian religious life. To define Hinduism is truly difficult. It has no definite founder or beginning, and within it the most extraordinary diversity of ideas about God, man and the world have flourished. There are two objects of faith which more or less distinguish Hindus: the Vedas and the caste system.

The Vedas are a large collection of holy scriptures, whose origins range from 1500 to 500 B.C. They include ecstatic hymns of praise to the gods, detailed analysis of religious ritual and deep philosophical discussions. They are considered to be revelations of absolute religious truth, possessing an authority like that of the Koran for Muslims. But as the contents of the Vedas are so much more diverse than those of the Koran, acceptance of the Vedas does not entail any particular theological belief.

We have already discussed the outlines of the system of caste or varna. From the Hindu standpoint this represented an established social order which was to be respected and preserved. By virtue of caste, people had their assigned roles in society, some to lead and others to serve. In the same way, men and women had their distinct roles. These divinely-ordained roles could not be set aside in the way that Buddha had done.

The most important aspect of the caste system was its conferral of religious authority on the brahmins. They enjoyed this status by hereditary right, but it is also the case that they were by far the best-educated group in India. Though some, like Buddha, might challenge their authority, it was accepted by the vast majority. However, the brahminical authority supported a great diversity of philosophical beliefs, for the brahmins themselves were a very diverse group. Some were ascetics, while others clung to the ancient rituals. A great many became secularized. That is, they gave up their priestly functions though retaining the prestige of their high-caste birth. These secular brahmins often played significant roles as advisors and ministers to the kshatriya kings.

Hinduism permeated ancient Indian life, as it still does. Its very diversity enabled it to adapt effectively to the challenges that presented themselves. Even in the reign of Ashoka, Buddhism did not seriously threaten Hindu dominance. Indeed, the Buddhist religion survived because it was able to take root beyond

India. Precisely because it was not so imbued with distinctively Indian customs, Buddhism was more "exportable." In India itself, Buddhism slowly dwindled away. By 1100 A.D. it was virtually extinct in the land of its birth, its once great monasteries in ruins.

The story of Indian philosophy, therefore, is primarily the story of Hindu philosophy. Two epochs may be distinguished in that story. There was the period of great visionary religious philosophies, and there was the period of the scholastic philosophies which systematized and rationalized the earlier visions. In each period there were orthodox (i.e., Hindu) teachings and non-orthodox (such as Buddha's). Vigorous controversy was the order of the day, as these philosophies clashed.

In the end, however, what the Indian philosophers agreed about is more important than their areas of disagreement. By Buddha's time a solid core of generally-accepted principles already existed. He probably did more than any other individual to disseminate these principles to India and the world. But before him there had been Jains, brahmin ascetics and others who believed much the same as was in the Four Noble Truths. These principles, though they have different origins, form a remarkably coherent and compelling set of ideas. We will now examine them in detail.

III. THE FOUR BASIC IDEAS OF INDIAN PHILOSOPHY

REINCARNATION. The notion that we may return to this world as another person or an animal is still one which strikes most people in the Western world as quite strange. If your friend confided to you that he or she had come to believe in reincarnation, you might even think you had cause to worry about this person's mental stability. Most of us need to make a real effort to appreciate this idea in the Indian context, to see it as Indians do: something utterly natural and in keeping with the order of the world.

The first and foremost condition for belief in reincarnation is recognition of the reality of the soul. By *soul* we mean an intangible entity which is distinct from the body and which somehow provides life to the body. It is natural to believe that the soul, as the very principle of life, cannot itself be subject to death. Of course, that is precisely what many religions and philosophies do believe in: an immortal soul which transcends this life and which expresses the essence of our being. What distinguishes Indian belief is the notion that the soul's destiny lies on this earth rather than in some otherworldly heaven or hell. Heavens and hells are not absent from Indian belief, but they provide nothing more than temporary stays between reincarnations.

Indian philosophy holds that the soul, having left this world at death, is drawn back for reincarnation. There is a cycle of birth and death—samsara—which endlessly repeats. A particular body is in no way essential for the soul. It is only a temporary habitation, mere clothing which the soul wears out and then casts off. The idea (in other religions) that the soul would permanently reunite with its body in the afterlife is considered nonsensical. Any given body has only a brief, almost accidental, association with the soul.

Just when the idea of reincarnation became so entrenched in Indian thought, and why, is hard to say. Certainly, by Buddha's time, it was entrenched. Yoga (to be discussed in detail shortly) may well hold the clue the origin of reincarnationist belief in India. An ancient Vedic text speaks of yogis in the state of trance: "Our yoga has taken us beyond ourselves—thus we are able to ride the winds. You mortals behold our bodies and no more." (Rig Veda, X, 136)

This passage indicates that when a yogi sat down and went into trance, the body became an empty shell. The soul was liberated from the body and could freely roam the world, or "ride the winds." At the end of the trance, the body would come alive again as the soul re-entered it. We see quite a strong suggestion here of the reincarnationist view of how the body and soul are related.

This is amplified by the ancient Indian belief that men and gods alike, by their yogic power, could enter into other life forms with their souls. The yogi could literally become a bull, a snake or an eagle. So this gives more credence to the notion of the soul migrating from one body to another. The theory of reincarnation is just a generalizing of these yogic processes. All souls migrate, it was concluded. The yogi differs from others only in the ability to direct this. For the rest of us, soul transference is a process occurring spontaneously without our full understanding. The soul naturally moves on when its present body is no longer "habitable."

Historians of thought have always been intrigued with the question of whether the Indian belief in reincarnation is somehow tied to a similar idea found in Pythagoras, Plato and other ancient Greek philosophers. Pythagoras, the earliest of these, lived about 500 B.C.—about when reincarnation was taking hold in India. It is hard to believe that the simultaneous presence of this idea in two cultures was purely coincidental. But, on the other hand, it is not possible to discern at such an early date the link by which transmission might have taken place. If there was a transmission, it was almost certainly from India to Greece rather than the reverse. For the roots of the idea in India can be traced back to the ancient yogic tradition, as we have just seen.

KARMA. The word *karma* originally meant "action" in Sanskrit (the classical language of India), but gradually it was imbued with a special moral and spiritual meaning. Karma was not so much the action itself but a certain power in the action which insured that appropriate consequences would ensue. Thus, we can speak of a *law of karma* by virtue of which good actions lead to good results for the doer, and bad actions to bad results. Indian philosophers frequently use the analogy of the seed and the fruit. When a certain seed has been planted, the fruit which comes of it must be of a certain kind.

As with reincarnation, the origins of this idea are not completely clear. Probably, it grew up in the context of the elaborate Hindu ritualism that flourished in the centuries just before Buddha. The brahmin priests who performed these rituals believed them to possess an infallible efficacy, not even depending of the will of the gods to whom they were addressed. As long as the *action* of the ritual was performed exactly in the required manner, the result would follow. The law of karma simply generalized this principle of inevitable result to *all* actions.

When the ideas of reincarnation and karma were combined, they took on a new and extraordinarily powerful meaning. The reward-punishment processes of karma were seen as taking place primarily through reincarnation. To put it quite simply: one's reincarnation depended on the moral character of the previous life. The condition into which a person was born was no accident. Being a brahmin or a kshatriya was a reward for good deeds; being a shudra or untouchable (or a woman of any caste) was a punishment.

The law of karma thus provided an excellent way of justifying the existing social order and discouraging revolt. Hindu theorists were not slow to exploit it. There is a work known as the *Laws of Manu* written about 200 B.C. It gives an account of the ideally ordered society, describing the four varnas, emphasizing the subordinate position of women and insisting on the four ashrams (stages of life—see page 52). Manu relentlessly stresses the need to abide by the restrictions of caste and gender. The only hope of improving one's lot lies in the acceptance of present status, thereby earning good karma for the next reincarnation.

Other thinkers, like Buddha, did not see the law of karma as justifying the restrictive social order. But even they acknowledged the general principle that the circumstances of the present life are the reflection—the *fruit*—of how we have lived previously.

With regard to the law of karma, there is one especially puzzling question: What makes it work? It is not easy to see how all the souls of the world can be guaranteed of receiving a reincarnation which is exactly as deserved. The idea that comes naturally to mind is that God must be the enforcer of the law of karma. Only He could know the condition of each soul, and only He would have the power to bring about the appropriate result.

Surprisingly enough, this is not the explanation which Indian philosophy gives for the law of karma. Instead, it is believed that karma operates by a power inherent in the actions themselves. As we just saw, the ancient rituals did not depend on the gods for their working. Likewise, our normal actions directly produce effects in the soul, and these in turn lead to the deserved reincarnation.

There are two key factors in the soul that are central to karma: desire and ignorance. We have briefly discussed them in connection with Buddha's Wheel of Becoming. Now they must be more closely scrutinized. Desire is the propelling force for all reincarnation, and it is able to play this role by reason of its close links to action. There is a clear reciprocal relation between action and desire. Desires lead to actions, obviously; there could hardly be an action without desire to motivate it.

At the same time, actions lead to desires, for when we act in response to a desire, we reinforce it.

These simple psychological facts, which nobody could deny, are the basis for all the manifestations of karma. In the course of a lifetime, each person's soul will be shaped by certain patterns of desire and action. One person may be a glutton who lives for the pleasure of eating. Another may be a miser who is consumed by the desire for money. Yet a third may be devoted to some nobler pursuit, such as the quest for knowledge. In death these three—and all of us—face a common predicament: the separation of the soul, with all its desires, from the body.

Here is a most important truth to be reckoned with: desires are indeed the property of the soul (or mind). They cannot reside in the stomach, the sex organs or any other unconscious bodily part. But the body, while not being the actual possessor of desire, is indispensable for its fulfillment. That is the dilemma facing the soul at the death of the body. It has various desires, for example, the desire for food; but it cannot satisfy this desire except by using the body to get food, to consume it and finally to digest it.

It might be objected that the desire for food will necessarily disappear, once the body is gone, since it is the body that has a physical requirement for food. But this misconstrues the nature of desire. Desire is directed toward the *psychological* gratification which comes with various activities. Our addiction to this mental state can and will linger even when its physical basis is no more.

Thus, the soul is drawn irresistibly to be reborn in another body, some newly conceived body that is "available for occupancy." And all this takes place without the intervention of God. The soul's own instinct is to seek a new reincarnation.

The difficult issue that remains is why the body chosen for rebirth should reflect the good or bad karma of the soul. If the soul governs its own reincarnation, then there seemingly should be only good reincarnations. Here the other chief factor mentioned above—ignorance—comes into play. Passionate, animalistic desires will drive the soul recklessly to some ignoble rebirth. In its *ignorance* the soul fails to see the implications of its choice. Blinded by desperate need, it will seize upon whatever body is most obviously suitable to its desire. In this way, the soul of a glutton might be reborn in a pig, or a vicious criminal might reincarnate as a wolf.

If desires are kept somewhat more under control, a better result may be expected. Rebirth as a brahmin would be the result of a calm, contemplative life, for this temperament is conducive to the brahmin's mission of religious learning. One who led a life of devotion to duty would become a kshatriya, for he is the one who defends justice and keeps order.

The self-enforcing character of karma must once again be stressed. There is no need for God to take a hand in this process of allocating souls to their proper destinies. Each soul will instinctively find its own proper level.

LIBERATION. Together, the ideas of reincarnation and karma provided a sweeping and coherent picture of life. Throughout the universe, each living thing is in the midst of an immense spiritual journey. There is no beginning to this, for souls are uncreated. Every soul has forever been proceeding in samsara, each reincarnation determined by its predecessor. This beginninglessness is hard for many to conceive, but we must appreciate how central this is to the Indian way of thinking. If the soul *began* in some particular state, there would be no karmic explanation for it. In order for karma to prevail absolutely, each life must be preceded by another *without beginning*.

Does samsara have an end? That is the question which became more and more urgent for Indian philosophers. Certainly, there was no reason why samsara had to end. The soul could very well continue in its course forever. It might have good reincarnations and bad ones, but never, in the natural course of events, would any permanent state be attained. Again, the rigorous character of karma is the determining factor. Whatever reward or punishment is won through karma must be limited; the effect must be proportionate to the cause. Thus, each life exhausts the karmic effects of its predecessor, even as new karma is laid up. As the Buddhists would say, it is a wheel that turns and turns.

In this perspective samsara assumed an aspect of futility. It appeared to be an endless struggle to maintain or improve one's place, which seemingly led nowhere. If one was reborn a brahmin, one had to measure up to the exacting duties of this religious calling—or else face "demotion" to a lower caste. The ideal of escape, of *liberation* from samsara now took hold. Buddha called it *nirvana*, Hindus called it *moksha*; but what they aspired to was the same: to die and not to be reborn.

How could this be accomplished? That was a topic of endless debate. One thing was clearly understood, though. Liberation could not be achieved by karma; that is, it could not be achieved by the morality of one's actions. One ancient text expresses it thus: "The world that was not made [i.e., the indestructible higher state of being] is not achieved by what is done." (Mundaka Upanishad, I,ii,12). Most Indian philosophers—Buddha being a prominent example—believed that knowledge of higher truth would set the soul free.

To students of Indian religion, the primacy of the goal of liberation has always been a puzzle. Most of us cling so greedily to life, it is hard to comprehend a philosophy which wants nothing more than to be rid of it. Understand that we are not talking about suicide here. That is a frustration with present circumstances of life rather than with life itself. (And, in the Indian view, it only leads to another reincarnation, probably a worse one.)

Many theories have been advanced as to why this rejection of life gained such a hold in Indian philosophy. Some have pointed to the Indian climate, which involves a season of brutal heat followed by torrential rains. But many other places have harsh climates without having produced this philosophy. Some point to the widespread Indian poverty, but this involves a grave historical misunderstanding. India may well be poor today in relation to the Western world, but this was definitely not so in ancient times. India was then a land of fabled wealth, possessing a sophisticated urban culture founded on the agricultural bounty of the Ganges valley. It was precisely in this prosperous time that the ideal of liberation came to prominence.

When all is said and done, we can only cite those considerations previously discussed to explain the primacy of liberation. The theory of endless samsara imparted a weariness and a pointlessness to life. In the framework of the problem posed by the joint action of karma and reincarnation, there was no solution but liberation.

One more point needs mentioning, in order to better understand the social context of liberation. It has never been a universal practice or aspiration in India. The liberation seekers, whether Hindu, Buddhist or otherwise, have always been an elite minority in their religious communities. The quest for liberation requires a drastic reorientation of one's life. Not many people have ever been willing to do this. Most are content to seek nothing more than a good life followed by a good reincarnation.

Thus, religion in India exists on two levels. On the higher level there is the goal of liberation. On the lower, the goal of a good reincarnation. This is sought through good works, done in the context of a normal life of personal and social commitments. Naturally, the great majority are on this level. If mindful of liberation at all, they see it as something to be postponed to some future reincarnation.

YOGA. As noted before, the origins of yoga go back to the Indus civilization some four thousand years ago. There is no telling just what the practice of yoga consisted in at that time. Somehow yoga survived when practically every other aspect of the Indus civilization was erased. Today yoga is best known in the form expounded by Patanjali (about 100 B.C.). He formulated the ancient discipline of yoga in a particularly coherent and practical way, and, ever since his time, he has been the chief guide for yogis, i.e., those who practice yoga.

Whatever purpose yoga may have served for the Indus people, it had become by Patanjali's time the chief discipline for attaining liberation. We cannot really appreciate the meaning of liberation in India without examining the techniques of yoga. There were many forms of yoga, but Patanjali's, which is termed the *raja-yoga* ("king of yogas"), is singled out for detailed discussion.

The *religious* purpose of yoga must be kept in mind. Many people in the United States practice yoga for the enhancement of physical health, and it can perfectly well serve such a purpose. But in the true and complete yoga, this is only a preliminary to spiritual development. In fact, the physical disciplines comprise one of three general phases of Patanjali's raja-yoga, being preceded by the moral phase and followed by the mental. Patanjali identifies a total of eight *limbs* or stages: the first two are classed as moral, the next two as physical and the last four as mental. They are limbs in the sense that our arms and legs are limbs: providing a means of moving toward liberation.

Avoidance and Practice are the two moral limbs. They consist in refraining from immoral actions and applying oneself to what is beneficial and wholesome. This component of yoga is not much different from what would be upheld in the morality of many cultures. For example, Patanjali instructs us to avoid greed and lust. He names piety, contentment and cleanliness as virtues to be practiced. The importance of the moral phase lies in its value as a preliminary discipline. One must first gain moral self-mastery before undertaking the more distinctive components of yogic discipline.

The third limb is Posture, which Patanjali define as "effortless stability." By this phrase he means to refer to certain positionings of the body which can be held for long periods without discomfort. There are a great many of these postures, some having application to specific bodily ailments such as backache or constipation. It is somewhat puzzling, on the face of it, that seekers of liberation should concern themselves with the needs of the body. But there is a perfectly coherent reason for this. The yogi must remove whatever might be a source of distraction in the higher (mental) stages of the discipline. So the body is to be made, as far as possible, free of pain and discomfort.

The most important posture is the lotus, in which the yogi sits perfectly straight, legs crossed, each foot resting on the opposite thigh. Just as the lotus flower sits fixed on the surface of the water, the yogi in this position attains a perfect bodily stability. Each part of the body is held in place with no room to shift or squirm. This is the ideal posture for meditation. The body is kept so still that it will not disturb the mind.

Breathing is the fourth limb of raja-yoga. Its immediate aim is simply to slow down the process of breathing. Normally this takes place at a much faster pace than is really needed. The yogi will take in breath very slowly, hold it for a while and then slowly exhale. This can be done by anyone; it only requires paying attention to one's own breathing. The trick is to get the slowed pace to carry over into the normal unconscious breathing.

Slowing down the respiratory process is not an end in itself. It is thought that this makes it possible to calm all of the body's inner functioning. Physiological functions like heartbeat, which cannot be directly controlled, will slow down in tandem with breathing. Thus, in the fourth limb, there is an immobilizing of the internal body, just as the third limb immobilized the body's external aspect. In each case there is the same underlying consideration. If the body, inside and out, is made perfectly still, it will not distract the mind.

There is a further consideration as well. Yoga presupposes that every person is endowed with an enormous energy. One may almost call it a god-like power. In normal living this energy is continually being dissipated in various activities. If a person can just be perfectly still, this power is concentrated. Then, as we will see, there are extraordinary consequences.

With the fifth limb raja-yoga moves into the all-important mental phase. This limb is called *Restraint*. It involves the control of the sense organs. Normally, we are quite taken with the multitude of sights, sound, smells, touches and tastes which present themselves. The mind will notice these as they occur, one after another.

Restraint blocks the entry of these sense data. The physical organs continue to function, but the transmission of their data to the mind is cut off.

We experience this sort of thing all the time. Suppose you are watching TV or speaking on the phone. Someone in the house calls out to you, but you don't hear it. The other person's voice was loud enough. Your physical mechanism of hearing vibrated as usual in response to the voice. But your mind did not notice because it was absorbed in something else.

Yoga's aim here is just to be able to induce this kind of sensory blockage at will. Rather than occurring haphazardly, restraint will be a technique consciously applied in focusing the mind. It is not an easy task. In the mental phase, we have reached a higher order of difficulty, far exceeding anything in the earlier limbs. The fifth limb can only slowly be mastered, in conjunction with the final three limbs.

They are Concentration, Contemplation and Trance. Collectively they are referred to as *Meditation*. These three limbs are actually just different levels of the same accomplishment. They require, to an ever intensifying degree, training the mind's attention on a single object. As the body was held still in stages three and four, now the mind is brought to a halt. The mind is in a state very comparable to that of the eyes when they stare at something.

At these stages the great obstacle is what yogis call the "monkey mind." This is the mind's tendency to be continually jumping from one thought to another. Everyone has experienced this: one thought leads to another, and that to a third and then a fourth, so that in a few moments the mind is thinking something altogether different from what it began with. To deal with this problem, one must force the mind to stay on a single idea. The idea should be something quite simple, say, the color red.

The mind *will* wander off within a moment or two as a person begins this discipline. It is so restless and so easily bored. Self-conscious thoughts, concerns about one's own attempt to practice yoga, are particularly intrusive. Each intrusion must be noticed as soon as possible so that the mind can be refocused.

Thus, we have Concentration, the beginning of yogic meditation. Be aware that this concentration is something rather different from what is usually implied by the word. Ordinarily, to concentrate would simply be to keep the thoughts within a certain general area. A student concentrating on a chemistry exam would be thinking only about chemistry rather than about sports or work or personal problems. By contrast, yogic concentration is a stoppage of the very process of thinking. The mind is held still as it "stares" at a certain idea. This is by no means a state of unconsciousness. The mind is awake and alert but unmoving.

As already indicated, to progress to limbs seven and eight is merely to lengthen the period of concentration. Initially, it cannot be sustained for even three or four seconds; but eventually it must persist for hours. The precise demarcations are not specified, but as a rough estimate one can say that if the mind can be held still for an entire minute, the transition from Concentration to Contemplation has been made. If the mind can be stopped for an hour, Trance has been attained. Such achievements are hardly imaginable for the mind as we generally experience it.

Meditation (that is, the sustained practice of the final three limbs) is said by Patanjali to have astounding effects. This is what was alluded to before when we spoke of the godlike power that yoga is trying to tap. The so-called psychic powers now emerge. Patanjali gives a long list of them, including telepathy (the ability to see into others' minds), psychokinesis (the ability to move objects by mind alone) and clairvoyance (perception of events in distant times and places). These powers are viewed by us moderns with much skepticism, though a few scientists have thought them worth investigating. Whatever the scientific verdict may be, Patanjali was firmly convinced of the reality of the psychic powers. He saw them as the inevitable by-product of the yogi's prolonged meditation.

It is very important to understand exactly how these powers are supposed to operate. In general, Indian philosophers think of knowing as a process in which the mind is absorbed into its object. (This makes an interesting contrast with Western epistemology, which tends to see the object as somehow absorbed into the mind.) In yogic meditation, the absorption of mind into object is carried to perfection. Normally, the mind is spread among many objects, in particular its own bodily states. In trance, all the mind's attention is concentrated into a single object, while the body has been abandoned, a mere shell. (Remember that Vedic passage on page 65.)

In telepathy, for example, the yogi knows another's thoughts by virtue of being in that person's mind. The yogi knows them in the direct and unmistakable way that the other person knows his own thoughts. Likewise, the yogi practices psychokinesis through being inside the object to be moved. The yogi possesses clairvoyant knowledge by being mentally present in the time or place known.

Having considered the powers at length, Patanjali goes on to make it absolutely clear that they are not the purpose of yoga. What use would these powers have other than the fulfillment of desire? But yoga wants to overcome desire, not to find more efficient ways of satisfying it. More precisely, yoga wants, through meditation, to raise the mind to that fullness of understanding known as enlightenment. In the wake of this achievement, all desire will be rendered meaningless.

Truth, not power, is the ultimate goal of yoga. The psychic powers can pose a real threat to this, insofar as they tempt the yogi to their exercise. Any use of the powers is dangerous and should be avoided. Even if there was an ostensibly good purpose, such as averting tragedy through the foreknowledge of natural disasters, display of the powers would lead the yogi to pride and selfishness, and ultimately to his spiritual downfall. Note that the powers cannot be avoided, according to Patanjali. Once the mind has reached a certain level of meditative penetration, the powers are at one's disposal. The temptation to use them must be resolutely resisted.

In Indian folklore there is a belief that testifies to this attitude. It has to with the origin of demons. These beings are thought to be nothing other than yogis gone wrong. They are yogis who have acquired the psychic powers and succumbed to the temptation of using them. The powers corrupt the yogi and gradually turn him into a malicious, depraved being. As a demon he will haunt the world, wreaking havoc, until finally the powers are dissipated by his reckless self-indulgence.

IV. THE ERA OF VISIONARY PHILOSOPHIES

In the period lasting from about 600 to 100 B.C., India was blessed with a multitude of visionary, charismatic religious teachers. Some, like Buddha, are well known by name. Others remain shadowy figures behind works they anonymously authored. We will first consider two *orthodox* philosophies, adhering to the dominant Hinduism: the ancient philosophy of the Upanishads and the strikingly different philosophy of the Bhagavad Gita. Then, there are the non-orthodox philosophies: Jainism, Buddhism (in two distinct forms) and Carvaka.

1. Orthodox (Hindu) Philosophies
The Upanishads: Brahman and Atman

If any system of thought can claim to be the quintessential Indian philosophy, it is the teaching of the Upanishads. They are a set of about twelve books, of which the earliest are probably the most ancient philosophical works preserved anywhere. The Upanishads form a part—the latest part—of the Vedas, the holy scriptures of Hinduism. The earlier portions are almost entirely of a liturgical and ritualistic character, while the Upanishads take a new departure. They clearly derive from brahmin ascetics who were becoming ever more prominent in Indian spiritual life. The names of these ascetics are mentioned occasionally, but for the most part they are mysterious figures whose lives (unlike Buddha's) are unknown.

The word *Upanishad* is derived from the Sanskrit *upa-ni-shad* meaning "sit near to." This refers to the fact that the Upanishads contained mysterious, secret doctrines that were not to be given out to the public. They were reserved for chosen pupils who sat hear to the master and were imparted these truths only after a long period of preparation.

The philosophy of the Upanishads developed out of the context of the Vedic sacrifice rituals. These, as already noted, were the special property of the brahmin priests, who had developed them to a formidable complexity. The rituals were believed to have enormous power by which the gods could be literally compelled to grant favors of vigor, wealth, power and every form of worldly success.

Unlike Buddha and other rejecters of Hindu orthodoxy, the sages of the Upanishads did not question the efficacy of these rituals. Instead, they challenged the motives that were behind them. In the spirit of the ascetics, they dismissed the impermanent satisfactions which the rituals procured. In the Katha Upanishad, the god Yama seeks to bribe the youthful Naciketas with an abundance of worldly goods, including fine chariots and dancing maidens, but the young man answers with scorn:

Transient—those things which belong to mortals, O Yama.
They only wear out the senses.
Even a full life is brief indeed!
Keep those chariots, keep the dance and song.
Not with wealth is a man to be satisfied. (I,1,26–27)

The most that can be gained by the rituals is a temporary stay in heaven:

> Those deluded men, regarding sacrifices and meritorious works as most important, do not know any other good. Having enjoyment in the heights of heaven won by good deeds, they enter this world again, or even a lower one. (Mundaka Up., I,2,10)

What fascinated the authors of the Upanishads about the rituals was not their material rewards but the mysterious power which they somehow tapped. This power was greater than that of any known god. It was given the name *Brahman*. This must be sharply distinguished from the caste designation *brahmin*, though, of course, the terms are related. Brahm*an* was the power inherent in the ritual of the brahm*ins*.

Brahman is, indeed, God, but this deity is altogether different from what most religious persons have cherished. The essential fact about Brahman is that it is not a person. The word *person* is not to be taken as equivalent to *human*. It refers to a psychological rather than a biological fact. More specifically, a person is a being possessing understanding and responsiveness. In this sense, many others besides humans might be persons: for example, aliens from a distinct galaxy who bore no physical resemblance to us. If they understood us and interacted with us, they would be persons.

God, in the Judaeo-Christian-Islamic conception, is definitely a person. He knows His creation with perfect understanding, and He responds to it with perfect compassion. The Bible and the Koran continuously testify to these qualities. Brahman, on the other hand, is devoid of such characteristics. Consider this analogy by which the creation of the world is explained:

> As from a blazing fire sparks of like form issue forth by the thousands, even so the many kinds of beings come forth from the Imperishable [Brahman], and to It they return. (Mundaka Up., II,1,1)

Creation is here a spontaneous, chaotic process involving no concern or even awareness on the part of the Creator. No more than the fire cherishes its sparks can we be loved by Brahman. It did not create us as a loving father; It does not watch over us. It is simply a power producing and controlling the world.

The contrast with the Biblical-Koranic view is truly profound. From that standpoint, God is a wise and loving maker, a master craftsman who infuses every part of creation with beauty and purpose. In this perspective, the material world cannot rightfully be held in contempt, for it is God's handiwork. By contrast, this world is, for the Upanishads, a mere overflow of the divine energy. There is no plan or justification for its existence. There is no real answer to the perennial question "For what purpose are we here?" Certainly, the pursuit of liberation from this world is much more comprehensible in such a perspective.

If God is not a person, then the Upanishads' conception of our relation with God must be very different from what is found in other philosophies. One cannot pray to Brahman, for It does not hear or answer prayer. One cannot obey Brahman, for there is nothing which It commands. Neither love nor fear makes any sense in relation to It. There is nothing to do but *know* Brahman, and in this knowledge our own being is transformed, as will soon be discussed.

Why would such a notion of God ever come to prominence? To many, Brahman seems so cold and lifeless in contrast to a loving personal God. We must realize that people form notions of God in accord with their own ideals and values. Where power is idealized, God will be seen as a being of absolute, despotic power. Where love is idealized, God will be seen as a being of boundless, compassionate love. And where (as in India) detachment and tranquillity are idealized, God will be seen as Brahman, a deity with no feeling or response toward creation.

To this extraordinary concept of God the Upanishads join an equally remarkable notion of the human self, or *Atman*. The self is far more of a mystery than we ordinarily realize. "It is hidden in things; it does not shine forth." (Katha Up., I,3,12) Originally Atman meant "breath" and was thought of as a vital power hovering within things while they lived—something like a soul. But in the Upanishads Atman has come to be something utterly different from the soul. The clearest explanation is given in the Maitri Upanishad:

> Truly, the seers proclaim this Atman to be here, in the midst of bodies but unaffected by good or bad karma. It cannot be seen or taken hold of. It lacks any sense of "I." It may seem to be active and changing. In reality, it does nothing and changes not at all. It is pure, steadfast, unagitated, fixed in contemplation, abiding in itself.
>
> There is another self, a lower self, which *is* affected by good and bad karma. This one rises and falls in the course of reincarnation. He wanders about, obsessed with contrasting qualities [such as pleasure and pain] . . . Now the higher self [Atman] is like a drop of water on a lotus leaf, but the lower self is affected by nature's qualities. He is bewildered, and this prevents him from seeing the God that dwells within. Borne along and defiled by the stream of qualities, wavering, confused, distracted and full of desire, he thinks "I am he," "This is mine." Thus, he binds himself with himself, like a bird in a snare. (II,7; III,2)

What is particularly noteworthy in this passage is the unambiguous declaration that Atman does not partake of the process of reincarnation. It must not be identified with the soul. That "lower self" just described is the soul, experiencing the good and bad fruits of earlier deeds. The soul may also be referred to as the *mind*.

Atman's essential characteristic is its stability. It remains steadfast while the body and the soul are continually undergoing change. It lies at the core of our being, a refuge from the insecurities of normal life. One of the most powerful messages in the Upanishads is the call to be aware of this pool of tranquillity that lies within each of us.

In order for Atman to become our refuge, body and mind both must be renounced as alien and irrelevant. Obviously, this is far more easily said than done. It would be a huge feat of self control to look on the problems of one's own body as mere external events. One would have to speak of some affliction—say, a migraine headache—as something that was just happening, not something happening to *me*, i.e., to Atman.

To look on the processes of the *mind* as external to me (when it is the mind which is doing the looking) is pretty well beyond comprehension. But this is precisely what the Upanishads conception of liberation requires. It is the resounding affirmation that I am *not* body, I am *not* mind, I *am* Atman.

This mysterious Atman has a further meaning which carries it far beyond the individual. It is not just something within us. The great sage Yajnavalkya is quoted as saying:

> Worlds . . . gods . . . creatures . . . all things whatsoever—they have no value of themselves but only by virtue of Atman within them. It is the Atman that should be discerned and contemplated. By this discernment and contemplation, all is known. (Briharadaranyaka Up., II, 4, 5)

This teaching of Atman is presented still more dramatically in a series of analogies which Uddalaka explains to his son, Svetaketu. Uddalaka describes how bees mingle the nectar of many flowers to produce honey. This common essence of the honey obliterates all the distinctive characteristics of the nectars that made it up. Likewise, there is a common essence pervading the world. Uddalaka says:

> That which is the subtle essence—this whole world has it for its Atman. That is truth, that is Atman. That art thou, Svetaketu. (Chandogya Upanishad, VI, 9, 4)

Several more analogies are given, each pointing to the hidden essence in all things. For example, the salt which is dissolved in water: it cannot be seen or touched, but it is present nonetheless. Similarly, there is in all things a power which cannot be seen, and that power is one's own Atman. As Uddalaka repeats, "That are thou." These words (in Sanskrit: *tat tvam asi*) are thought to be the most profound and revealing sentence in the entire Upanishads. Like the note of a conch shell being blown, the holy saying resounds at the conclusion of each of Uddalaka's analogies.

Atman is not just my self, then. It is the self of everything that exists. And, most importantly, this self is not something divided up, so that what is in me differs from yours and his and hers. It is the same pure, unchanging, indivisible Atman that is in all things. Now it should be evident that this Atman, which is the self of all things, must be identical with that all-pervading power we earlier referred to as Brahman.

The Upanishads explicitly make this identification, affirming that the statement "I am Brahman" represents ultimate truth. Whoever knows this becomes fully and consciously that all-pervading power. Conversely,

> Whoever sees God as distinct from himself and worships this *other* Being—such a one is ignorant. (Brihadaranyaka Up., I, 4, 10)

For the Upanishads enlightenment means seeing the absolute unity of all things. Differences that appear are the result of a superficial view that fails to see the inner self in all. The distinction between the knowing self and the known object is eliminated, since the same Atman is both seer and seen.

> Where there is duality, there one sees the other, smells the other, tastes . . . speaks to . . . hears . . . touches . . . thinks of . . . knows the other. But where everything has become just one's own self, by what and whom should one see, smell, taste, etc.? (Brihadaranyaka Up. IV, 5, 15)

The Mundaka Upanishad (III, 2, 8) compares enlightenment to the condition of rivers which have flowed into the ocean. The waters of each river have lost all individual shape and character, as we must lose all individual identity in the knowledge of Brahman and Atman.

All this cannot fail to evoke a recollection of the Sufis and their concept of fana (annihilation). Like the Sufis, the sages of the Upanishads sought to negate the separateness of our individual existence. Each group emphasized the need for a teacher (shaikh/guru), and each made some use of yogic techniques. We must keep in mind the all-important difference that the Sufis sought union with a personal god, while the Upanishads centered on the impersonal Brahman. Thus, the Sufis' passionate love for God could have no place in the Upanishads' scheme of salvation.

The Bhagavad Gita: Karma-Yoga and Bhakti-Yoga

The Bhagavad Gita is one of the most beloved and influential works in Indian literature. Technically, it does not possess the status of a revealed scripture such as is enjoyed by the Upanishads and other parts of the Vedas. But in practice it is regarded with the utmost veneration and has played a considerable role in shaping Indian philosophy.

The title *Bhagavad Gita* means "Song of the Blessed One," the Blessed One being the God Krishna. It is the account of a lengthy dialogue that is supposed to have taken place between Krishna and his friend, Arjuna. The Gita was written about 200 B.C., and was set in the context of an earlier story, the epic poem *Mahabharata*. The latter is the long and complicated story of how five brothers (one of whom is Arjuna) are cheated and humbled but eventually put right the wrongs they have suffered. The brothers are kshatriya rulers over vast kingdom, but their own cousins manage to take it over by playing on a weakness for gambling in the eldest brother (not Arjuna).

The Gita begins at the point when a climactic battle is about to take place. Arjuna and his brothers, with their thousands of allies, face their wicked cousins with an equally large army. Arjuna, the mightiest warrior on the field, stands in a chariot in the middle of his side's battle line. Slowly, he surveys the whole scene; and suddenly, he is overcome by emotion at the prospect of all the carnage about to occur. With him in the chariot is Krishna, his driver. Krishna is an old friend of Arjuna's who has come to aid in this battle. At this point the divine status of Krishna is unknown.

Arjuna confides his misgivings to Krishna:

> I see no good that can come of slaying my own kinsmen in the battle. I do not long for victory or pleasures. Of what real value are these things, or even life itself? Those for whom we might desire them are standing here, ready to lay down their lives.
>
> I would not consent to kill these kinsmen of mine even for the rule of the whole universe. How much less for the sake of some earthly kingdom? What satisfaction can be ours after we have slain these wicked cousins of ours? If we kill them, it will only pile new sin upon the old. . . .
>
> Far better would it be for me if these cousins, with weapons in hand should slay me, while I stood unarmed and unresisting. (Chapter I, verses 31–33, 35–36, 46)

With these words, the Gita tells us, Arjuna casts aside his weapons and sinks down on the seat of his chariot, overwhelmed by sorrow. His idealistic sentiments are, in fact, an expression of the principle of ahimsa (non-violence), which Buddhism and Jainism popularized in India. Arjuna's reaction to the impending slaughter bears a striking parallel to the Buddhist emperor Ashoka's horror at the bloody victory which his armies had won.

It is disappointing, perhaps, to learn that the Bhagavad Gita is devoted to showing that Arjuna's feelings, however noble, are misguided. After Arjuna has spoken his piece in Chapter One of the Gita, Krishna responds in the remaining seventeen chapters. He patiently instructs Arjuna in the folly of his thinking. A whole barrage of reasons are given to show Arjuna why he is wrong, but Krishna's central theme is caste duty. Arjuna, it will be recalled, is of the kshatriya caste. As such he has the inborn duty to defend justice and social order. It is morally right that he play this role in society, as every other person must fulfill the role that he or she is born with.

Here we see a profound difference between Hinduism (as expressed in the Bhagavad Gita) and its adversaries, such as Buddhism. Because Hinduism upholds the social order, it has difficulty in espousing a pure and thorough ahimsa. Society cannot be protected without exercising a certain amount of violence, and kshatriyas are the ones who must carry this out when the circumstances require. From the Gita's standpoint, which is very representative of Hinduism in general, it is completely unacceptable that Arjuna shirk his role in this battle. Though Buddha is never mentioned by name, it is quite clear that his example of neglecting caste duty is strongly disapproved of.

KRISHNA AND ARJUNA

A modern depiction of Krishna and Arjuna at the beginning of the Bhagavad Gita. Krishna stands ready to comfort and instruct His despondent friend. [Bhaktivedanta Book Trust]

The Gita defends its insistence on caste duty by putting forward a particularly rigid interpretation of how the law of karma works. Krishna explains it as follows:

> If you, in your conceit, think, "I will not fight," your resolve will have no effect. You are compelled by nature. That which you foolishly shrink from doing will be done by you even against your will. Your own actions [in the previous life] have bound you to this. (Chapter XVIII, verses 59–60)

On this view, each one is born to a certain caste with tendencies which, like the action of a coiled up spring, cannot be permanently repressed. We have established these tendencies in a previous life, and now they must come out.

Thus, Arjuna is deluded to think that he even has the choice of practicing ahimsa. He must go forward with this battle. His chief concern, according to Krishna, must be to do so in the proper frame of mind. That state of mind is one of detachment: "Do your duty as a sacrifice, free from all attachment." (III, 9) This involves "renouncing the fruits" of actions, as Krishna phrases it (II, 47). What he means is that Arjuna must fight the battle simply because it is his duty, without any desire for what he might gain from victory. To state it quite simply: Arjuna must fight *without caring whether he wins or loses.*

The emphasis on duty with detachment enables the Gita to put forward a way of liberation different from what Buddha and many others had followed. Buddha had insisted that the liberation seeker must go forth from his home, renouncing family and possessions. Every distraction from one's spiritual endeavor has to be eliminated. The Gita denies that this is necessary, offering what is termed the way of *karma yoga*.

Karma yoga is the pursuit of liberation through action. The Gita proclaims that this can be just as valid a way of seeking liberation as the more traditional yoga based on knowledge. Right action can be a means of liberation, provided it is done in the spirit of detachment. Then the soul will not be tied down; its desires will not be reinforced. The idea of karma yoga is put forward as an antidote to what many Hindus saw as a disturbing trend in ancient Indian society. Buddha and many others had exemplified the trend, namely, dropping out of society to seek liberation.

The Gita is clearly mindful of the disastrous consequences which would follow if the most energetic and dedicated members of society dropped out. It is saying, with its teaching of karma yoga, that one need not choose between liberation and social duty. Both can be accomplished if only the right attitude is achieved.

In the end, it is a much broader issue than Arjuna's problem of whether the kshatriya's duty must be carried out. Important as that may be, it is just one aspect of the general issue of social duty. Every person is born into a certain social context. We have responsibilities as members of a family and a community. These responsibilities should not, cannot and need not be abandoned in favor of the quest for liberation.

We have dwelt at great length now on this social message that the Gita is conveying. But there is actually another aspect of the Gita's teaching that is far more important. This is related to that fact which was mentioned a while back but then ignored: the fact that Krishna is God. As the Gita proceeds, His divine nature becomes more and more the center of attention. In the light of this, a new concept of liberation, different from anything we have yet discussed, emerges.

The following passage is the first in the Gita where Krishna clearly divulges who He really is:

> Though I am unborn and indestructible, though I am the lord of all creatures, nonetheless, while remaining established in my divine nature, I take on worldly being through my mysterious power. Whenever there is a decline of righteousness and a rise of unrighteousness, then I reincarnate myself. (IV, 6–7)

It is evident that Krishna is an altogether different deity from the Upanishads' Brahman. Krishna *is* a person, so concerned for our welfare that He takes on human form (becomes an *avatar* in the Hindu terminology). As a person, He is an appropriate object of love and worship. In fact, such devotion, which the Gita calls *bhakti*, becomes the principal means of liberation.

The karma yoga which we were just now discussing is subsumed under bhakti yoga. That is, the actions of moral and social duty are seen as acts of devotion to Krishna. They are performed simply because Krishna wants us to perform them. Everything we do, says the Gita, should be in honor of Krishna:

> Whatever you do or eat or give, whatever disciplines you perform, let it be an offering to Me. In this way, you will be free from the entanglements of good and bad karma. With your mind firmly established in renunciation, you will be free and attain to Me . . .
>
> Those who take refuge in Me, however lowborn—women, vaishyas, shudras—they all reach the highest goal. How much more, then, the noble brahmins and kshatriyas? You find yourself in an impermanent and sorrowful world. Therefore, worship Me, fix your mind on Me, be devoted to Me, make all your offerings to Me, adore Me. By this discipline you will indeed come to Me. (IX, 27–28, 32–34)

This passage may be regarded as the very heart of the Bhagavad Gita. It is remarkable in that it prescribes the pursuit of liberation by bhakti yoga for all humans, regardless of caste or sex. Even more remarkable is the concept of liberation. It is not, as in Buddha's teaching and the Upanishads, a repression of all desire and feeling. The Gita urges us to *redirect* our desires, not eliminate them. We must see the perfect beauty of Krishna, and then we will be able to turn away from this "impermanent and sorrowful world."

In its striving to love God, the Gita shows some resemblance to the Sufi way. Like the Sufis, the Gita points to the possibility of mystical experience in which the true nature of God is beheld. In Chapter XI, Arjuna begs Krishna to discard His human disguise and manifest His divine form. Krishna, because of His special love for Arjuna, complies with this request, and the author of the Gita struggles to express in words what is then seen:

Wearing divine garlands and raiments, with divine perfumes and ointments, made up of all wonders, resplendent, boundless, with face turned everywhere. If the light of a thousand suns were to blaze forth all at once in the sky, that might resemble the splendor of that exalted being. There Arjuna beheld the whole universe, with its manifold divisions gathered together into one, in the body of the God of gods. (verses 11–13)

However, the Gita does not teach the Sufi idea of annihilation in God. It was the Upanishads which came close to Sufism on that point. The Gita, for its part, believes in an eternal relation of servitude to God. The devotee never disappears or merges into God.

2. Non-Orthodox Philosophies

Jainism: The Ancient Way

Jainism has been called the world's oldest living religion, and this claim may well be right. In its present form, Jainism derives from the revered teacher Mahavira, who was an older contemporary of the Buddha. We have already seen how Buddha was influenced by the Jains in the early years of his spiritual quest. The approximate dates of Mahavira's life are 600 to 525 B.C.

Mahavira was not, and did not claim to be, the founder of Jainism. For his religious inspiration he cited a long series of *tirthankaras* ("crossing-makers"). It is not clear when the various tirthankaras lived, but the tradition is at least several centuries older than Mahavira himself. Jains compare the quest for liberation to the crossing of a swift and dangerous stream. Mahavira and his predecessors were credited with having found the ford by which this torrent could be traversed.

Jainism has always been notable for the extreme character of its discipline. Mahavira and his disciples used to go about naked to show their indifference to worldly customs. They would practice severe mortifications of the body in order to be rid of its urgings. They were completely dedicated to the principle of ahimsa, scrupulously avoiding harm to any living thing. (A Jain monk will strain water before drinking to save any tiny organism who may be present; he will dust off his path before treading it, so as to gently remove any unseen creatures.) The culmination of the quest for liberation is *sallekhana*, in which the Jain monk starves himself to death after having gotten rid of all bodily desire.

The basis for these practices was a clearly articulated metaphysics. All reality, according to the Jains, is *jiva* or *ajiva*. Jivas are souls. They have the capacity for thought, perception and feeling, and they give life to whatever body contains them. Ajivas are bodies. They may be human, animal or plant bodies; or they may consist in various simple physical substances: air, water, etc. Every ajiva is associated with a jiva. That is, every part of the material world is alive. This is why the practice of ahimsa assumes such awesome proportions for the Jains.

The jiva does not in any way benefit from its involvement with ajiva. The Jains see this involvement as a literal mingling of the two substances. By virtue of this, the natural clarity of the jiva's thought is clouded and distorted, and it is physically held down on this earthly plane. The rigorous physical disciplines which the Jains perform are methods of "de-contaminating" the jiva. Conversely, a life of physical indulgence leaves the jiva still more polluted and burdened with ajiva. If the jiva can be purified, then it will rise into a higher spiritual plane.

In that spiritual world, Mahavira and all the other purified ones may be found. Each liberated jiva exists in a state of splendid isolation, enjoying the clarity and bliss of its own consciousness. This isolation is one of the most striking aspects of the Jain philosophy, for most people would find quite unattractive the prospect of being eternally cut off from everything else. In the Jain view, however, the perfect isolation allows the jiva to perfectly express its own nature, undisturbed by any external influence.

This emphasis on the soul's need for isolation explains precisely why ahimsa is so important for the Jains. Harmful, hurting actions create a bondage between jivas. Whoever is a victim of violence feels hatred for the perpetrator; and a cycle of violence and counter-violence is set up, in which the jivas are tangled together. It is very important to appreciate this way of thinking. The motive of ahimsa is *not* loving kindness toward other living creatures. It is more a matter of *respect* for these life forms, a willingness to let them proceed on their own way.

One final point in the Jain philosophy is most interesting: the absence of any God who creates and rules the universe. The world, with its innumerable jivas and ajivas, exists from all eternity. There is no higher power to give it direction or to offer aid and comfort to creatures. Such a God would, in fact, be incompatible with the Jain ideal of liberation. An individual jiva could never attain that desired state of complete independence if it were the creature and subject of God.

Hinayana Buddhism: The Analytical Approach

Hinayana (known to its own adherents as *Theravada*, the "Doctrine of the Elders") is the developed, systematic form of Buddha's original teachings. These teachings were the fruit of an acute *mindfulness*. Buddha firmly believed that if we could just be perfectly attentive to the world around us and to our own minds, profound insights would result.

We would discern that what appears simple is actually complex, and that what seems attractive is actually delusory. *Analysis* is the key: we must mentally take apart the objects of our experience in order to know them clearly.

Two doctrines are particularly central to the Hinayana viewpoint: Dependent Origination and the Three Characteristics. Dependent Origination teaches that all things are produced by causes; they originate in a state of dependence on other things and processes. A plant, for example, derives from a seed; but there are also soil, sunshine and moisture making their contributions. All of these are conditioned by a multitude of earlier causes, so that the causation of any particular entity is infinitely complex.

For the Hinayanists, the causal perspective is essential to the deepening of one's spiritual life. Looking within the mind, we can discern the arising of various mental states: greed, lust, anger, just to name those of most concern. Anger is a particularly good example. Once developed, it is extremely difficult to control. But if a person can detect it as it is just beginning to form, if a person can see the causes that are nurturing it, then counteracting factors can be introduced.

Dependent Origination also has profound implications for our general philosophical outlook. It is a principle allowing of no exceptions. The very nature of all things is that they arise and are sustained by causes. Existence, in this view, is not stable or enduring; it has a kind of pulse-like character, surging up as its causes assert themselves.

This view completely negates the possibility of a Supreme Being. We have already seen that Buddha was an atheist. Now the philosophical basis for his position is evident. God, if He exists, would necessarily be uncaused. Otherwise, He would have limitations and dependencies incompatible with His status as Supreme Being. But Dependent Origination asserts that nothing is uncaused.

The teaching of the Three Characteristics may be considered the culminating truth in Hinayana. It tells us exactly how to analyze the reality of material objects and of our own selves. The characteristics are Impermanence, Painfulness and Lack-of-self. They are marks of all existing things by which we can understand the futility of clinging to anything. If one could truly grasp these characteristics, the objects of desire would become repugnant and all sense of personal gratification would be negated.

The impermanence of things consists in their instability. Whatever seems solid and enduring in an object is simply a delusion born of the failure to analyze it closely enough. Take a brick, for example. It certainly seems solid and virtually indestructible. But, in reality, there are continual, imperceptible changes taking place in it. These changes occur by reason of the *atoms* that constitute all material reality. The notion of atoms—indivisible units from which larger objects are constructed—was taken up by several schools of Indian philosophy as well as by certain philosophers in ancient Greece (who bequeathed the term to modern science).

Hinayana's view differed from other philosophical theories of the atom by insisting on its radical instability. Each atom exists for just a single moment, a tiny fraction of a second. It is *dependently originated* by some earlier atom; and in its moment of existence, it generates a successor to itself. Thus, a certain continuity is provided. Moreover, as vast numbers of these atoms are collected, material objects as we know them appear. Such objects give an impression of being solid and lasting, but this is contradicted by the underlying reality of the atoms.

When this impermanence is clearly understood, the futility of desire is obvious. Anything that we might crave is continually undergoing change, losing whatever qualities may originally have spurred our desire. Death—or any other form of destruction—is simply the culmination of a process of dissolution and decay that is taking place at every moment. To see things as impermanent is to see them as inherently unreliable, as betraying any hope for satisfaction that we may repose in them.

This is precisely the insight to which Buddha led the bereaved mother Gotami. She saw that she had been wrong to be so attached to her son, given the fragility of all life. This is one of the most important teachings of Hinayana Buddhism and must not be minimized or overlooked. Loving human relationships are not a source of ultimate fulfillment and meaning in our lives. Contrary to what so many religions and philosophies have taught, these relationships are a delusion for the soul and an obstacle to its spiritual progress. Remember that Buddha himself set the example on this matter when he abandoned his own family.

One who sees everywhere the mark of impermanence is able to attain a state of calmness and detachment. Many Buddhists believe that Buddha himself, by virtue of his paranormal powers of perception, could actually see the atoms in their perpetual flux. We ourselves may hope for some of this insight by diligent mindfulness on the nature of things. In the direct perception of this impermanence, all the illusory hope of holding onto things will be quenched.

The second characteristic, Painfulness, has a function very similar to the first. Indeed, it is largely a result of the first in that the impermanence of things is often a source of pain. The word *pain* is to be taken in a very broad sense, embracing every kind of physical or mental affliction, discomfort and disagreeableness. Hinayana teaching, as also expressed in Buddha's First Noble Truth, is that painfulness greatly exceeds pleasantness in any object or situation. Thus, it is futile to regard life as a kind of game in which one seeks to get the most pleasure with the least pain. Such a game is doomed to end in failure.

In justification of the teaching of painfulness, there is a relentless emphasis on the undesirable features of whatever seems to be attractive. The human body is a notable example of what is subjected to this kind of analysis. We are urged to look beneath the superficial beauties that it may possess and reflect upon the blood, mucus, bile, urine, excrement, etc. Even those few pleasant qualities displayed on the body's exterior are soon lost. Buddhist meditation manuals take a grim delight in noting the effects of the aging process on appearance and vitality, and they dwell in grisly detail on the still more drastic effects that set in after death. Meditation about the present and future condition of the body is very definitely intended as an antidote to be kept ready-at-hand against the onset of sexual desire.

The pleasures of eating are fought by the same tactic. We are invited to contemplate the realities of the process:

> Crushed by the teeth and smeared with saliva, the chewed food becomes a mixture from which all visual beauty and good odor have disappeared; and it reaches a state of extreme repulsiveness, like a dog's vomit. And in such a condition one has to swallow it down ... After it has reached the stomach, the food remains in that region, which is like an unwashed cesspool, pitch dark, traversed by foul-smelling winds. Upon being digested, the food becomes excrement, or else urine.

Such lurid meditations will strike many people as one-sided and unhealthy. Hinayana's reply is that this approach is the essential correction required for our normal instinct to ignore the unpleasant. We must train ourselves to see the ugly side of life precisely because that is what we do not wish to look at.

In Painfulness as in Impermanence, Buddha is believed to have had supernatural powers of perception. He could and did see the totality of the world's suffering. The human tendency is to insulate ourselves from the sight of suffering. We all know in the abstract of the starvation and disease that are rampant in the world, but it is too disturbing to actually look at them. Buddha did look directly and calmly at all of it, and so must we. Our great besetting problem is illusion-making. We remain attached to the world because we picture it as a place containing beauty, contentment and stability. Craving is overcome when these deceptions are supplanted by the realities of painfulness and impermanence.

The third characteristic, Lack-of-self, has a rather different function than the first two, and it is considerably harder to explain. Impermanence and Painfulness pertain to the *object* of desire, portraying it in such guise as make us no longer desire it. Lack-of-self involves the *subject* of desire, i.e., that which (supposedly) experiences it. To most, this experiencer seems an obvious and basic reality; but Hinayana teaches that it is a complete delusion.

Many people never give a thought to what they are talking about when they use that ubiquitous little word "I." Consider these two statements:

> I am sitting down
> I am thinking about philosophy

They presuppose a certain entity to which both the physical and mental states belong. When these next statements are made,

> I will be standing up
> I was thinking about the weather

there is the further implication that this entity persists through time. It is the same self that was, is and will be. Hinayana, reaffirming the principle of impermanence, insists that no such entity can exist. Only the passing physical and mental states exist. There is no self which possesses them or experiences them.

Considerable care is taken in the description of these states, which are the sole reality of a human person. They fall into five categories: bodily processes, sensations, perception, cravings and thoughts. They are known as the *five heaps*, as each one encompasses a great many different processes that will be manifesting themselves at a given moment. For example, a certain person will now have a great multitude of perceptions: seeing, hearing, touching many things. Each of these will be tied in with various events in the other four categories. Hearing the bird's call, for example, is the result of the body's proximity to the bird, and this hearing may well evoke thoughts of some kind.

By the principle of Dependent Origination, physical and mental states are continually being brought into being. But it is not "I" who originate or control them. They are merely the result of the complex interaction of earlier processes. In this network of causal relationships, the whole being of a person is comprised. By causal continuity, it extends from one moment to the next, and from one reincarnation to the next. There is no permanent self in all this, just the appearing and disappearing processes. An ancient Buddhist verse sums it up:

> Only suffering exists, not the one who is suffering
> There is not an actor but only acting
> Nirvana exists but not the one seeking it
> The [Eightfold] Path exists but not the traveler on it

In the light of all this, we would do better to say "There is a sitting" and "There is a thinking about philosophy" rather than speak of "I" doing them. That way, the separateness of the two events would be emphasized, and the notion of a continuing, unifying self is suppressed. Now this may seem absurd. How, one asks, could there just be sitting or thinking "on their own" with no one to do them? The Buddhists answer that it is just our language, with its subject-predicate structure, which makes us think this way. Grammar requires that the predicate *think* be attached to some subject, but reality is otherwise.

There remains the question of what purpose this teaching serves. How will an understanding that a person is only the five heaps contribute to our spiritual awakening? Those familiar with the history of European philosophy may recognize that this teaching is very similar to one held by the great British skeptic, David Hume. It certainly did not lead to spiritual awakening in his case, and it is not easy to see how it might do so for the Buddhists.

The essential point is this: if there is no self, then there is nothing on behalf of which our desires might be fulfilled. Consider what this would mean in a particular instance of desire. I am hungry, or, in the Buddhist rendition, there is a craving for something to eat. This craving will be followed by certain actions and, in favorable circumstances, by certain taste-perceptions along with sensations of pleasure. But all these are discrete events. In none of them, singly or collectively, can "I" be found. The craving, seen as a distinct event belonging to nobody, contains no reason for its fulfillment. It resembles a case of Peter being hungry, Paul eating and John being full.

The futility of desire when there is no self is still more evident when it is a craving for intangible objects such as status or power. In these cases the process of fulfillment is far more complex, and the assumption of an enduring self is far more essential. Take the particular case of power. If a person is nothing more than a collection of dependently originated processes, where can power reside? Power implies that there is a desire and that there are actions stemming from this desire which cause it to be fulfilled. The desire and the actions must be "mine" so that the result can express "my" power.

Maybe this will be somewhat clearer if we draw an analogy between the concept of the self and the concept of the nation-state as developed in the philosophy of G.W.F. Hegel. This scholarly German professor unwittingly provided an ideological basis for a host of modern nationalistic political movements, of which the most extreme and diseased was Nazism. Hegel saw the state as an entity existing in its own right. It was not just a collection of people living on a certain territory. It was a kind of super-person, enduring through the generations. Individual citizens were the property of the state, existing for the state.

Now it should be quite clear that this belief in the state is not just some academic matter for scholars to argue over. By maintaining that the state transcends its own people, Hegel and his followers made credible the concepts of national glory and national destiny. These became legitimate objects for which individual citizens could and should sacrifice themselves. Conversely, holding that the state is no more than its people removes the basis for the nationalistic struggles which took place in the name of the state.

A Buddhist would say that the notion of self is illusory in just the manner of this concept of the transcendent state. Self and state are not just mistaken notions; they are dangerous. They sustain destructive strivings which would not exist if the realities in question were analyzed and understood as they really are. What we call the self is really just the five heaps. The self's power and glory are just as spurious as the state's.

One other matter calls for attention as we close this discussion of Lack-of-self. There is a truly striking contrast between this Buddhist teaching and the Hindu philosophy of the Upanishads. In the latter we saw the concept of self (Atman) exalted to the highest degree. This self, though mysterious, was undoubtedly real; it was to be cherished as the basis for our liberation. Now we see Buddhism treating self as a pernicious error.

Actually, the difference is a little less than meets the eye. The two philosophies have this much, at least, in common. They agree that the changeable body and soul cannot, together or separately, be the self. They further agree in condemning the egoism that results from identification with the needs of the body and soul. In both theories, nothing is truly "mine." (Remember that passage from the Maitri Upanishad, quoted on page 75.) Their disagreement, which is serious enough, is about whether there is something beyond the body and soul. The Buddhist philosophy has an abiding distrust of any such transcendental entity, while its Hindu opponent finds its essential meaning in the higher realm. The Buddhist philosophy is content to dwell on patient analysis of the world around us, while the other delves into deeper mysteries.

Mahayana Buddhism: Bodhisattvas and Emptiness

Mahayana involved truly revolutionary developments in Indian religion and philosophy. Its origins are obscure, and there is no one person to whom its beginnings can be attributed. Mahayanist ideas gradually arose among the sangha and in the larger Buddhist community. As we will see, certain elements of Mahayana gave it a strong popular appeal. By about 200 BC, this new form of Buddhism had emerged as a recognized alternative to Hinayana.

Mahayana is definitely at variance with the known teachings of Buddha, and its adherents have been at considerable pains to explain this fact. They speak of Buddha's *upaya*, "skill in means." This expression refers to the gift that he possessed of finding the right technique for communicating with his listeners. Buddha, say the Mahayanists, had an incomparable knack of discerning exactly what teaching or practice would be most suitable for anyone with whom he dealt. Thus, he taught different doctrines to different people. The great majority of his listeners were at a very elementary stage of spiritual development, and Buddha formulated the Hinayana to accommodate their limitations. To a small elite, in a private setting, something more difficult could be imparted. This, of course, was the Mahayana.

Certainly, the Mahayanists had a point in suggesting that theirs was the more challenging form of Buddhism. This is true both of their moral ideal, as exemplified by the *bodhisattva*, and of the underlying philosophical theory, as expressed in the *sunyavada* (emptiness teaching). It was the doctrine of the bodhisattva that gave rise to the designation *Mahayana*, literally, the "Great Way." A bodhisattva is understood by Mahayanists to be a being of perfect compassion. Feeling a boundless pity for the suffering of other creatures, this being defers personal liberation. As long as other beings suffer, the bodhisattva shares that suffering and makes every possible effort to alleviate it.

In contrast to Mahayana there is Hinayana, the "Small Way." (Keep in mind that this term is of Mahayanist coinage and not at all what the "Hinayanists" use to refer to themselves.) The Small Way is directed to the pursuit of one's own liberation. By the Hinayanaist reckoning, there is no purpose served by one person's emotional involvement with another. Hinayana cites Buddha injunction to "be lamps to yourselves", while Mahayana insists that no one can be truly liberated until all are liberated.

A passage in the Hinayanists' own scripture expresses exactly what their opposing co-religionists had in mind when they chastized the "selfishness" of the Small Way:

> When the wise man drives away sloth by strenuous effort, climbing the high tower of wisdom, he gazes sorrowless on the sorrowing crowd below. The wise person gazes on the fools, even as one on a mountain peak gazes at the dwellers on the plain(*Dhammapada*, II, 8)

The sentiment expressed here is quite in keeping with the Hinayana quest for detachment and imperturbability, but it is completely alien to the way of the bodhisattva. The essence of that way is compassionate involvement with others. The bodhisattva cannot see the suffering of others without being moved. Of course, we are all compassionate to some extent; but the bodhisattva has carried this attitude to the farthest extreme. The most painful sacrifices will be made, even for animals.

For example, there is the story of the bodhisattva who let himself be eaten by a starving tiger. He could easily have escaped the weakened animal but chose to surrender his life instead. Even more amazing is the sacrifice recounted in another story:

> As a bodhisattva meditated in the seclusion of the forest, a woman approached him, desirous of having sexual relations. [Such incidents are common in Indian religious folklore and are usually met with a stern rebuke.] The bodhisattva had taken a vow of chastity and would have to endure millions of years' torment in hell for violating it. But he could not bring himself to inflict any disappointment on the woman, and so he did as she wanted.

From this we may gather that the bodhisattva has a complete disregard for his own welfare. Any amount of personal sacrifice is justified if some good, even a trivial good, can be performed for another.

Whence come these remarkable beings, the bodhisattvas? They are, for all practical purposes, gods—but self-made gods rather than beings eternally enjoying that status. Every bodhisattva has endured, like ourselves, a countless number of human and animal incarnations. At some point, this being has made a vow of total compassion for the suffering of other creatures and thereby has become a bodhisattva. The karmic merit resulting from the fulfillment of this vow elevates the bodhisattva to a god-like condition. He acquires miraculous powers (akin to the yogi's psychic powers) and tirelessly devotes them to works of compassion. He is no longer in a human body but in a supernatural form suited to his powers.

In theory, the vow of a bodhisattva must be taken by us all. In practice, Mahayanists were generally content to worship the bodhisattvas and seek the blessings that they were so eager to bestow. This kind of religious belief had great popular appeal, and eventually Mahayana eclipsed Hinayana in the size of its following in India. As we saw, Hinayana had no use for the worship of gods. It promoted a spiritual ideal of self-reliance and detachment. Mahayana did not have a single, supreme God, like Allah or Krishna. But its bodhisattvas fulfilled many of the same emotional needs which those deities satisfy. Thus, it is not surprising that Mahayana grew so strong.

In passing, we may note a certain similarity between the Mahayana philosophy and that of the Bhagavad Gita. Each is a rebellion against a tendency in its own religion to a rather cold ideal of detachment and indifference. Against Hinayana and the Upanishads, the two later movements place real value on human feeling, whether bhakti or compassion. They also have in common a recognition of the human need for a personal god of some kind.

However, the story of Mahayana philosophy is only half told. There is still the theory of Emptiness to be accounted for. It is an extraordinarily strange and difficult teaching; and, *apparently*, it even invalidates the entire bodhisattva theory we have just studied. The teaching of Emptiness was first formulated in a series of works known as the *Prajnaparamita* Sutras ("Verses of Highest Wisdom") which date to perhaps 100 B.C.

These works teach that reality is *empty* in the sense of being devoid of any describable characteristic. The world is like a dream or the conjuration of a magician: mere appearance without any underlying substance. This way of thinking is actually not a complete departure from Hinayana. The latter had continually stressed how much of our view of the world is the spurious construct of the desire-crazed mind. It asserted that we must purge the mind of all false concepts and see only the true elements (which they called the *dharmas)* of reality. For example, we must do away with the concept of self and see only the five heaps.

The doctrine of Emptiness takes the position that these Hinyanist dharmas are themselves false constructs. The *Heart Sutra*, one of the most incisive of the Wisdom Sutras, reviews and dismisses practically all the fundamental Hinayanist teachings:

> Emptiness entails the non-existence of bodily processes, sensations, perceptions, cravings and thoughts [the five heaps] . . . There are not ignorance and the other elements of the Wheel of Becoming. There is not Suffering, the Cause of Suffering, its Stoppage and the Eightfold Path [the four noble truths]. There is no enlightenment, no attainment of liberation, no state of bondage.

Emptiness does not confine itself to the denial of specific Hinayanist dogmas. *Everything* in our conception of the world is illusory. The most ordinary and obvious objects in our experience have been conjured up in the mind and have no objective existence. There is no earth, moon, sun or sky. Even our own bodies are imaginary.

What could ever have led Mahayana to adopt such a mind-boggling viewpoint? The last sentence of that passage from the *Heart Sutra* provides a clue. Mahayana was grappling with a fundamental problem about how or whether liberation could be attained. It is a very basic problem, really, which may well have occurred to you already in reading this account of Indian philosophy.

To be liberated is to be rid of every concern and attachment; but to reach this state, must there not be an intense (and essentially selfish) desire for it? There seems to be a contradiction inherent in the quest for liberation. It is a desire for desirelessness. The other Indian philosophies, by and large, gloss over this problem. They say that desire for liberation is not a problem, that it is only the other desires that must be done away with. Mahayana confronts the issue head-on. How is it possible to get from samsara to nirvana, given that everything we do is motivated by selfish desire and thus reinforces selfish desire?

Mahayana's noble ideal of the bodhisattva does not truly solve this problem. It is said that the bodhisattva acts only for the happiness of others. Can such a being as this truly exist, completely devoid of selfish concern? Would there not be some personal gratification that the bodhisattva felt from his works of compassion?

Would there not be some selfish calculation that his own salvation is gained by devotion to the salvation of others?

Buddha's old concept of the Wheel of Becoming provides another perspective by which to grasp the difficulties involved here. We see ignorance, desire, rebirth and suffering linked in an endless cycle. Can it really be escaped, if each element gives rise to another? Mahayana draws the daunting conclusion that it cannot be escaped. Samsara is a trap in which we are caught by the self-perpetuating nature of the Wheel. There is no way from samsara to nirvana; there is, as the *Heart Sutra* puts it, no enlightenment and no attainment of liberation.

But the Sutra also tells us that there is no bondage, and that is the true key to making some sense of all this. We must understand that the entire domain of samsara is an illusion. The Wheel is an illusion. We have never been in bondage. If it *were* real, we would never be able to escape it. By the same token, nirvana must be eternally real. If it did not already exist, it could never be brought into existence. Here is how another one of the Wisdom Sutras expresses it:

> One who has set out on the way of the bodhisattva should think in this manner: "All beings I must lead to nirvana; and yet after beings have thus been led to nirvana, no being at all has been led to nirvana." And why? If to a bodhisattva, the notion of a being were to occur, he would not be a bodhisattva. (*Diamond Sutra*, Ch. 17)

The passage is one of confounding irony and paradox. It speaks of the bodhisattva; but in the end, it tells us that every being (including the bodhisattva) is unreal. Make no mistake about that. Emptiness entails the non-existence of the bodhisattva along with everything else in this world. The whole panorama of samsara—struggling souls and compassionate ones alike—is a grand hallucination. It must be so, or else nirvana could not exist.

Thus, we are in the strange position of finding that these two chief teachings of Mahayana—Bodhisattva and Emptiness—contradict one another. But it is not quite as bad as that. Mahayana tries to resolve the contradiction by advancing the notion of two levels of truth. Bodhisattva is a provisional truth. It is an ideal to look up to and to emulate, a method by which we can make ourselves ready for a greater understanding. Emptiness is this greater understanding, the final truth. In this Emptiness there is just nirvana. Not beings, thoughts, feelings of any kind but just nirvana in its perfect unity and tranquillity.

The Carvakas: Dissenters Against the Core Beliefs

Standing out from all the other Indian philosophers is a small, obscure group known as the Carvakas. To the spirituality and religious commitment of the others, the Carvakas opposed a staunch worldliness, dismissive of any higher reality. Those principles, like karma and liberation, which are fundamental in the other philosophies meet with sarcastic rejection by the Carvakas.

Materialism is the Carvakas' basic doctrine. They deny any kind of reality other the physical which we can see and touch. In particular, they deny all gods;

and they deny that humans possess any reality besides that of their bodies. This latter point immediately raises an objection as to how intangible processes like thinking can be carried out by mere matter. If the body can think, then why not a stone or a clod of earth. But clearly, those things possess no capacity for thought.

The Carvakas have an interesting answer to this objection. They draw attention to a familiar (in India) phenomenon. When betel, areca-nut and lime are ground up and blended, the resulting mixture has an intense red color. None of the components is red, but their combination somehow attains this color. This, say the Carvakas, is how we must understand the arising of thought in the human body. Certain material elements, in themselves devoid of thought, are able to produce it in combination. Thinking, as we might express it today, is a special kind of chemical reaction.

In this way the Carvakas resolutely denied the reality of any kind of soul, which would be the seat of our mental life and which would experience the karmic consequences of our present actions in a future life. When we die, our existence is completely ended. Thus, there is no justification for the moral and spiritual disciplines which religions advocate. This leads the Carvakas to a philosophy of total hedonism: nothing is valued but our own sensual gratification.

Here is how one of the traditional accounts of the Indian philosophies expresses it:

> There is no world other than this, no heaven and no hell. The realm of God and such as that are invented by stupid impostors belonging to the other schools of thought. The only heaven lies in eating delicious food, enjoying the company of young women, wearing fine clothes, perfumes, garlands, sandal-paste, etc. The only hell consists in the troubles caused by enemies, weapons, diseases. And the only liberation is death. (*Sarvasiddhantasamgraha*, I, 8–10, quoted from Radhakrishnan, *Sourcebook*, page 235)

Note how the passage expresses not just disagreement but contempt toward religious ways of thinking. To the Carvakas, it was the height of stupidity to give up the pleasures of life in order to pursue liberation. Recall how Gautama the Buddha renounced his own priviliged life to become a homeless beggar. Seeing the suffering around him, Gautama could not any longer find enjoyment in what he had.

The Carvakas oppose this way of thinking with their analogy of the rose and the thorns, which is the perfect expression of their hedonism. The enjoyment of a rose may be marred by the painfulness of the thorns, but it would be foolish to throw away the rose on this account. The liberation seekers, shrinking from the painfulness of life in general, are exactly like the one who deprives himself of the pleasure of the rose. The Carvakas willingly acknowledge that life does contain its "thorns", but our only sensible option is to face the problems of life, trying to keep them at a minimum while we have our enjoyments. They do not hesitate to brand the liberation seekers as lazy cowards, using their religious calling as a pretext for avoiding honest work.

The Carvakas held in equally low esteem the brahmin priesthood with their elaborate rituals. These rituals were nothing more than a hoax meant to hoodwink the general public. To prove this, the Carvakas cited the case of a certain ritual in which a cow was sacrificed. The ritual had been criticized by those who abhorred harm to any living thing, and the brahmins hastened to meet this criticism by assuring everyone that the poor cow would immediately be transported to heaven. The Carvakas pounced on this rationalization. If the cow goes to heaven, they asked, why not sacrifice one's own father so that he may enjoy this wonderful fate? According to them, the case shows the cynical dishonesty of the priestly profession. They do not themselves believe in their rituals; they only use them to make a living off the gullible.

Who were the authors of this bold dissent, when did they appear, and what retaliation did they provoke? Little is known of these matters. A few names are mentioned. In particular, there is a certain Brihaspati who is referred to in the ancient accounts of Carvaka teaching. His name means "master of prayer," which shows him to have been a brahmin—though, of course, a very untypical one. But no details of his life are known. We do know that the Carvakas were present in India by Buddha's time. As Buddhist scripture relates, they added their discordant voices to the vigorous religious discussion which was then taking place.

However, the Carvakas had no religious zeal to weld themselves into a coherent and enduring movement, so their appearances in Indian history are sporadic and elusive. It does not appear that they were subjected to any persecution. That, in general, is not the Indian way. The simple truth is that the Carvakas' ideas were too far removed from the mainstream of Indian thought to be taken seriously. It is a fascinating fact that these ideas were expounded in India at all, but they cannot be said to have exerted any real influence on the development of Indian philosophy.

V. PHILOSOPHIES OF THE SCHOLASTIC PERIOD

The term *scholasticism*, taken quite literally, refers to teaching that is suitable for *schools*. As applied to philosophy, the term connotes a rigid and dogmatic approach. The scholastic philosophy is systematic, argumentative, attentive to detail, and, above all, quite sure of itself. The scholastic style of philosophizing is very conspicuous in the history of European thought beginning with (but not confined to) the Middle Ages. Less widely known is the scholasticism prevailing in the later periods of Indian philosophy. In the scholastic period the visionary utterances of such works as the Upanishads and the Bhagavad Gita are supplemented by drier, more pedantic formulations. Precisely because so many different views had come to prominence in the earlier age, the various partisans needed to clarify, qualify and justify what they were saying.

Note that for most of these scholastic philosophies, particular works from the visionary era constituted the point of departure. Few of these systems were truly new, least of all in the minds of those who formulated them. These later thinkers saw their task as the preservation and vindication of the earlier teachings.

Indian scholasticism articulated itself through collections of verses called *sutras* or *karikas*. These stated the doctrines and arguments in an extremely concise manner. As an example, take these two verses which come at the beginning of the *Samkhyakarikas*, a work expounding (in some seventy-two verses altogether) the views of the Samkhya school of philosophy:

1. Suffering, in its three forms, gives rise to philosophical inquiry, which seeks to bring it to an end. The objection is made that this is pointless, since there are empirical means to remedy suffering. But we reject these means as uncertain and temporary.

2. The attempt to destroy suffering by means of the Vedic scriptures is also deficient. For the rituals associated with these scriptures are impure and devoid of any lasting and assured effect. Superior to these is our school's discernment of the evolved, the unevolved and the knower.

In these lines (which are even more concise in the Sanskrit original) various points are alluded to. The first verse provides the Samkhya disciple with criticisms to direct against the Carvakas. The second is aimed at a school of philosophers known as the Mimamsas. The evolved, the unevolved and the knower comprise the essentials of the Samkhyas' own position. These karikas presuppose a well-developed system of oral teaching. The Samkhya student would learn them by heart in order to have ready-to-mind all the objections, counter-objections, illustrations and enumerations that his school could deploy against its adversaries. The karikas themselves do not really explain points, but they serve to remind a student of explanations imparted in the course of oral instruction.

The scholastic era in Indian philosophy can be said to have started around the beginning of the Christian era, and this kind of philosophizing flourished in India for well over a thousand years. In what follows we will examine six of the many different scholastic systems, in roughly the order that they came to prominence. With one exception (Madhyamaka), these philosophies are all "orthodox" in that they accept the Hindu scriptures. This is a reflection of the fact that during the scholastic era Hinduism was ever more effective in overcoming its philosophic rivals. But Hinduism itself was extraordinarily multi-faceted, as these philosophies show.

1. Samkhya: Prakriti and Purusha

Samkhya was the first scholasticism to appear and the first to decline. Its inspiration was in certain schemes of classification that are suggested in the Upanishads. In keeping with the spirit of scholasticism, Samkhya carried out the classification far more precisely and consistently. The word *samkhya* means "enumeration" and refers to a listing of twenty-five *tattvas* or "realities" into which all existence can be classified. This enumeration is not for some idle theoretical or academic purpose. The attainment of liberation depends upon our precisely making the discrimination among these tattvas.

Two of the twenty-five tattvas are of paramount importance: *prakriti*, the primeval stuff, and *purusha*, the knowing self. The latter is inspired by the Upanishads' concept of Atman. The former is something quite distinctive of Samkhya. It is a dynamic, creative reality in which the remaining tattvas are contained as potentialities. Samkhya gives a thorough account of the order in which these potentialities are evolved into actualities. We omit the details of this presentation, noting only that the evolution on one side produces the physical world and on another side give rise to various mental and physiological capacities. In this way, the human body and the human soul are precisely accounted for.

Evolution out of prakriti is a process that eventually reverses itself. The various tattvas are "devolved" or merged back into prakriti, which is exactly as it was at the beginning: undifferentiated, or "unevolved." The entire sequence of events constitutes a cycle that endlessly repeats itself. The unevolved and the evolved states eternally alternate with one another, on a truly vast time scale. Billions of years ago, all of our souls came out of prakriti, along with the physical materials for our bodies. These souls will pursue their samsaric courses for further billions of years, until dissolution into prakriti again takes place. Then, after yet more billions of years, prakriti will begin the cycle anew by differentiating itself into the other tattvas. There is neither beginning nor end to the cycles, though (as we will see) individual souls may effect their own termination.

If you are asking yourself *why* all this continues to happen through such aeons, you are asking exactly the right question, as far as the Samkhya philosophers are concerned. But we are not quite in a position yet to examine the answer they devised.

Prakriti is believed to contain three basic elements, known as the *gunas*. They are literally the "threads" from which all reality is woven. Through the dynamic interaction of the gunas, the entire evolutionary process can be explained, and all its products can be defined. The gunas are sattwa, rajas and tamas. They can be loosely characterized as light, energy and matter, respectively. Sattwa is expressed in the psychological component of evolution, and tamas in the physical. Rajas plays the role of a propelling power, fueling both sides of the evolutionary process.

When prakriti is in its unevolved state, the gunas are in a state of equilibrium. They are perfectly balanced against one another, so that each one's distinctive characteristic is cancelled out. Thus, prakriti in itself is without any discernible qualities. Once the equilibrium is disturbed, qualities appear, reflecting a preponderance of one or another of the gunas. Where sattwa is dominant, there is the soul. Where tamas has the ascendancy, bodies are manifest. And in all processes of activity, the energy of rajas is at work.

Now to the pivotal question. What disturbs the equilibrium of prakriti, causing yet another cycle of cosmic evolution to begin? It is the purusha, the other of the two fundamental tattvas, which is responsible. But it does this, not through direct action, but by providing a purpose for the evolutionary cycle. This is the central truth of the Samkhya system, and we must now consider just what the purusha is.

Like the Upanishads' Atman, purusha represents the true self. It is an entity of perfect calmness and stability, standing apart from all processes of change. It is not composed of the gunas, and, above all, it is not to be identified with the sattwa-constituted soul. The great difference between the Samkhya conception of purusha and the Upanishadic idea of Atman is that purusha is multiple rather than one. Each living creature has it own purusha, with its own distinctive spiritual condition. These purushas are not merged into a single all-embracing divine principle. That is, there is nothing corresponding to Brahman in the Samkhya system.

Each purusha is utterly passive. It simply contemplates the world from the perspective of the particular soul and body with which it is associated; but it does not take action of any kind. The purusha is so absorbed in this contemplation that it entirely forgets itself, even as someone watching a play might be so fascinated with the plot as to momentarily forget all about his own life.

That is why the evolutionary cycle proceeds. It is the means by which each purusha can become aware of itself. As the details of cosmic cycle disclose themselves to the mind, it becomes clear that there must be something beyond prakriti which constitutes the cause and purpose of this endless process. In the state of equilibrium, prakriti itself has no tendency to evolve. If there were only prakriti, the souls absorbed in it would remain forever in a state akin to deep sleep. For the purushas' sake, the other tattvas do emerge, they persist, and finally, in exhaustion, they sink back into prakriti to await the next cycle. On a grand scale, it repeats our own daily cycle of activity and rest.

The Samkhyas use the example of the cow's milk. Independent of her knowledge or control, the milk is formed in her body for the sake of the calf. The reality of the calf is proven, so to speak, by the existence of the milk. Likewise, the prakritic activity reveals purusha to us. But note that purusha in no way exerts force on prakriti to initiate this activity—just as the calf in no way provides the energy for its mother's milk production.

If an individual soul comes to understand the reality of purusha in this way, then samsara is ended for it. The particular purusha associated with this soul is now free, no longer engrossed in the functioning of its body and soul. Those two, for their part, have no further reason for their existence and are permanently dissolved into prakriti. The *Samkhyakarikas* have a particularly striking image for this:

59. As a dancer stops dancing once she has performed for her audience, so prakriti stops, once she has displayed her true nature before purusha . . .

61. I believe there is no one more bashful than this prakriti who, upon the realization "I have been seen" never again shows herself before purusha.

To "see" prakriti in its true nature is simply to see it as an objective reality distinct from purusha.

There is one matter we must not gloss over in this discussion. Where precisely does this seeing take place? It is most certainly *not* purusha which sees this truth, for it is a passive, unchanging observer. The purusha cannot be said to come to know anything or to disentangle itself from anything. The change to enlightenment can only take place in the soul, that product of prakriti's sattwa guna. By coming to grasp the evolutionary process and its underlying purpose, the soul knows purusha and thus brings to an end their mutual bondage.

Though Samkhya did not remain an active school for long, its influence on later Indian philosophy was enormous. It set the pattern for the new scholastic style of philosophizing, and it contributed many important concepts to the general stock of philosophic ideas. Particularly noteworthy here are the guna doctrine and the theory of cosmic cycles. The great majority of later Indian philosophers accepted both of these even as they rejected the central Samkhya thesis about the nature of liberation.

2. Madhyamaka Buddhism: The Theory to End all Theories

Until about 600 AD Buddhism continued to be a thriving movement in India, and it attracted to itself some of the most gifted philosophic minds. Mahayana gradually gained the ascendancy over Hinayana, so that its teachings became the subject of scholastic elaboration. Buddhist philosophers were especially anxious to elaborate and defend the theory of Emptiness, and this most certainly gave them a good deal to puzzle over.

One important group of Mahayana philosophers were the *Vijnanavadins*. Their name designates them as proponents of the "consciousness doctrine." They denied all objective reality, insisting that there was nothing but the mind and its ideas. Their teaching was roughly similar to one put forward much later by the British philosopher George Berkeley. In Vijnanavadins' case this idea was the natural outgrowth of the Emptiness theory and its emphasis on the deluded nature of our ideas about the world. If our ideas are indeed so mistaken, then we may as well dispense with the view that there *is* an objective world for them to be about.

Nevertheless, the Vijnanavadins' way did not suit some other Mahayanists because it did affirm the absolute reality of the mind. Affirming the reality of anything violated the spirit of Emptiness, according to these others, who are known as the Madhyamikas. It probably is fair to say that they did achieve the most consistent and coherent philosophical rendition of Emptiness. Certainly, theirs was the most extreme version of it.

The word *madhyama* means "middle", and so our philosophers are literally the "proponents of the middle doctrine." This is an allusion to the famous Middle Way which Buddha taught, the way between the extremes of self-indulgence and self-torture. But the Madhyamaka philosophy went far, far beyond that practical teaching. Their middle way was between "It is" and "It is not." That is, their way refused to accept either of the alternatives for a given question.

Buddha had, in fact, provided an example which was a direct and meaningful inspiration for the Madhyamaka approach. This was in his answer (or rather his failure to answer) the question of what would happen to a liberated person after death. (See page 62.) On several occasions Buddha had explicitly ruled out any possible answer to the question. "It would be wrong to say that the liberated one still exists, and it would be wrong to say that the liberated one does not still exist." This formulation certainly did leave nothing to say on the question, not to mention the fact that it defied our normal logic, which would insist that *one* of the two possibilities must be true.

What Buddha said of this one matter, Madhyamaka now proceeded to say with respect to every question: that all of the alternative answers must be ruled out. This approach was carried to perfection by Nagarjuna (about 150 AD), who may be considered the founder of Madhyamaka philosophy. His method is admirably easy to state (though fiendishly difficult to understand in its actual execution). Systematically refute every one of the philosophical positions that can be taken on a given point. In this way, the whole intellectual landscape will be cleared. Emptiness is achieved in the complete silencing of one's attempt to describe reality in any way. One is enlightened by virtue of this literal emptying of the mind. (But Nagarjuna himself will not express it this way, since he does not affirm the existence of the mind—or anything else.)

In his major work, the *Mulamadhyamakakarikas*, Nagarjuna takes up the questions of philosophy, one after another, applying this method. We will mainly confine ourselves to the question he considers in his very first chapter, a question of consuming interest to all Indian philosophers. What is the relation between cause and effect? There are two primary possibilities here. Either the effect is contained in the cause, or it is distinct from the cause. These Indian philosophers designate these as, respectively, *satkarya*, "existing effect [in the cause]" and *asatkarya*, "non-existing effect [in the cause]"

These possibilities require some careful explanation. The Samkhyas were notable for having taken the first position. Their view was that the emergence of entities from prakriti could not be understood unless these entities were already present in it. They liked to use the example of the oil which is produced by pressing the sesame seed. How, they asked, could the oil be brought forth unless it was already in the seed? This is impossible, according to Nagarjuna. If the effect already existed in the cause, there would be no need for it to *be* caused. The oil may already exist in some form in the seed, but it does not exist in its completed form; the causation of that form is what Samkhya cannot explain.

Opposing the Samkhyas were (among others) the Hinayana Buddhists who maintained that the cause and effect are completely distinct. Causation is understood in the coordination of two events, A and B. If we systematically observe that

"Given the occurrence of A, there follows the occurrence of B", then A may be said to be the cause of B. This is certainly a more common and natural view of causation than the Samkhyas'.

But Nagarjuna finds it objectionable. What basis for the causal link can there be? When is this link created? If A becomes the cause of B after B already exists, then it is unnecessary. But if A is the cause of B before B exists, that is impossible. How can something be considered a cause when its effect is non-existent? B is either existent or non-existent at every moment, and so there is no time at which A can become B's cause.

Thus, both Satkarya and Asatkarya are refuted, and there is no way to comprehend causation. Suppose now that one denies that there is causation at all, holding that things arise in a completely random way. That view is also absurd. We are left with no basis for believing that things actually do come into existence. Every way of making sense of their coming-to-be proves incoherent. The phenomena of the world are, as Nagarjuna likes to say, like the creations of a magician. They appear, but there is no rational basis for their appearance, and so we must say that they are illusory.

There is a certain resemblance between Nagarjuna's approach here and Al-Ghazali's critique of the Muslim philosophers' belief in causation. But note that Ghazali's discussion revolved around the issue of whether the cause of something could be rationally known. Nagarjuna's problem is deeper than that. It is the issue of whether such a thing as causation is possible at all.

In Chapter XV of the his *Karikas*, Nagarjuna gives further support to his theory of emptiness by attacking the possibility that entities could have any kind of characteristic. Such a characteristic would be, in his terminology, *svabhava*, "own-being." But any quality in an object exists in relation to a multitude of conditioning factors. Even if we cannot rationally explain this conditioning process, it unmistakably presents itself to us.

Take the round shape of a ball, for instance. There are various forces which create this shape and manifest it—these are basically the forces holding the ball together. So the ball is not round of itself; roundness is not part of its svabhava. And the same analysis can be made of every single one of the ball's qualities. It has *no* svabhava; it is just a blank waiting for other things to imprint qualities upon it.

What is said of the ball can be said of all other objects as well. They are all devoid of svabhava. But if each thing is a void in itself, how can any qualities ever be brought into being?

Imagine a village in which the each person's wealth consists solely in promissory notes from other members of the community. Thus, Brown has no tangible assets, only IOUs from Black, White, Green, etc. But they don't have any tangible assets either, only more IOUs. It is conceivable that our village will be the scene of vibrant economic activity, with continual trading in these IOUs. But a rational observer will say that it is all a sham. The wealth of this community is nothing but an illusion.

This is exactly how it stands with our world, according to Nagarjuna. There is no basis in svabhava for any of the characteristics we see manifested around us. The world in its entirety is an illusion, exactly like what some magician might conjure up. The peace of nirvana will manifest itself when all the plurality and change of the illusory world have been "emptied" out of the mind.

It is a most extreme and uncompromising position. There were certainly other schools in Indian philosophy who recoiled from this illusionism, and now we will consider one of them in particular.

3. Nyaya: Defending Common Sense

Nyaya means "logic", and that was originally the predominant interest of the philosophers of this school. They developed *syllogisms*, or patterns for sound reasoning. They carefully surveyed the various means, such as perception, for gaining right knowledge. They analyzed the phenomenon of error in order to understand where our quest for knowledge goes wrong.

Nyaya was founded on the belief that knowledge *is* attainable. The representatives of this philosophy firmly believed that human beings are in possession of the basic means for acquiring it. The need is simply to sort out good intellectual methods from bad ones.

For this reason, Nyaya strongly opposed those schools which taught that all or most or our normal understanding of the world is deluded. Their criticism was not just directed toward Nagarjuna's extreme illusionism. They also objected to philosophies like Hinayana or Samkhya which believed that certain crucial parts of our normal belief structure were mental contrivances. Nyaya took its stand on the proposition that what a normal person believes about the world is basically right.

To defend this viewpoint, Nyaya developed its own distinctive metaphysics. It was a metaphysics which held that the world displays a comprehensive order. Everything can be classified into an elaborate system of categories. There are exactly seven kinds of reality. The first of these, substance, has nine subdivisions. The second, quality, has twenty-four. And so forth. There is nothing which does not have its clearly defined place.

It is somewhat reminiscent of the Samkhyas, with their twenty-five tattvas. But the tattvas belong to phases in a cosmic evolutionary process; they represent a *dynamic* scheme of classification. While Nyaya accepts the Samkhya belief in cosmic cycles, it does not accept Samkhya's characterization of the specific phases of this process. Its primary interest is in eternally valid types of reality, and so its categories are *static*.

We will now look at some of the particular entities that appear in the Nyaya system of classification. We need to understand just what made the postulation of these necessary in the context of Indian philosophy. It will become evident that Buddhist philosophers (Hinayana and Mahayana) are the Nyayas' main adversaries. They had denied the reality of what, in the Nyayas' view, was essential to a sound view of the world.

Space and time are good examples to begin with. Nyaya counts them as two of the nine basic substances. This means that they are to be considered independent, objectively-existing realities. In addition to the concrete things of this world, there are the eternal frameworks of space and time in which these things are situated. In contrast, Buddhist philosophers held that space and time are purely relational. That is, they have no intrinsic reality; they are creations of the mind by which the objects of our experience are put in order. To a Buddhist, for example, space is just "nothing"; there is no need to suppose the reality of space above and beyond the objects in space.

The dispute here is closely paralleled by a later controversy in Western thought. Newton believed the objective reality of space to be essential for understanding the physical world, while Leibniz and Kant denied that there was an absolute space.

Another point of Nyaya-Buddhist dispute which has a counterpart in Western philosophy is the issue of *universals*. A universal is a general property which is found in all members of a given class. For example, all dogs have *doghood*; all pots have *pot-ness*. These terms by which we refer to the universal qualities are certainly meaningful (though often rather awkward). The question is: do they refer to anything that actually exists? The Buddhists said No. The universal is simply a mental device by which we put similar things together. Nyaya insisted that universals do objectively exist. When we look at the pot, we can actually perceive pot-ness in addition to the pot itself. From the Nyaya standpoint, it was essential that these universals exist. Otherwise, the classifications by which our world is made intelligible would have no basis. Things would not really belong in the same category unless they shared a given universal.

The Nyayas' primary tool for understanding the structure of the physical world is the concept of the atom. These are the *indestructible* bits of matter from which all material objects are constructed. There are light atoms, air atoms, water atoms and earth atoms—they supply four of the nine kinds of substance in the Nyaya system. Notice how different the Nyaya atom is from that which is featured in the Hinayana philosophy. The Hinayana atom is a momentary flash of being. To comprehend it is to know the utter instability and unreliability of the world around us. The Nyaya atom, on the other hand, exists forever. It may be joined to other atoms, or it may exist in separation; but its intrinsic characteristics remain the same.

In fact, the Nyayas use the theory of atoms to give their own distinctive version of the Samkhya theory of cosmic cycles. The primordial condition at the beginning of each cycle is one in which all the atoms are separated from each other. When the atoms are combined into larger objects, the world as we know it emerges. Then, after the passage of incalculable time, the objects dissolve back into their constituent atoms, and the world awaits the beginning of a new cycle.

The discussion of the cosmic cycle brings up another point of vital importance. You will recall that the Samkhyas had a rather peculiar explanation of why a given cycle begins. It was the non-sentient prakriti's somehow responding to the purushas' need for liberation. Nyaya considers this absurd. There must be some direct power exerted upon the world in its incoherent state, a power which will (as the Nyayas see it) inaugurate the process of joining atoms together. This power can only come from some supremely powerful God who chooses to begin the cycle again. God will do this in order to facilitate the liberation of individual souls.

Samkhya had explicitly rejected this possibility, maintaining that there could be no reason why a perfect divine being would need or wish to involve Himself in such a way. Nyaya insisted that there was no other way of explaining the cycle. Note that the Nyaya philosophy does not hold that God is the cause of the atoms' *existence*, for they are eternal and uncreated. God is merely the explanation why the atoms combine and later dissolve.

God, to the Nyayas, is an example of a self, and we must now discuss the general meaning of this category in their philosophy. Every living thing possesses a self, though there is a profound difference between finite selves and that infinite self which is God. Nyaya vigorously reaffirmed the reality of self against Buddhist criticism. In Buddhism, self is the prime example of an erroneous concept which the mind has concocted. In the specific version of Hinayana, there are really just the momentary processes, known as the five heaps. The delusion of self is projected onto these processes, much as one might draw a continuous line connecting a series of disjointed dots. Nyaya argues that memory and moral responsibility cannot be accounted for unless we suppose that there *is* continuing self to which the processes belong.

Nyaya holds that even those Indian philosophies which believe in the self are sometimes seriously mistaken about it. The opponents they have in mind are Samkhya and the Upanishads. The Samkhyas bring out the issue very clearly. They insist on the essential *disconnectedness* between the self and the phenomenal world. The self (purusha) is a pure consciousness. It does not really have desire or pleasure or pain. It becomes mistakenly bound up with these through its false association with a soul in the phenomenal world. Enlightenment consists in the dispelling of this illusory association. The view is much the same in the Upanishads, though there it involves a single Atman rather than a plurality of purushas.

Nyaya holds, by contrast, that the self is not disengaged from its own mental states. It is "I" who think and feel and desire. These states are forms of consciousness, and consciousness itself is just a property that the self may or may not possess at any given time. We must appreciate this position as one more instance of Nyaya's determination to vindicate the standpoint of common sense.

One intriguing question which emerges from all this is: if the world is such a tidy place as the Nyayas believe, why should we wish to be liberated from it? Though they do avow that their philosophy is a quest for liberation, it is somewhat difficult to believe that this really is an overriding concern for them (as it clearly is for most of the others). It is a philosophy that is so deeply tied to the world as it is normally experienced. Added to this is the fact that Nyaya has a singularly unappealing concept of exactly what liberation is. It is simply the self's permanent loss of consciousness. The liberated self no longer experiences pain, pleasure or anything. It is in what we would nowadays call a "persistent vegetative state."

Whether for this or other reasons, the Nyaya metaphysics did not, in the long run, prove very influential in Indian philosophy. Nyaya was valued more for its logic than for its general account of the nature of reality. In later times, the members of the school themselves reverted to an exclusive preoccupation with logic.

4. Mimamsa: Upholding the Ancient Ritual

Mimamsa (or Purva Mimamsa, as it is more fully known) is one of the most difficult Indian philosophies to explain. The difficulty does not come, as in the case of the Mahayana philosophy, from the abstruseness or complexity of its ideas. The basic idea of the Mimamsa philosophy is really quite simple. It is just totally implausible from the standpoint of someone living in the modern world.

This extraordinary idea, around which the whole Mimamsa philosophy centered, was that the Hindu scriptures, the Vedas, had existed forever. They had existed in this world, reverently passed on from one generation to the next by the brahmin priesthood. In fact, the Mimamsas were exclusively concerned with the earlier portion of the Vedas, which pertained to the ancient rituals. Thus comes the name *Purva Mimamsa*, which means "earlier interpretation." They largely ignored the later portion, the Upanishads, whose philosophical devotees we will be considering in the remaining two sections.

The Vedic rituals had already been declining in popularity by 500 BC. The Upanishads consider ritualism to be an inferior kind of religion (See p. 73.), and the non-Hindu philosophies attacked it even more forcefully. Nevertheless, the rituals were preserved; and the Mimamsas, their philosophical defenders, continued to be a vigorous presence in Indian thought until at least 800 AD.

The belief in the *eternity* of the Vedic ritual tradition is what makes the Mimamsa philosophy so strange to us today. We are thoroughly imbued with the idea that things can be traced back to their origins. With good reason, we think we know something about the beginnings of the whole universe and of human life in particular. It goes totally against the grain of our thought to suppose that anything in the material world has been here forever.

Moreover, the Mimamsas insisted that our world had existed forever *in its present form*. They rejected the notion of eternally repeating cycles which the Samkhyas and most other Indian philosophers believed in. They could not accept the idea that the whole world would periodically dissolve into an incoherent state, for then the transmission of the Vedas would be interrupted.

The Mimamsa position becomes even more remarkable when we realize that they did not attribute the Vedas to any God. The Vedas are infallibly true, they argued, precisely because they are not the words of a God. If divine authorship were the basis of Vedic authority, then one would have to show the existence of God and prove somehow that these scriptures were actually communicated by

God. These tasks, particularly the latter, would pose insurmountable difficulties which would end up compromising the infallibility of the Vedas.

From this we see that the Mimamsas had a completely different attitude toward their scriptures than what is encountered in any other religious philosophy. The Koran and the Bible, for example, are valid in the eyes of their believers *because* they come from God. Since God is all-knowing and truthful, these scriptures are to be believed. The Mimamsas deliberately forfeit any support that their scriptures might receive from such a consideration. The Vedas exist eternally *without any author*; this confers on them an inherent validity.

Let us try to enter into the Mimamsa world view in order to get some notion of the basis for their confidence in the Vedas. For the sake of argument, accept the idea that our world has always been here, and accept that the Vedas have always been preserved in each generation. As a basis for this, assume that there are plausible historical records which trace the Vedas back through millions—not just thousands—of years. And so we not implausibly project from millions of years to "forever."

Now consider some particular Vedic injunction such as "Perform ritual X and you will receive reward Y in heaven"—this is actually typical of the Vedic passages that concern the Mimamsas. This injunction cannot be verified, for we are not in heaven. But if it has been passed on forever, with no origin, does that not give it a certain authority? Would one not be tempted to say that this truth, by virtue of its eternal presence, was somehow inherent in the very nature of the world? At any rate, that is how the Mimamsas felt the truth of their Vedas to be vindicated.

They developed a rather sophisticated epistemology (theory of knowledge) to lend further credence to this viewpoint. They held that truth in general was a function of the inherent characteristics of a mode of knowing, not of any external circumstances. Let me explain this by the example of perception. What is it that validates some normal perception, such as my seeing of house right in front of me? Other Indian philosophers, notably the Nyayas had maintained that this perception was valid provided certain conditions were met: the eyes must be healthy, the house sufficiently close, obstructing factors must be absent, etc.

The Mimamsas pointed out how problematic this approach was. We justify the first perception by certain other perceptions of the circumstances. But then these perceptions have to be justified, and we are caught in an infinite regress where justification is never obtained. Much better, they say, to posit that the perception in valid by its very nature. Of course, perceptions go wrong from time to time, as, for instance, when one "sees" a snake where there is only a coiled up rope. (This is favorite example in Indian philosophy.) The Mimamsa point is that a perception must be considered valid unless there are some special circumstances that make it invalid. It is, if you will, a case of "innocent until proven guilty."

As applied to the Vedas, this principle means that their truth is established, since there are no external circumstances which could invalidate it. If they had an author, then one could ask: is this author credible, is this author in a position to make these statements? As there is *not* an author, there is no basis for challenge.

On their fundamental belief in the eternity and infallibility of the Vedas, the Mimamsas built a coherent philosophy of life. The early representatives of the school did not believe in liberation at all. Their concept of religious salvation was *heaven*, gained by the performance of the required rituals. The later Mimamsas fell in with the general belief in liberation, but even then they insisted on ritualistic *actions* rather than enlightened *knowledge* as the means of obtaining it.

5. Shankara's Advaita Vedanta: Reality and Illusion

The name *Vedanta* means "end of the Vedas" and thus refers to the Upanishads, the final portion of that vast body of scripture. The Mimamsas may have ignored them, but there were many others who found the Upanishads to be a profound source of philosophic inspiration. Thus, there were many schools of Vedanta philosophy.

Foremost among these is Advaita Vedanta, which is largely the creation of one man, the great Shankara (about 788–820 AD). No other philosopher has attained an eminence in India equal to his. It may be said that in Shankara's thought, the Indian mind found a system of ideas that was uniquely satisfying. To a large extent, the success of his philosophy was the result of his willingness to make use of ideas from other philosophies. The cosmology of the Samkhyas, the logic of the Nyayas, the devotionalism of the Gita—all these had a place in Shankara's system. As we will see, there was also extensive borrowing from a source he would never have willingly acknowledged, namely, Mahayana Buddhism. But the place of all these borrowed materials was rigidly circumscribed by the nature of the Advaita philosophy, to which we now turn.

Advaita is literally "non-dualistic", and it expresses the fact that Shankara holds reality to consist in a single, undifferentiated unity. There is no duality of principles, such as with the prakriti and purusha of the Samkhyas. Shankara finds this non-dualistic way of thinking in the Upanishads' notion of the single ultimate reality referred to as Brahman. The fact that this Brahman is identified with Atman, the one true self in us all, reinforces the non-dualism.

But Shankara adds something which was not in the Upanishads. This is the idea that everything other than Brahman-Atman is an illusion. The entire phenomenal world that we experience is false. There is only the underlying reality discerned by enlightenment: Brahman-Atman. This doctrine is not taught by the Upanishads. They hold that phenomenal reality is derivative, superficial and unimportant—but not illusory.

It is perfectly clear where Shankara got this notion, though he would not have admitted it. The idea was inspired by the Mahayana teaching of Emptiness. The more important question is: why did he feel the need to import this idea into his philosophy and to convince himself that it was truly the teaching of the Upanishads? Remember that in the Upanishads, the aim is that the true self

(Atman) transcend the afflictions of this world and experience unity with Brahman. It is taken for granted that this involves some kind of *change*.

That is what poses the problem for Shankara. The one essential property of Atman is that it is unchanging. If that is so, then how can it undergo the process of being liberated? Atman is whatever it is *eternally*. It is not really true to say that Atman separates from the material world and unites with Brahman, though we inevitably fall into this way of speaking. In reality, Atman and Brahman are *always* the same.

For Shankara, as for the Mahayanists, the problem of escaping from samsara is insurmountable, since (as he would put it) is is a change which must somehow affect the unchanging Atman. The solution can only be to proclaim the illusoriness of samsara and (what is really the same thing) of all change. The unchanging perfection of Brahman is the only reality. Any change that we perceive is an illusion.

Of course, there are differences between Shankara and the Mahayanists. They believe in Emptiness, by virtue of which *every* quality we might wish to impute to reality is false. Brahman is *not* empty, according to Shankara. There are three absolute truths which may be spoken of it. First, it is being: not "has being" but "is being." There is nothing at all other than Brahman; it is the totality of existence. This position is strikingly similar to ibn-Sina's description of the Necessary Being. With each philosopher the idea is that particular modes of being—even such cherished religious qualities as being-wise and being-just—cannot be attributed to God, strictly speaking. God is just pure being, being as such.

The second truth about Brahman is that it is consciousness. This is not an additional property augmenting what has already been stated in the first truth. By virtue of the fact that it is being, Brahman is also consciousness. It is the nature of being to reveal itself, and to manifest things is the essential function of conscious-ness. In this aspect Brahman most clearly shows the character of Atman as described in the Upanishads. It is a pure, empty awareness, containing in itself no thought or idea. When shining into the mind, this light of awareness will illuminate the mind's thoughts; but the mind and Atman are quite distinct, as the Upanishads taught.

In the third place, Brahman is bliss. This property is, again, not a new charac-teristic but merely the expression of what has already been described. Brahman, in its stable condition of pure self-awareness, is necessarily a state of bliss. Just as the consciousness of finite minds comes from Brahman, so whatever joy we experience is the result of momentarily tapping into the sustained, infinite bliss of Brahman.

Thus, with these three affirmations, Shankara distinguishes his view from Mahayana, which refused to predicate any quality of the ultimate reality. But every-thing we perceive other than being, consciousness and bliss is illusory. If one sees a red, round, shiny object, all that is really there is simple being, not redness or any of the other qualities. The being is real but not the being-red, etc.

Shankara uses that analogy of the snake and the rope to explain himself. In fact, this image is one of the keys to understanding his thought; so we will explore

RAMAKRISHNA, MEDITATION POSE AT DAKSHINESWAR

Ramakrishna (1835–86), perhaps the most revered Hindu saint of modern times. His life testifies to the enduring vitality of the ancient ideals of Indian spirituality. At the time the photo was taken, Ramakrishna was in a state of yogic trance. [Ramakrishna Center of New York]

it very carefully. Imagine a rope coiled up in a dark corner. Someone looking at the rope supposes that there is a snake. The image of the snake is, so to speak, superimposed on the rope.

In the same way, the image of the phenomenal world is conjured up. On the pure being of Brahman we superimpose all the false modes of being. Just as the rope must be there in order for the snake to be seen, so Brahman is essential as the basis of the illusion. But Brahman is totally distorted in our normal perception of it. Just as seeing the snake gives rise to needless fears, our perception of the phenomenal world creates a multitude of false concerns and frustrations.

The supremely difficult question for Shankara's philosophy is: where does this illusion come from? If Brahman is the only reality, what can there be to distort it? Brahman, like the rope, is a purely passive substratum; it cannot distort itself. But there is nothing other than Brahman. This is exactly where the snake-rope analogy breaks down. In that situation, there is an external observer and some kind of filtering medium. Thus, the rope, as presented through the medium to the observer, can be distorted. Advaita Vedanta firmly denied the existence of any such realities additional to Brahman.

And yet there must be some explanation for the illusion. What Shankara proposes is *maya*. This word originally meant, roughly, "mysterious divine power." It was seen as a faculty belonging to the various gods, which they would exercise from time to time. For Shankara maya is something quite different. In no sense does it belong to Brahman. It is an alien power causing Brahman to appear with characteristics other than its own. Maya conjures up all the illusory objects of our world, along with our minds to perceive them. That last point is essential to grasp. For Advaita, the ideas and feelings in our minds are just as illusory as the sticks and stones of the material world. They are not really occurring at all. The only reality is the passive, unchanging being of Brahman; all else is the work of maya.

It is easy to see that maya does not provide a very compelling solution to the problem of how the world-illusion originates. One could point out: if maya causes the illusion, then it must exist, and so Brahman is no longer the only reality. But Shankara would respond: maya doesn't really exist, though it isn't non-existent either. His position is that maya is in some mysterious, inexplicable condition between being and non-being. It is very hard to fathom what this might mean; and Shankara, to his credit, does not imagine that this is a truly convincing answer. In our present state of delusion, he says, no philosophical explanations will ever be entirely satisfactory. That is precisely why we must rely on the Holy Vedic scriptures as our guide and on yogic experience as the fulfillment of our religious quest. In that fulfillment there will only be Brahman. The world-illusion, having dissipated, will no longer need explanation.

Pending this culmination, there is still the problem of how to cope with this illusory world. This is a matter to which Shankara gives careful attention and on which he delivers a striking answer. As long as one continues to believe in this illusory world, one is intellectually obliged to believe in a God as its wise and benevolent creator. Shankara refers to this God by the generic name of *Ishwara*, "the Lord." Through devotion to Ishwara—just what the Bhagavad Gita had prescribed—the soul can be purified and raised to the point where it is capable of seeing Brahman.

It must be clearly understood that Ishwara *is* an illusion. There is no such loving, personal God as He. But He is a useful illusion. He provides the spiritual focus by which we can begin to extricate ourselves from the present state of bondage and delusion. Here is a key to appreciating the power of Shankara's philosophy in India. He tended to the spiritual needs of all. There was the ultimate truth of Brahman for the spiritual elite, and there was the lower truth of Ishwara, the Lord, for others. Shankara even composed moving hymns of devotion to the Lord so as to inspire people to worship Him.

Shankara's practical side is also shown in his organizational activities. He adopted a policy which at the time was quite controversial in Hinduism: the founding of monasteries. We have seen how important the sangha (monastic order) was for the spread of Buddhism. In every generation the Buddhist monasteries beckoned to young men—many of them from Hindu families—who were frustrated with the cares and burdens of normal social life, as Buddha himself had been. Traditional Hinduism had frowned on this, insisting that each person must fulfill family and civic responsibilities before concentrating on the personal spiritual quest. The arch-conservative Mimamsas were particularly emphatic in condemning monasticism and upholding marriage as a sacred institution.

Shankara defied Hindu custom and adopted the Buddhist way. He left home when quite young and never took up the duties of a householder (though he did return home to officiate at his mother's funeral, which most renouncers of the world would never have done). Shankara instituted monastic practices which are still thriving in India today. This policy had the effect, as he himself undoubtedly desired, of weakening Buddhism. The young men who had formerly been drawn to that religion could now take up the monastic life without abandoning Hinduism. By making the monastery an integral part of Hindu spirituality, Shankara hastened the disappearance of Buddhism from India. It is truly amazing that he could find time in his short life for all these organizational activities, along with his vast output of writing.

6. Ramanuja's Visistadvaita Vedanta: Brahman as a Personal God

The philosophy of Ramanuja offered a very different interpretation of the Upanishads from Shankara's. His version of Vedanta is termed *Visistadvaita* meaning "qualified non-dualist." Ramanuja affirms that reality is one but insists that this unity is qualified, that is, differentiated. In the context of this qualified non-dualism, a totally different conception of Brahman was proposed, and with it, a notion of religious salvation that owed much more to the Bhagavad Gita than to the Upanishads.

The core of Ramanuja's philosophy is the belief that Brahman is a benevolent personal God who creates and rules over the world. We, as creatures of Brahman, remain ever distinct from Him and subordinate to Him. However, we are united to Him in the sense that we cannot exist independently of Him. It must be said that Ramanuja's conception of Brahman does not really accord with the general teaching of the Upanishads. He himself intuitively senses this and devotes much energy to laborious reinterpretation of various Upanishadic passages. To a certain extent, he does succeed in fitting them into his view. The truth is that the Upanishads are often vague, mystifying and inconsistent, so they lend themselves to different interpretations.

Ramanuja's teaching is best explained by reference to an analogy which he often invokes: body and soul. They constitute a unity, but their status is quite unequal. The soul is the life of the body; without the soul the body cannot function or even exist. This is how we must understand the relation between God (Brahman) and the created world. He is the soul of our own souls and of everything else in the phenomenal world. He eternally sustains and governs our existences. That is why this philosophy can be described as non-dualistic. Reality does not consist of many things. There is just a single thing, but that single entity contains within itself great complexity.

In the spirit of this analogy, we can also understand Ramanuja's concept of liberation. It cannot be merging of the individual self into Brahman, as the Upanishads seem to teach. There cannot be fana (annihilation) of the individual self, as the Sufis taught. Our individual selves will always remain distinct from God, as the body must always differ from the soul. In liberation the Self will exist in a state purified of all worldly desire and completely absorbed in the love of God. Like the Bhagavad Gita, Ramanuja insists that it is primarily through bhakti (devotion) rather than knowledge or deeds that we attain liberation.

He directs forceful criticism at some of the vulnerable points in Shankara's philosophy. For example, there is the teaching of consciousness. Shankara says that Brahman is a state of pure, empty awareness without any object. Ramanuja considers this quite impossible. Consciousness, he says, is always a relation between a subject and an object. There is never just the act of consciousness by itself; there is always, in addition, the possessor of consciousness and the object which consciousness knows.

Ramanuja is also well aware of the problems with the concept of maya which we have already discussed. Where can this maya exist, he asks. It cannot reside in our finite minds, for they are the creation of maya (according to Shankara). Neither can it exist in Brahman, for Shankara holds that to be pure, luminous knowledge. If we say (as Shankara does) that maya does not truly exist but rather stands between being and non-being, that is an incoherent position without meaning.

Ramanuja articulated his position with great dedication and logical dexterity. His Visistadvaita has not attained quite the eminence in later Indian philosophy as Shankara's Advaita, but it has run a very strong second.

REVIEW QUESTIONS FOR INDIAN PHILOSOPHY

1. Describe the spiritual crisis which overcame Gautama as a young man. Why was he unable to enjoy what he already possessed?

2. Why did Gautama's father object so strongly to his son's leaving home to become an ascetic? How did Gautama respond to this objection?

3. Explain Gautama the Buddha's teaching of the Middle Way. How did he came to adopt this position?

4. To whom was Buddha's religious teaching addressed? Why is this so significant?

5. Explain the teaching of the Wheel of Becoming.

6. Explain the contrast in the religious roles of Jesus (as seen by Christians) and Buddha. Use the story Gotami and the Mustard Seed to illustrate Buddha's position.

7. Describe the circumstances of Buddha's death. How did it reaffirm his basic religious principles?

8. Describe the place of Hinduism in Indian history and culture. How can Hinduism be defined? How does this relate to the brahmins?

9. How were the ideas of reincarnation and karma used to justify the existing social order in India?

10. Explain the two key factors which make the law of karma work.

11. What is liberation, and why was it so ardently sought by the Indian philosophers?

12. Explain the two levels on which Indian religion exists.

13. Explain the various stages of Raja-yoga. How do they contribute to the ultimate goal of liberation?

14. Give examples of the psychic powers in yoga. In what way are they thought to be achieved? What attitude is taken toward them?

15. What is the Upanishads' conception of Brahman? How does it differ from the Judaeo-Christian-Islamic notion of God?

16. Explain the Upanishads' concept of Atman. How is Atman related to Brahman?

17. What is Arjuna's dilemma at the beginning of the Bhagavad Gita? How does Krishna resolve the dilemma for him?

18. Contrast Buddha's way of handling social responsibility with the Gita's principle of karma-yoga.

19. Explain the Gita's principle of bhakti-yoga. How does it involve a concept of liberation different from that given by Buddha and the Upanishads?

20. Explain, with examples, what is meant in saying that Hinayana takes an analytical approach.

21. What is the teaching of Dependent Origination, and why is it so important in the Hinayana quest for liberation?

22. Define the Three Characteristics. How does each one contribute to the elimination of desire? Be particularly careful to explain the nature and impact of the third characteristic, Lack-of-self.

23. Compare the Upanishads and Hinayana on the Self.

24. How does Mahayana explain the variance between its doctrines and what Buddha publicly taught?

25. What do the terms *Hinayana* and *Mahayana* actually mean? Relate this to the teaching of the Bodhisattva.

26. What is the teaching of Emptiness? What led Mahayana to hold this teaching? How is it reconciled with the teaching of the Bodhisattva?

27. Explain the Carvakas' materialistic account of thinking.

28. How did the Carvakas use the analogy of the rose and the thorns to attack the seekers of liberation?

29. Describe the style of philosophizing which is called "Scholastic."

30. Describe the cycle by which the world evolves and then devolves in the Samkhya system. What causes the beginning of each cycle?

31. How did Buddha's way of dealing with the fate of the liberated person at death provide an inspiration for Nagarjuna?

32. Explain Nagarjuna's arguments on causation. How does he refute the idea that things possess svabhava, and what are the implications of this?

33. What is the basic stance of the Nyaya philosophers? Relate this to their position on space, time, universals and God.

34. How does the Nyaya view of the world-cycle differ from Samkhya's?

35. How did the Mimamsa philosophers defend the idea that the Vedas are infallibly true?

36. How does Shankara's philosophy differ from that of the Upanishads, and where does he derive this difference?

37. Explain each of Shankara's three truths about Brahman.

38. Explain Shankara's analogy of the snake and the rope.

39. What problem is maya supposed to explain in Shankara's philosophy? Why doesn't it succeed very well in doing this?

40. What is meant in speaking of Ramanuja's Non-Dualism as "Qualified"? How does he use the analogy of body and soul to clarify his account of our relationship with God?

III. CHINA

A Note on the Spelling and Pronunciation of Chinese Names

You have probably had your fill of cumbersome and unfamiliar names in the first two sections of this book. I am sorry to say that the situation will become even worse in this section. The writing and phonetics of the Chinese language are completely different from those of English, and this poses a severe problem—which has yet to be satisfactorily solved—for rendering Chinese words into English.

Throughout this section, I will use what is called the pin-yin system, which is the one officially sanctioned by the Chinese government. This has the disadvantage of using certain consonants for sounds which are not at all what a speaker of English would expect. This is especially true of "q" and "x."

There are other ways of representing Chinese sounds in our Roman alphabet, of which the Wade-Giles is by far the most commonly encountered. Much, if not most, of literature available on China has made use of the Wade-Giles system. This is so different from the pin-yin that it will sometimes be very difficult to recognize the same word. For example, xian (pin-yin) and hsien (Wade-Giles) are the same word.

The following incomplete table is meant to provide you with a little assistance in dealing with these annoying problems.

Pin-yin Version	Wade-Giles Version	Pronunciation (Closest English Equivalent to the Chinese Pronunciation)
q	ch`	ch
x	hs	sh
r	j	r
zh	ch	j
z	tz	dz
d	t	d
b	p	b
g	k	g
t	t`	t
p	p`	p
k	k`	k

Keep in mind that in many cases, the closest English equivalent is not really very close at all.

One Chinese word that is especially useful to take notice of is *zi*, which, in our present context, means "master" or "teacher." This will be founded tacked onto the name of practically every one of the early Chinese philosophers.

I. CONFUCIUS

Confucius (whose name is a Westernized version of *Kong Fu-zi*, meaning "Master Kong") was born in a time of prolonged crisis for China. The dates of his life (approximately 550–475 B.C.) coincide almost exactly with those of Buddha's, though it is quite impossible that the two civilization builders could even have known of each other's existence. He was born in the middle of the Zhou dynasty (1027–249 B.C.), the longest but one of the most chaotic in Chinese history.

Confucius' China already possessed an ancient and impressive civilization. The Zhou dynasty had been preceded by the Shang (about 1700–1027 B.C.), and that by the little known Xia (about 2100–1700 B.C.). Still earlier was a semi-legendary time of culture heroes and sage-kings. By Confucius' time many traditions and social norms had become well entrenched, and Confucius himself was thoroughly imbued with these. The family was of supreme importance, and its concerns had priority over any individual needs. There was a rigid distinction between "gentlemen" (*jun-zi*) and "commoners" (*xiao-ren*). The gentlemen comprised a hereditary aristocracy, with many different ranks, all the way from powerful princes down to petty officials. The commoners were mainly peasant farmers, though they also included merchants and skilled craftsmen. However, Chinese of all classes had a clear sense of themselves as a single people, sharply distinguished from the "barbarians" that surrounded them.

The unity of China is precisely what had been disrupted in the political crisis of the Zhou dynasty. This dynasty had begun as a vigorous and effective regime. It exercised a rather loose control over the entire country through a feudal system, which set up dukes, counts and barons to govern the various parts of the country. The Zhou rulers had reserved a strategic central domain for themselves to directly rule.

By 700 B.C this system was in tatters, and it only grew worse in the subsequent centuries. The Zhou king had lost all authority beyond his own shrunken domain, and the feudal lords now governed as independent rulers. There was perpetual conflict among them, as they jockeyed for position, unhindered by any higher authority. The number of feudal states, which had originally been above a hundred, stood at about twenty in Confucius' day. The smaller and weaker were constantly being gobbled up by their stronger neighbors. Meanwhile, basic social order had deteriorated. Highway robbery reached epidemic proportions, as gangs of thieves were continually ambushing unprotected travelers.

Relations between the different states were conducted with utter ruthlessness and lack of principle. Within each state it was little better, as rulers faced frequent subversion or rebellion from their own underlings. The common people suffered grievously as they were taxed to support the princes' ostentatious life styles and continual war making. Through it all there was a widespread conviction that this state of affairs was neither natural nor necessary. There was a deep yearning for unity and stability, combined with strong belief that some way to attain them could be found. This is where Confucius' China differs so profoundly from Buddha's India. In the latter men of wisdom had generally given up hope that worldly problems could be solved.

Confucius himself surveyed the situation from the perspective of a gentleman, born to privilege and status. His family was not wealthy, and they no longer enjoyed hereditary right to a specific official position. But Confucius clearly belonged to the upper level of society. This is very evident in the confidence with which he conducted himself, throughout his life, dealing with the high and the mighty.

One clear reflection of Confucius' class status is the fact that he was so well educated. It is not known precisely how or from whom Confucius acquired this education. Formal schooling was still uncommon at that time. It may be that his learning came mostly from his own diligent independent study. In any case, he learned a great deal. He once said of himself, "In a village of ten families you will certainly find people as loyal and faithful as I, but you will not find one who loves learning as much as I do." (*Analects* V, 28—the *Analects* are the collected sayings of Confucius compiled by his disciples shortly after his death. The book is our primary source for an understanding of his thought and character.)

Confucius' learning included all those refinements that were appropriate for a Chinese gentleman. He was an accomplished musician, a keen lover of poetry and a diligent student of history. But he paid no attention to magical arts like divination and geomancy, which were already flourishing in China. And he did not venture to speculate about the nature of God or the universe, as so many philosophers have done.

The one subject which most absorbed Confucius was *li*. This is a term of broad and deep meaning, for which there is no English equivalent. It includes religious ceremonies which we might call "liturgy", but also social customs which we would call "manners" or "etiquette." In the conduct of official state business, it encompasses what we refer to as "protocol." Confucius was deeply devoted to the li, regarding them as the essential means to an ordered and harmonious life. He probably knew them better than anyone else in China, and he was widely acclaimed for this knowledge.

It does not appear that there was ever a moment of enlightenment for Confucius such as Muhammad and Buddha experienced. There was not some sudden insight or decision which changed the course of his life. Instead, there was a continuous deepening of his moral and political convictions, combined with an unwavering determination to carry them into effect.

These convictions centered on how to deal with the deplorable conditions then prevailing in China. As one might expect of someone with his vast store of traditional learning, Confucius saw the existing problems as the result of a deviation from the values and customs of the past. China had once been tranquil, harmonious and well governed—at least in Confucius' rather idealized view of it. The need was simply to return to these ancient ways.

Confucius looked to many venerable figures as exemplars of the wisdom and virtue that were needed. Among them all, the Duke of Zhou particularly stood out. This eminent figure had lived at the beginning of the Zhou dynasty, when it was still in a thriving condition. He was the brother and trusted advisor of the first Zhou monarch. When his brother died, leaving an infant son to succeed him, the Duke assumed the post of regent and governed faithfully until his nephew was old enough to take the throne. The duke's loyalty and dutifulness were a shining example which stood in stark contrast to the tawdry behavior which characterized the later part of the dynasty.

The Duke of Zhou provided more than a noble example. As the Zhou dynasty took power, he put forward a theory which served as the guiding principle for Confucius' own ideas on the subject. The Zhou had come to power by overthrowing the Shang, a dynasty which had become cruel and oppressive in its declining years. The Zhou had raised the standard of rebellion and had prevailed against the superior forces of the Shang. This could only be the work of God or *Tian*, as the Duke of Zhou referred to Him. Tian had disapproved of the last Shang ruler and so had transferred his power to a new dynasty.

The key concept in the Duke theory is *mandate*, which may be defined as "entitlement to rule." The mandate was Tian's, to confer and to take away, as He thought best. Tian's intervention to overthrow the Shang was not overt. He did not appear to anyone or send a prophet to announce His decree. But all the same, He had been involved. The victory of Zhou showed that they had now received the mandate.

What the Duke's theory really stressed is that the moral character of a dynasty was essential to its retaining the mandate. The Duke was reversing the old principle of "might makes right." Mere power, he insisted, does not give anyone the right to rule. If that were so, Shang might have continued to govern forever. The operative principle is that "right makes might": morality is an essential condition for receiving the authority to rule. The power of Tian stood as the guarantee that right would prevail.

It is hard to say whether the Duke realized that this doctrine might eventually be turned against his own family's dynasty. That is certainly what Confucius, with utmost respect to the Duke, understood it to mean. In his view, the Zhou dynasty had long since lost the mandate. The later rulers were far below the founders of the dynasty in moral quality. Events had confirmed this in the steady decline of the Zhou regime to political insignificance.

Hence, there was no question, in Confucius' mind or anyone else's, of restoring the Zhou to greatness. Its time was finished. The question was: who would follow the Zhou? That is, who would receive the mandate to establish a new dynasty? The tragedy, as Confucius saw it, was that among all the potentates of China, great and small, there was no one who showed any true worthiness. Confucius could see nothing but grasping, conniving, unprincipled ambition. His frustration was such that he even (not very seriously) contemplated the possibility of going to live among the barbarian tribes. (*Analects*, IX, 13)

As far as Confucius was concerned, the root of China's problems was the depravity of its ruling class. The so-called "gentlemen" were not really gentlemen at all. Here we encounter one of the salient aspects of Confucian thought: a tendency to shift the meaning of words from the descriptive to the normative. To put it more simply: Confucius wanted to use moral criteria to determine the application of words. This is known as the Rectification of Names, and its most famous statement is *Analects* XII, 11:

> Duke Jing of Qi asked Confucius about government. Confucius replied, "Let the lord be a lord; the subject a subject, the father a father, the son a son." The Duke said, "Excellent! If indeed the lord is not a lord, the subject not a subject, the father not a father, the son not a son, I could be sure of nothing anymore—not even of my daily food."

To dwell on just one of the names Confucius cites. A father, in the truest sense, is not he who has physically begotten someone. To really be a father, one must live up to an exacting set of moral responsibilities to one's offspring.

The name *gentleman* is most certainly another which Confucius wants to rectify. There is probably no topic which Confucius discusses more frequently in the *Analects*. For example,

> IV, 10. A gentleman in his dealings with the world shows no partisanship. Wherever he sees right, he takes sides with it.

> XV, 18. A gentleman is distressed by his own lack of capacity. He is never distressed at the failure of others to recognize his merits.

> XV, 31. A gentleman, in his plans, thinks of the Way. He does not think how he is going to make a living.

It is obvious that Confucius does not intend these statements to be descriptions of how the Chinese upper class actually behaved. When he speaks of the gentleman, he always means the *true* gentleman.

There is a discussion in *Analects* XII, 19, which gives further meaning to Confucius' belief that the ruling class needed to reform itself. A powerful lord asked what might be done to curb lawlessness, suggesting that putting criminals to death would be the most effective measure. Confucius indignantly replies:

> You are here to govern. What need is there to kill? If you desire what is good, the people will be good. The gentleman, in his essential power, may be compared to the wind, while the essential character of the commoners is like the grass. Whichever way the wind blows, the grass will bend.

The passage should not be taken to mean that Confucius was unconditionally opposed to the use of capital punishment. He probably would have approved it in the case of certain incorrigible individuals. But he certainly did not see it as an instrument of social policy. Those bandits who were waylaying travelers did not, in general, deserve execution. Their crimes were the symptoms of a social disorder created by bad leadership.

The passage also raises the question of just how Confucius looked upon that vast class of commoners. It is tempting to suppose that he, so conscious of his own aristocratic status, would have viewed them with snobbery or even contempt. But this is contradicted by what we have just read and by many other passages. Confucius felt compassion for the sufferings of the common people and anger toward the failed leadership which had caused these sufferings. Moreover, he believed in an inherent capacity for goodness possessed by *all* human beings. That goodness needs only the nurturing of good example in order to manifest itself:

> . . . If their betters practice the *li*, the people will be ashamed to show disrespect. If their betters cultivate justice, the people will be ashamed to be disobedient. If their betters cultivate good faith, the people will be ashamed to lie. (XIII, 4)

Mind you, Confucius was no democrat. In his wildest dreams, he could not have contemplated a society in which the distinction between gentlemen and commoners was erased. Political power must be concentrated in the hands of a worthy ruling class, not dispersed among the people.

> The common people may be made to follow the Way but not to understand it. (VIII, 9)

But note how this passage, even as it denies to commoners the understanding needed to govern themselves, affirms that they are capable of *doing* the good.

Confucius had, therefore, a very clear idea of what a good and stable social order should consist in. Throughout his life he cherished this vision and yearned to put it into effect. Though he certainly did not suppose that Tian had directly spoken to him, he did have a firm conviction that he was an instrument for the realization of Tian's purpose. This sustained him through many trying times. Once, in an incident that has never really been explained, he was surrounded by an angry mob as he traveled by carriage. He remained perfectly calm.

> . . . Does civilization not rest now with me? If Tian wishes to destroy civilization, why has it been entrusted to me? If Tian does not intend to destroy civilization, what have I to fear from these people? (IX, 5)

In truth, there was little that Confucius could do to remedy the political situation. He was from the lower ranks of the gentlemen and could not hope to inherit political power. His father had been a soldier, but this profession had no appeal whatsoever to Confucius. In spite of his vast education, Confucius initially earned his living in a variety of rather humble ways. Among other things, he was in charge of a government supply depot in his native state of Lu. His skill and efficiency in carrying out these responsibilities were duly noted, but he himself found no satisfaction in the work.

Confucius was never able to fulfill his political ambitions, but eventually he did find a profession that suited him: teaching. His becoming a schoolmaster took place almost accidentally, most likely when he was in his mid-thirties. As he had already acquired a reputation for great learning, younger men were drawn to him. They were mostly idealists, like Confucius himself. They were eager to make the world a better place, and they knew that to do this they needed a knowledge of China's vast traditions.

In all probability, there never was a school in our modern sense. There were no classes, examinations, grades or degrees. Confucius simply received students in his own home and held very open-ended discussions on topics that were relevant to the education of a gentleman. Many of the sayings in the *Analects* are excerpts from these discussions. They make it clear that Confucius was a teacher who encouraged questions and was willing to hear the opinions of others. It is doubtful whether he ever gave a sermon or a lecture, as Muhammad and Buddha were accustomed to do.

In this way Master Kong (as his students knew him) was able to make a modestly comfortable living. His students paid him tuition insofar as they were able. He took pride in the fact that he never turned away a student, however poor, who truly wanted to learn (*Analects*, VII, 7). This should not be taken to mean that any of Confucius' students were commoners. Those impoverished persons who became his disciples (including the one among all his students whom he regarded most highly) were, in all probability, gentlemen whose families were down on their luck.

Of course, a gentleman "does not think of how he is going to make a living", as we have already noted. Master Kong valued his teaching, not as a livelihood, but as a means of inspiring others with his moral and political ideals. He certainly succeeded in winning a small but dedicated corps of disciples. It was these disciples (probably no more than a hundred, altogether) who eventually compiled the *Analects*. Many of them became teachers in their own right. The Confucian philosophy was preserved and soon became (but not in Confucius' lifetime) a widespread and thriving movement.

Confucius could not foresee the ultimate success of this movement. He was deeply frustrated at the failure of his ideas to win support from those who held power in his own state of Lu. He undertook a series of travels—probably in his fifties—to seek support (and possible political employment) elsewhere. Accompanied by a few of his students, he visited a number of the Chinese states—those independent states which were so frequently at war with one another.

He managed to gain interviews with a number of rulers and ministers of state. He was generally listened to with respect, as he was an imposing man, eloquent in personal conversation. But nowhere did Confucius find any real enthusiasm for his political philosophy. Living in such harsh and brutal times, his listeners could not bring themselves to believe that moral reform would suffice to bring peace and order. As we will see, there were other philosophers who seemed to have a much

CONFUCIUS BY THE FLOWING STREAM

Confucius, with his students, by a flowing stream. This particular occasion is described in Analects, IX:16. Confucius is exclaiming, "It keeps flowing like this, day and night." For him and for other Chinese philosophers, water possessed an almost mystical significance. Precisely what he meant by these words has always been debated by Confucian scholars.
[HarperCollins]

more practical solution. So it was that Master Kong returned to Lu to resume his routine of teaching, a routine that persisted to the end of his life.

We have seen that Confucius saw political problems in very personal terms. That is, he believed that everything wrong with China could be traced to the moral failings of the ruling class. He and his followers never tire of stressing this basic truth: one must regulate one's own character before seeking to regulate society. To complete our account of Confucius and his teaching, we must seek a fuller understanding of what the character of a gentleman (a *true* gentleman) consists in.

The basis of this character is the virtue of filial love, in the unique form that Chinese civilization has conceived of it. Filial love is simply love for one's parents, combined with an appropriate respect and obedience. Just what this entails is a truly vast subject. Suffice it to say that for the Confucians, the most important moral obligation that anyone has is to his parents. They have given us our very lives; anything else we receive can only be secondary to that. No one who has failed with regard to the duties of filial love can be considered a good person. Other good works cannot redeem this failure.

The responsibilities of filial love are delineated primarily with respect to sons rather than daughters; for sons are to remain at home and carry on the family name, while daughters are married into other families. As long as his parents live, a filial son is expected to be attentive to their needs and obedient to their wishes. After they have died, he must carry out prolonged and exacting rituals of mourning. For all the rest of his life, he must cherish their memory and strive to do nothing that would dishonor them. Most certainly, he must marry and raise a family of his own, for to let the family line die out would be to consign the parents and all one's ancestors to oblivion.

Other moral responsibilities are subordinated to filial love. When there is conflict between it and some other duty, we must set aside the other. There is a revealing discussion of this point between Confucius and one of his disciples in *Analects* XVII, 21. It concerns those mourning rituals which a son was expected to perform for either of his parents. These required that the son retire into his home for a period extending into the third year after the death. All normal activities would be suspended, and the son would live as a virtual recluse, eating only the coarsest food and dressing in the plainest manner.

Confucius' student thought this somewhat excessive. "Surely," he argued, "one year is long enough. If a gentleman gives up his work for three years, his endeavors will be useless." The point of the objection must be carefully appreciated. The student was not so much complaining of the inconvenience of the mourning regime. Rather, he was concerned about how the gentleman's role as a leader in society would be diminished through his having to be secluded for so long.

But Confucius was having none of it. He asked, "Would you, then, after one year be able to enjoy eating good rice and wearing your finery?" "Yes, I would," answered the student. "Then do so, by all means," exclaimed the Master, "but the gentleman in mourning finds no relish in good food, no pleasure in music and no comforts in his own home. That is why he does not eat the good rice or wear the finery."

Filial love is thus considered to be the natural expression of our deepest feelings. It must not be set aside for the sake of something else, however worthy. Indeed, all our other moral feelings and commitments are built upon it. One of Confucius' disciples, quoted in Analects I, 2, puts it this way:

> ... A gentleman works at the root. Once the root is secured, the Way unfolds. To respect parents and elders is the root of *ren*.

The word *ren* has special significance for Confucians. It signifies a complete goodness which expresses itself through a loving kindness in all our human relationships. There is no higher praise that can be bestowed than to say that someone has attained ren. And filial piety is the essential prerequisite for the development of ren. One may say that the meaning of human love is learned through the relationship with the parents. A helpless child, receiving its parents' care and nurturing, will naturally respond to that love. This is how we all learn how to love (or how we should learn it). Whatever kindness or benevolence we ever show to anyone is derived from that learning experience.

Other family relationships also hold great importance for Confucius. He was deeply concerned about harmony among brothers, and insisted that younger brothers must defer to the eldest. Such deference is essential to maintaining the unity of the family, and only through unity can the status and dignity of the family be preserved. Reverence for the ancestors is another principle by which the importance of the family is affirmed. As we will see, there were important rituals through which this reverence was expressed.

Underlying it all was this simple truth: the individual person does not really matter; the individual's needs and interests must be subordinated to those of the family. It is a very hard principle to comprehend in Western society, which is so oriented to the individual. Western societies prize the rights of the individual. They are not merely sanctioned in the laws but also enshrined in popular culture with its affirmation of self-gratification, self-esteem and self-fulfillment.

Now we turn to the discussion of a different aspect of the Confucian gentleman's morality, one that has been a great puzzlement to many. While Confucius was severely demanding of himself and others, he allowed for a considerable flexibility in carrying out moral principles. He set no store by laws or commandments as a basis for morality. The diversity and complexity of the situations we encounter will not allow of this. The gentleman must possess a highly developed moral sensibility that will enable him to respond to the uniqueness of each situation. Any rule, such as "Tell the truth", will need to be broken from time to time.

A good example of this is to be found in *Analects*, XIII, 18. There, Confucius was informed about the case of an "upright" young man who had reported his own father's crime of stealing a sheep.

> I would *not* call that upright. A son should conceal his father's misconduct, and a father his son's. That is what I would call upright.

One way to express the Confucian principle is to say that "the end justifies the means." What exactly do these words signify? They state that the purpose (end) of an action can excuse whatever measures are needed to achieve that purpose. In simpler terms: what is normally bad becomes good, if there is a good enough reason for it. Many people would regard this end-means idea as a very dubious one, characteristic of those who have no real principles at all. But to Confucians it is just plain common sense. In the case just considered, Confucius approved deception as a means of preserving the family's honor. He certainly did not sanction dishonesty in general, but in this particular case the end justified the means.

No rule can be held sacred; that is what Confucian flexibility requires. There is a story about Shun, a legendary sage of pre-dynastic times, which illustrates this very well. The noble Shun's father, as it happened, possessed a character completely opposite to his son's: a lazy, quarrelsome, irresponsible drunkard. This did not by any means exempt Shun from the duties of filial piety. Shun patiently bore the many burdens and indignities that his father heaped upon him.

Eventually, in keeping with custom, the father arranged a marriage for his son; but, in a fit of irrational anger, he suddenly withdrew his permission for the wedding. Shun was in a quandary. Filial piety obliged him, on the one hand, to obey his father, but, on the other, to marry and continue the family line. In these extraordinary circumstances, he chose to go ahead with the wedding.

From the Confucian standpoint, it is most important to recognize that there is no specific rule which could have told Shun how he was to resolve this painful dilemma. He could only consult his own moral instincts and make his decision. The gentleman's extensive education—in such areas as poetry, history, even music—is meant to equip him with the intuitions needed to face the infinite variety of moral situations.

There is one final component of the Confucian gentleman's personal values that we must explore in depth. That would be the *li*, the many rituals, which were the main component of Master Kong's own expertise. It is not easy for an outsider to understand why these li were so cherished. Confucius believed that the ruler's correct performance of them would be the most effective means of inspiring the people's awe and obedience. He believed that ordinary gentlemen's practice of li would serve to induce a spirit of civility and harmony throughout society.

Many of the li have an apparently trivial character. We are told, for example, that Confucius would not sit on a mat that was not straight (X, 9). The devotion to these li suggests fussiness and superficiality rather than nobility. Let us take one especially prominent ritual and try to understand what it meant to Master Kong and his followers. This is the practice of bowing, which is called for as a token of respect in many different circumstances. Physically, bowing is just a lowering of the body. But the act can never be purely physical. The mind is bound to feel an attitude that corresponds to the body's lowliness, namely humility or respect. To Confucians this harmonizing of body and mind is a perfectly natural process (which modern psychology tends to confirm).

The important point is that these li were never mere external displays. They were powerful instruments for conditioning the feelings of all those who took part in them. The bowing that Confucians engaged in was not some meaningless routine. It was a continual reinforcement of the mutual respect which they held to be essential for social harmony.

The ancient ritual of ancestor worship is another example of a li which holds great meaning and importance. At one time this ritual was exactly what its name implies: a religious act of communing with the spirits of the dead. For many ordinary Chinese it continued to be this. Confucius, however, was skeptical of the possibility of life after death. In *Analects*, XI, 11, he expresses the view that we are quite unable to know whether there is or is not a future life. Under these circumstances, he could not, while performing the ancestor worship, have seen himself as literally speaking to the departed ancestors.

What was his understanding of the ritual, then? As with bowing, we must first examine the precise physical nature of what was done. Members of the entire extended family would be gathered for this ceremony. Offerings would be made in honor of the ancestors, whose presence was symbolized by plaques on which their names were inscribed. Throughout the ceremony, a strict priority of older before younger was followed. In the minds of all participants, the ritual would reinforce the transcendent importance of the family. The unity of the family through the generations would be reaffirmed, along with the differentiation of roles within it.

Thus, the ancestor worship had no supernatural significance for Confucius. Its true purpose lay in the minds and hearts of the living members of the family, not in some mysterious domain of departed spirits.

To conclude this section, we can do no better than quote Confucius' own summation of his life, as given in Analects, II, 4:

> At fifteen, my mind was set on learning. At thirty my character had been formed. At forty my doubts were resolved. At fifty I knew what Tian had decreed, and at sixty I was resigned to this. At seventy I was finally able to follow my heart's desire without transgressing moral principles.

As Confucius died in his early seventies, these reflections must have come near the very end of his life. The most striking part of this little autobiography is the reference to Tian's decree. We have already seen his belief that human affairs were ultimately presided over by Tian. As a younger man, Confucius clearly had hoped that he might be Tian's instrument in reforming China. He had not seen that hope fulfilled in his lifetime but had finally been reconciled to this. In the end, he was at peace. It is impossible to say whether Master Kong knew or even suspected how spectacularly his hope would be fulfilled in later generations.

II. AFTER CONFUCIUS

The movement founded by Confucius grew with surprising speed. His followers were soon to be found nearly everywhere in China. They called themselves, not Confucians, but *Ru*, "Scholars." They followed Confucius in devoting themselves to the study and preservation of the ancient Chinese traditions, especially the li. One cannot help but compare them to the Brahmins in India, though the Ru were certainly not a caste, nor were they priests in any sense. But the Ru, like the Brahmins, were honored for their knowledge. They were the prime culture-bearers of their respective societies.

The growing numbers and status of these Scholars did not, for now, entail any significant political power. The Confucian vision of a reformed society remained unrealized. The Ru flourished because the princes of ancient China deemed them to be a useful adornment to their regimes, much as the monarchs of Renaissance Europe were glad to patronize artists and scholars. The li may have possessed a deep moral meaning to the Confucians, but for others they were only for display.

Meanwhile, other philosophers, with views very different from those of Confucius, came to prominence. The later part of the Zhou dynasty (from about 400 B.C. onward) is known as the "Period of a Hundred Schools" because there were so many competing philosophies. The social conditions were so unstable and so demoralizing that thoughtful persons were bound to seek a better way. An extraordinary variety of viewpoints emerged. In no other period of Chinese history has such diversity existed.

The first notable opponent of Confucius was Mo Zi, who lived from approximately 470 to 390 B.C. He and the movement he founded constitute one of the most remarkable chapters in the entire history of philosophy, though his ultimate influence in China was negligible. Mo is so different from Confucius in every way—background, temperament, ideas—that we almost may think of him as the "anti-Confucius."

In the first place, Mo Zi was a commoner, a craftsman of some sort, probably in one of the building trades. He advocated a principle of "elevating the worthy", by which he meant raising talented commoners (like himself) into the ranks of the ruling class. As far as can be determined, Confucius was not absolutely opposed to this, but he did not think of it as a realistic possibility. (As we will see, later Confucians, reacting to the changing conditions of Chinese society, did fall in line with Mo's thinking on this point.)

Mo was of a very utilitarian outlook and condemned the li as useless and wasteful. He could not see any practical value in these ceremonies. He was particularly critical of elaborate funeral services, which were a major component of the li. Mo accused the Confucians of using these ceremonies for their own enrichment:

> Whenever there is a death in a rich family, they are overwhelmed with joy, saying, "This is our chance for food and clothing!" (*Mo Zi*, Section 39)

While Confucius had encouraged his students to think for themselves, Mo demanded "Identifying with One's Superior", by which he meant unquestioning obedience. While Confucius took a very disdainful attitude toward superstitions, Mo firmly believed in ghosts and other spirits, viewing them as enforcers of morality. Both men saw themselves as carrying out Tian's plan; but to Confucius, Tian was a lofty and remote figure, who made His will known to us in a very limited and indirect way. Mo, on the other hand, boldly proclaimed:

> The will of Tian is to me like a compass to a wheelwright or a square to a carpenter. [Recall that our philosopher had first-hand experience of these things.] The wheelwright uses his compass, and the carpenter his square to measure for the world, saying, "What fits these measurements is right, what does not is wrong."...How do I know the right and the wrong? Because I measure them by the clearest standard in the world, the will of Tian. (Section 26)

Confucius strongly disapproved of the militarism that was rampant in Chinese society. He believed that moral force rather than armed force was the key to establishing peace and order. Mo, by contrast, took the approach of "fighting fire with fire." He founded a military order which placed itself at the disposal of weaker states that were threatened by their aggressive neighbors. Drawing on his own professional background, he developed techniques of fortification and other methods of defensive warfare.

Most importantly, Mo advocated the principle of *impartial love*. He maintained that favoritism in love was the source of all conflict among states or families. It is natural for men to love their own states and families the most, but this natural tendency must be repressed for the sake of social harmony. Defying the Confucian notion of filial love, he insisted that we should be just as concerned for other people's parents as for our own:

> Let us examine for a moment the way in which a filial son plans for the welfare of his parents. When a filial son plans for his parents, does he wish others to love and benefit them, or does he wish others to hate and injure them? It stands to reason that he wishes others to love and benefit his parents. Now if I am a filial son, how do I go about accomplish this? Do I first make it a point to love and benefit other men's parents so that they will in return love and benefit my parents? Or do I first make it a point to hate and injure other men's parents, so that they will in return love and benefit my parents? Obviously, I must first make it a point to love and benefit other men's parents, so that they in return will love and benefit my parents. So, if all of us are to be filial sons, can we set about it any other way than by loving and benefiting other men's parents? (Section 16)

By these remarkable ideas, Mo Zi managed to gain a small but dedicated following. His military order actually succeeded in winning a few battles, but he stood no chance of stemming the general tide of military aggression. The Chinese—not merely the Confucians—found his ideas to be utterly impractical and simplistic.

Moreover, he was ridiculed for his plodding, monotonous literary style. The ability to write elegantly has always been highly prized in China, much as the ancient Greeks valued oratorical ability. It is vitally important to be able to express oneself concisely and with a certain subtlety. Mo Zi's writing is given to belaboring the obvious and is loaded with pointless rhetorical questions. I deliberately quoted the last passage extensively and verbatim so that you could experience for yourself this style that was found to be so unsatisfactory.

The Mohist movement was later divided into several contending groups. It survived right down to the end of the Zhou dynasty, and some of its later representative made important contributions to logic and scientific method. The movement disappeared for good in the cataclysmic events surrounding the rise and fall of the next dynasty, the Qin (221–207 B.C).

Much more serious opposition to Confucianism emerged in the form of Legalism and Daoism. In particular, Legalism gained a far greater influence than any other philosophy in the last centuries of the Zhou dynasty. The most important Legalist thinker was Han Fei Zi (died 233 B.C.), but the philosophy was already clearly articulated more than a century before his time. Various eminent statesmen were associated with this philosophy, most notably Shang Yang (died 330 B.C.). The latter epitomizes Legalism in its harshest form. He became prime minister of the state of Qin and ruthlessly applied Legalist principles to every aspect of the government's operations. As we will see, this proved to be of decisive importance.

Legalists attacked the Confucian idea that moral character is the basis of effective government. What we really need, they maintained, are good methods, not good people. Han Fei Zi pointed out that the typical ruler is rather mediocre, intellectually as well as morally. The real test of a political theory is whether it can enable such a ruler to govern successfully.

The method which is most central to Legalism is the rule of law—hence its name. Legalists believed that society would not be in order unless there were clearly defined laws, enforced by severe punishment. The contrast with Confucianism is truly profound. Recall that Confucius had an aversion to rules, believing that the gentleman must be flexible, reacting differently to different situations. With the Legalists, on the other hand, it was essential that there be rules, consistently and forcefully applied. Moreover, the Legalists recognized no distinction between gentleman and commoner; the laws applied equally to all subjects.

A very different kind of opposition to Confucianism came from the Daoists. The two chief philosophers of this school were Zhuang Zi (about 370–285 B.C.) and Lao Zi. The latter name (which means simply "the Old Philosopher") is a pseudonym for an unknown thinker who lived slightly later than Zhuang. The philosophy of Zhuang and Lao centered around the indescribable Dao, a principle which pervaded and controlled all things. The philosophy maintains that we cannot have tranquillity and contentment unless we bring ourselves into accord with this Dao.

Conformity with the Dao, as the Daoists saw it, meant withdrawing from the social and political "rat race" to a simpler existence. There is a revealing story in the *Analects* (XVIII, 6) of an encounter between Confucius and a couple of early Daoists.

Confucius was in the midst of his travels and had lost his way. He sent his disciple over to ask directions of two farmers, who were working in their field. However, they were not ordinary peasants but Daoists who had deliberately chosen this natural way of life. On learning that the traveler seeking information was none other than Master Kong, one of the farmers sarcastically asked how the wise Confucius could be lost. The other exclaimed to the disciple:

> The whole world is swept along by the same flood. Who can reverse its flow? Instead of following a gentleman who keeps running from one patron to the next, would it not be better to follow one who has forsaken society altogether?

Saying this, he turned away and continued his work. The chagrined disciple, no wiser as to the directions, returned to the Master and reported what had been said. Confucius ruefully said:

> One cannot associate with birds and beasts. With whom should I keep company if not with my own kind? If the world were truly following the Dao, I would not have to reform it.

The story, which is probably apocryphal, gives us a wonderful portrayal of the difference between Confucianism and Daoism. The former is a philosophy totally involved with human society; the latter calls us to go beyond the narrow, troubled human world and unite with nature.

We will need to study both Legalism and Daoism much more closely. For now we are only surveying the "Hundred Schools" Period. There are still other movements to be mentioned, in order to convey the philosophical richness of this time. For example, there were a school of so-called Cosmologists, who studied and classified the processes of nature. Rather than take refuge in nature (with the Daoists), the Cosmologists thought to understand it and apply its laws to human society. Their greatest contribution was to articulate the theory of the twin powers of yin and yang. This theory was already deeply embedded in Chinese thought, and we will need later to examine it in detail.

In addition, there was a school of thought known as the Logicians, who delighted in argument for its own sake. They put forward "proofs" for such statements as "A white horse is not a horse." Finally, there was a philosopher named Yang Chu, who shocked his contemporaries by saying that he would not give up a single hair of his body to save the whole world. Clearly, Yang was in revolt from the prevailing Chinese belief that the individual must be subordinated to some greater entity.

Meanwhile, there were important developments within the Confucian school itself. The key figures were Meng Zi (known in the West as Mencius) and Xun Zi. Mencius (about 370–290 B.C.) is acknowledged to be second only to Confucius himself as a shaper of the Confucian tradition. His most important contribution was on the subject of human nature. He insisted that human beings were essentially good in their natural endowment. Moral goodness is not something which must be forced on us. It is already present, waiting to be developed.

Mencius gives a compelling argument for this position:

> All people have the mind which cannot bear to see others' suffering. The ancient rulers had this mind, and it was expressed in their government. With such rulers and such a government, the whole country can be mastered as easily as making something go round in the palm of one's hand.
>
> Let me illustrate what I mean in speaking of the mind which cannot bear to see suffering. When people see a child falling into a well, they are immediately seized with alarm and distress. This is not because they wish to curry favor with the child's parents, nor is it because of a desire to be well-regarded by their neighbors. One who fails to feel a genuine concern in such a case is not even human in the true sense of the word...This feeling is the beginning of *ren*. (*Mencius*, IIA:6)

The chief point here is that people's reaction to the child's plight is completely natural, even instinctive. Mencius knows that with most people this compassionate instinct does not show itself too often. It takes a dramatic situation like the child's to bring out the best in us. But goodness is always present in us as a potentiality.

Note that Mencius uses the word *ren* here, signifying the noblest possibilities of human character. We do not all attain ren, but we all possess its beginning. If this "sprout" of ren is properly cultivated through a good Confucian education, it will grow to maturity. The true gentleman is precisely that one who is always mindful of his ren and striving to develop it.

There are two more of Mencius' ideas which are of major importance for the development of Confucianism. First, his insistence on the gentleman's right to exercise his own independent judgment; and secondly, his articulation of the harmonious and complementary relationship between gentlemen and commoners. Independence is something which Confucius had already stressed in his practice as a teacher. He had said, "The gentleman is not an implement" (II, 12), meaning that a gentleman is not simply to be used or controlled by anyone.

Mencius made it clear that this independence was especially appropriate when the gentleman assumed some kind of official post, as would be his natural aspiration in the Confucian view of things. Such a responsibility must be fulfilled with constant awareness of the moral and political requirements of Confucianism. The gentleman would never blindly obey those of higher rank. Even at the cost of his career, he would stand up for his principles. We will see exactly what this meant after the Confucians gained real power.

Here is how Mencius expresses the point:

> When the ruler regards his minister as his hands and feet, the ministers regard their ruler as their heart and soul. When the ruler regards his ministers as his dogs and horses, they regard him as a stranger. When the ruler regards his ministers as dirt and grass, they regard him as an enemy. (IVB:3)

He makes his point subtly but in such a way as to be clearly understood. If the ruler wishes to enjoy his ministers' loyalty, he must *respect* them. And respect means allowing them to exercise their own judgment and wield real power. Confucians used to speak of the principle of *wu wei* ("refraining from action"), which expressed their view of how the good ruler should conduct himself. He should stand apart from actual policy-making and let his ministers (chosen for their merits) run the government.

The relation between the two great classes, gentlemen and commoners, is also a matter of great importance for Mencius. In no way are these two groups in conflict. The gentlemen do not oppress or exploit the commoners, and the latter do not chafe under the authority of their betters. Each group is making its essential contribution to society. Mencius says:

> It is said, "Some labor with their minds and others with their bodies." Those who labor with their minds will lead, while the others follow. The leaders will receive their sustenance from the followers. (IIIA:4)

He is telling us that each group depends upon the other. The gentlemen would starve, were it not for the food provided by the commoners. But without the moral and political leadership of the gentlemen, the commoners will live in constant fear, unable to enjoy the fruits of their own labor. As Mencius saw it, this was precisely the situation that prevailed in China during his time.

Xun Zi, the other great Confucian of the late Zhou dynasty, lived shortly after Mencius, about 300–235 B.C. He vigorously disputed his predecessor's theory of human nature. He held what, I suppose, is the more realistic view: that humans are born with a collection of grasping, selfish desires. As a crooked piece of wood must be steamed and bent by the carpenter, so our nature must be reformed by the techniques of Confucian education:

> . . . As to the nature of man, when he is hungry he desires to be filled, when cold he desires warmth, when tired he desires rest. That is man's natural disposition. But now a man may be hungry and yet in the presence of elders he dare not be the first to eat...If a man follows his natural disposition he will show no courtesy, and if he shows courtesy, he is acting contrary to his natural disposition. From all this it is evident that the nature of man is evil and his goodness is acquired. (*Xun Zi*, Chapter 23)

It is the *li* which are particularly important to straightening our crooked nature. They are the essential tools for simultaneously moderating and expressing our natural desires. Xun discusses the matter at length in his Chapter 19:

> Whence do the rules of li arise? From the fact that men are born with desires, and when these desires are not satisfied, men are bound to pursue their satisfaction. When this pursuit is carried on unrestrained, there is bound to be contention . . . The ancient kings disliked this and set the necessary limits by codifying rules of li and righteousness . . . In this way it was made certain that desires were not frustrated, nor were things used up by desires.

The li also serve to reinforce class distinction, inasmuch as many rituals are appropriate only for gentlemen. Even the way in which the li are *understood* is a reflection of social status. Xun gives the example of praying for rain:

> If people pray for rain and it does rain, what does this mean? Nothing in particular, I would say. If they hadn't prayed, it still would have rained. The gentleman prays for rain, not because he believes that this will actually produce rain, but simply as an expression of his feelings. The common man, on the other hand, believes it to be supernatural. (*Xun Zi*, Chapter 17)

Xun is saying that all the li, even those which seem to be directed to spiritual powers, are really just for the sake of expressing and channeling our feelings—in this particular case, worry over a drought. But commoners will never rise to this sophisticated understanding, and that is fine with him. It keeps them in their proper places.

Xun Zi's views on li are entirely in keeping with the spirit of Confucianism. One cannot imagine Master Kong himself as doing anything other than endorsing them. But it an altogether different matter with regard to his negative appraisal of human nature. The ultimate judgment of the Confucians themselves was that Mencius was right and Xun gravely mistaken on this vital issue. This judgment seems sound insofar as it addresses the question of whose view is most in accord with the thinking of Confucius himself. The Master's vision of a harmonious society, with commoners gladly deferring to their rulers, really does seem to presuppose goodness, not evil, in human nature.

Xun's standing with his fellow Confucians was not helped by the fact that his two most gifted students both abandoned Confucianism in favor of Legalism. One of them was the great philosopher, Han Fei Zi. The other, Li Si, will enter our story in just a moment.

While these philosophical developments—Confucian and non-Confucian—were taking place, the political situation in China grew steadily worse. Slowly but surely the weaker states were weeded out in the ruthless struggle for survival. Gone were Confucius' beloved home state of Lu and, in 249 B.C., the pathetic remnant of the Zhou dynasty. About seven states remained, large powerful states with the capacity to wage truly destructive wars.

The state of Qin, under its Legalist government, was by far the most powerful. It had become a thoroughly totalitarian state, with its economy rigidly controlled and its people kept in fear by the harsh legal code. Xun Zi, when he paid a brief visit to Qin, marveled at how obedient the people were. His old student, Li Si, had become an important official there and was helping to orchestrate the state's resources for a final attempt to win complete power.

The other states understood their peril. They made a grand alliance to meet the common enemy, and together they possessed forces that far exceeded Qin's. But the Qin army was better trained and led, and it prevailed in the final campaign

(221 B.C.). The ruler of Qin took the name Shi Huang Di ("First Great Emperor") and inaugurated a new dynasty, named after the state from which it had originated.

The Qin dynasty was a regime unlike any that China had known in previous dynasties. In earlier times, even under stable and effective leadership, the central government had not attempted to exercise direct control over the entire country. By virtue of the feudal system, most of the country was governed by hereditary nobility. Legalism totally rejected this political system, inasmuch as it allowed ruling families to become entrenched and independent in their various domains. Li Si, now prime minister, set up a *bureaucracy*, a vast hierarchy of *appointed* officials. This hierarchy extended down to the smallest villages. Each official was directly answerable to his superior and could be dismissed at any time. In this way, the dissension and disloyalty which had plagued other regimes was to be eliminated.

The First Emperor and his energetic prime minister believed that they possessed, in the Legalist philosophy, the infallible instrument for effective governance. Confucianism and other subversive philosophies were suppressed. National standards were imposed (for the first time) with respect to weights and measures, currency and the writing system. Ambitious projects were undertaken, including the Great Wall. It was confidently expected that the new dynasty would last ten thousand generations. Earlier dynasties had failed precisely because they had lacked the techniques of Legalism.

Events soon made a mockery of this expectation. The First Emperor died in 210 B.C. The circumstances of his death are not known. He was not especially old—about fifty-five, probably—and foul play is a distinct possibility. The Emperor had many sons, and his sudden death set off a vicious struggle for the succession. Li Si conspired with others to put one of the younger sons on the throne, hoping to use him as a puppet. The conspirators soon fell out, and Li paid with his life.

Meanwhile, pent-up resentments at the harsh regime led to outbreaks of rebellion all over the country. By 207 B.C. the once invincible Qin army was shattered, the reigning emperor had meekly surrendered, and China was in the hands of various rebel chieftains. They contended for power, and one of them emerged victorious to become the founder of a new dynasty, the Han (202 B.C.–220 A.D.).

The founder of the Han and his successors saw clearly the failure of Legalism. They understood they must find some other political philosophy by which to govern. It was almost inevitable that their choice fell upon Confucianism. Though they had been subject to persecution under Qin, the Confucians had survived. They stood vindicated by the demise of their arch-rivals, the Legalists. They were ready and eager to provide both ideology and manpower for the new dynasty.

The remarkable fact is not that the Confucians took power at the beginning of the Han but that they kept it for so long. Through all subsequent dynasties, down to the first years of the twentieth century, Confucianism remained the official philosophy of the Chinese government. China's emperors committed themselves to ruling by Confucius' principles and to employing the adherents of these principles at all levels of the political hierarchy. Great, convulsive changes took place in China during the two thousand years of Confucian authority, including barbarian invasions and catastrophic rebellions. But through it all Confucianism remained constant. When barbarians conquered China (as the Mongols did in the thirteenth century), they found that they had to conform themselves to Confucian ways in order to remain in power.

Ironically, when it finally did take power, Confucianism found itself in a very different China than the one that Master Kong had inhabited, and this meant that his philosophy could not be implemented as he had envisaged it. For one thing, the feudal political system had lost all viability. Confucius believed deeply in that system as it had been instituted at the beginning of the Zhou. That is, he wanted the feudal power to be diffused through an aristocracy of gentlemen ruling in the various parts of the country. He had even called for the restoration of the many feudal states which had already been eliminated by his own time. At the beginning of the Han, an effort was actually to establish a feudal system; but this proved unworkable. The Confucians then took over the bureaucratic system of the Legalists and made it their own through the remainder of their long tenure in leadership.

It is important to understand just what this meant from a sociological standpoint. The old feudal system presupposed that each person was born to a certain position in society. Even within the class of gentlemen, there were sharp distinctions of status, which limited the career possibilities for someone like Confucius. *Social mobility* was almost non-existent. All this changed in the troubled times of the late Zhou and the Qin. Many of the old families of the nobility were destroyed, and many commoners took advantage of the chaos to raise themselves to a higher status, including the founder of the Han dynasty.

The Confucians accepted these changed circumstances. This is already evident with Mencius and Xun Zi. For example, the latter had written:

> Although a man may be a descendant of kings, dukes or high court ministers, if he cannot adhere to li, he should be ranked among the commoners. Although a man may be the descendant of commoners, if he has acquired learning, is upright in conduct and can adhere to li, he should be promoted to the post of prime minister or high court official. (*Xun Zi*, Chapter 9)

This attitude was still more evident with the Han Confucians. They fully adopted the principle of "elevating the worthy" which had originally been advanced by the anti-Confucian, Mo Zi. That is, they believed that political office should be open to any man who possessed the necessary ability and character. (Note that I say *man* and not *person*.) Confucius himself had actually prepared the way for this by always stressing the moral qualifications for being a gentleman. He clearly believed that mere birth did one make one a worthy person.

Eventually, during the Tang dynasty (618–907), the Confucians set up a system of civil service exams to institutionalize the principle of elevating the worthy. These exams were periodically administered throughout the country. They required students to write concise, elegant essays applying Confucian principles to practical questions which had been raised. Those passing the exam (generally 10–15%) were then eligible to serve in the government. It was a very effective way of recruiting talented people into public service, and it also insured the continuation of Confucian political dominance.

One must not exaggerate the significance of these policies. The distinction between gentlemen and commoners remained fundamental in Chinese society. From the Han onward, it was somewhat easier to cross this line of division; but one's birth still largely determined what opportunities were available. The exam system provided a chance to reach great political power—but only for those whose families could provide them with an education. Public education was extremely rare. There is also the fact that women were absolutely excluded from the exams and thus from the possibility of holding any public office. Later, we will explore the reasoning behind this, along with the general attitude toward women in traditional China.

While Confucianism was taking hold in China during the Han, something else occurred which was destined to change the course of Chinese history and philosophy. Somewhere around 50 AD Buddhist missionaries first began to arrive in China. The event was little noticed, and there is no certainty as to who these missionaries were or how they reached their destination. Buddhism was from the beginning a religion that did not restrict itself to any class or nationality, so it is no surprise that it eventually made its way to China.

The missionaries found China to be a rather unpromising field for conversions. Some of Buddhism's teachings violated the sacred precepts of filial love, for example, the exhortation to abandon one's family and enter a monastery. Buddha himself had disobeyed his father in entering the religious life and was thus a singularly inappropriate role model from the Chinese standpoint. Various other Buddhist teachings—from both Hinayana and Mahayana—struck the Chinese as abstruse and irrelevant. Only one Buddhist teaching really succeeded in capturing the Chinese imagination, namely the Mahayanist idea of compassionate bodhisattvas.

Thus, Buddhism grew very slowly in China. It had to adapt to an ancient, established culture very different from the one which had nurtured it. In philosophy, the Buddhist activity initially took the form of a massive translation effort to make the major treatises of Indian Buddhism available to Chinese readers. Around 600 AD, there was a shift toward the task of formulating new philosophies which would be more suitable for China. The Tang dynasty (618–907) saw the culmination of this process. It was a period when Buddhism enjoyed significant support from all segments of the population. Not only philosophy but also literature and the arts were dominated by the influence of Buddhism. In this book we will focus our attention on two of the most famous Chinese Buddhist philosophies, Hua-yan and Zen.

The one group who unrelentingly opposed Buddhism from the first were the Confucians. They could not forgive the violations of filial piety. They saw the

Buddhist monks as parasites on society, producing nothing useful with their religious exercises. They considered the teaching of reincarnation an affront to the family, as it maintained that we belong to a family for just a single lifetime and then move on to another. As we will later discuss, they were deeply disturbed by the moral implications of the Mahayanist teaching of Emptiness, which in various ways had been adapted into Chinese Buddhism.

Confucians also viewed Buddhism as riddled with irrational superstition, and this fact provides the background for a fascinating episode which took place in 819 AD. Showing just the credulousness that Confucians despised, some Chinese Buddhist pilgrims in India had acquired a relic which they believed to be a genuine tooth of the Buddha. This was brought back to China with great fanfare, and the Emperor, wishing to curry favor with his many Buddhist subjects, chose to pay special honor to this relic.

Han Yu, a high-ranking Confucian official, was disgusted with the Emperor's behavior and submitted a scathing memorial. (A memorial was a public letter of advice which officials had the right to submit to an emperor.) He chastized the Emperor for setting a bad example to the people. He continued:

> Buddha was a barbarian, who could not speak Chinese and wore outlandish clothing ... He did not understand the duties that bind sovereign and subject, nor the affections of father and son. If he were still alive today and came to Your Majesty's court as an ambassador, Your Majesty might receive him ... but you would have him quickly escorted to the border, dismissed and not allowed to delude the masses.
>
> How then, when he has long been dead, could his rotten bones, the foul and unlucky remains of his body, be properly admitted to the Palace? (quoted from *Sources of Chinese Tradition*, Vol. I, p. 373)

The Emperor, needless to say, was furious at this public rebuke. He demoted Han Yu and banished him to a remote province. But Han became a hero to later Confucians for having spoken out against the baneful Buddhist influence. The "Buddha-Tooth" Incident also provides an excellent illustration of that Confucian principle mentioned earlier: that a worthy Confucian official will show intellectual independence and speak out against what is wrong.

In the Tang, Han Yu was a rather lonely voice protesting the general admiration of Buddhism. In the next dynasty, the Song (960–1267), his implacable opposition to Buddhism became much more common. The Song Confucians were convinced that they must attack Buddhism more vigorously and purge Chinese society of its influence. To this end, they adapted and expanded the original Confucian philosophy. The result was *Neo-Confucianism*, which, in its various forms, is the last major development of traditional Chinese philosophy. In this book we will focus on the most influential of the Neo-Confucians, Zhu Xi (1130–1200), with brief attention to an opposing form of Neo-Confucianism developed by Wang Yangming (1472–1529).

III. BASIC IDEAS OF CHINESE PHILOSOPHY

As with Islamic and Indian thought, there are certain fundamental ideas which are almost universal in Chinese philosophy. They constitute points of agreement between movements which are otherwise bitterly opposed. Because they are so basic, they are sometimes taken for granted by the Chinese thinkers themselves. It is thus all the more important that we survey them now before saying any more about the specific Chinese philosophies.

Above all, we must try to identify the master idea, the idea which conditions and illuminates all the others. Allow me to explain what I have in mind. In Islamic thought, the master idea is clearly Allah, the one God. Everything else is related to that idea. For Indian thought, the idea of liberation or nirvana plays this role. Liberation is the supreme goal, and discussion focuses on such questions as: what exactly is liberation, why is it so important, how is it to be attained?

What idea is there in Chinese thought which possesses this kind of significance? I believe it is the concept of the yin and the yang, twin forces pervading the world and defining the nature of all things. The best known source for presentation of the yin and yang is the *Yi Jing* ("Book of Changes"). This ancient work was originally a divination manual, using a complex system of so-called hexagrams to predict the future. Each of the sixty-four hexagrams is a unique combination yin and yang. Even today, with many people throughout the world, the *Yi Jing* serves only for a rather unsophisticated fortune-telling. But a series of appendices attached to the book draw out deeper moral and metaphysical meanings. These appendices clearly show the profound explanatory power of the yin-yang teaching.

True, there is surprisingly little discussion of yin and yang in Confucius and most of the other early philosophers. Only the rather unimportant school of the Cosmologists explicitly gives central importance to the yin and yang. But the more closely one looks, the more one sees these ideas in the background, so obvious that no need is felt to discuss them.

Consider this table as an indication of both natural and human phenomena that can be classified in the categories of yin and yang.

YIN	YANG
Shade	Sunshine
Calmness	Energy
Earth	Tian
Cold	Heat
Night	Day
Water	Fire
Winter	Summer
Women	Men
Commoners	Gentlemen
Obeying	Commanding
Nurturing	Creating

Mourning	Rejoicing
Receiving	Giving
Superstition	Rationalism

The first and all-important characteristic of all the pairs named in this table is their interdependence. In many of the cases this is quite obvious: there could not be giving unless there were also receiving. In the Chinese view, that kind of interdependence exists in every single case. We will try to discuss most of them below and to give some idea of how all the yin-realities fall naturally together and likewise the yang-realities.

The basic relationship of yin and yang is what we must explore more deeply. They are *not* related as good and bad, nor is there any true opposition between them. This may seem strange, considering such entries as Mourning-Rejoicing; but it is undeniably so from the Chinese standpoint. Mourning is an essential and noble part of life; there could not and should not be a life of pure joy.

There is a harmony that prevails among all entities and all processes—that is the essential idea. Things form a natural community, with each playing its assigned and necessary role. In this way we can understand the subordination of the individual which, as already remarked (page 126), is so alien to Western thought. In the context of the yin-yang theory, *fitting in* is far more valued than *standing out*.

There are many ways to fit in: concern for family honor rather than personal gratification (Confucianism), submission to the natural order (Daoism), being an obedient and productive citizen of the state (Legalism). But almost always this precept: the individual exists in and for something greater. Yang Chu, with his refusal to sacrifice one hair of his body, is an exception. But it is an exception that proves the rule, since his philosophy was found by the Chinese themselves to be something absurd and repugnant. There is also a tinge of individualism in the Chinese Buddhist philosophy, but a discussion of that will have to wait.

There is an interesting manifestation of this emphasis on harmony over individualism in Chinese science. Joseph Needham has explained it at length in his monumental *Science and Civilization in China*. Western science has tended to be mechanistic, searching for explanation through *forces* operating in accord with inflexible *laws*. Whether the subject be gravity or genetics, you may observe that this kind of explanation is the Western scientist's quest. By contrast, traditional Chinese science focused on the classification of phenomena (not merely into yin and yang but into larger sets of categories as well). The aim was to present things as spontaneously functioning in an ordered harmony rather than as the subjects of a higher, imperious law. (See especially Volume II of Needham's work, pp. 273–91)

The idea of compelling law—whether natural, divine or human—is alien to Chinese thought. Obviously, Legalism is an exception; but again the exception proves the rule, as the Chinese consigned that philosophy to oblivion.

Now we can look at some of the specific pairings which are associated with the yin-yang theory.

YIN/YANG SYMBOL

The familiar symbol of yin and yang. The dark of yin and the light of yang thoroughly penetrate one another. One is inconceivable without the other. [PhotoDisc, Inc.]

SHADE-SUNSHINE. This might seem to be one of the more trivial entries on the above chart. But these two are actually the original meanings of the terms *yin* and *yang*. It can be seen in the history of the two Chinese ideographs representing yin and yang. The specific idea is of the shady and sunny sides of a mountain. One side is cool and dark, the other warm and bright. Most importantly, there cannot be one without the other. From this humble beginning the two concepts were expanded to cosmic proportions.

NIGHT-DAY, WINTER-SUMMER. These illustrate very clearly the cyclical nature of yin-yang manifestation. Night and winter are indeed expressions of the yin, involving coldness, darkness and inactivity; day and summer embody the contrasting qualities. But contrast is *not* opposition. The members of these pairs do not struggle with each other for dominance. Each has its time and then yields to the other in an eternal alternation. Nature would be incomplete and dysfunctional without the presence of both members. If there were only summer, for example, the earth would wear itself out with the perpetual growth and activity of living things. There must be winter as a season of rest, just as night provides the essential period of daily rest.

EARTH-TIAN. We have already seen something of Chinese belief about Tian, but the close pairing with Earth was not previously considered. One must understand that the original meaning of the word *tian* was "sky" or "the heavens." In ancient times, the sky was thought of as a great inverted bowl, arched over the vast, flat expanse of the earth. But sky and earth were not mere physical entities. Each was pervaded by a divine spirit. From the god Tian the benevolent powers of sunshine and rainfall were directed down upon the goddess Earth, impregnating her, so to speak. In this way Earth brought forth and nurtured all the living creatures.

It is immediately evident that Tian is *not* a supreme being in the manner of Allah or Krishna. Earth is his partner, not his creation. He is not a divine autocrat controlling all. Rather, he "fits in", "plays a role", like the rest of us.

Tian is indeed the ruler of the world, but he is ruler in the Chinese manner of wu wei (See page 134), not the activist manner of sovereigns in other cultures. A famous Chinese saying expresses it very well: "Tian does not speak." That is, he does not communicate with us through prophets or other means of revelation. There is no word of God, such the Koran, the Bible and the Bhagavad Gita are believed to be. Tian's creative activity has indeed endowed human beings with a moral purpose, but they themselves must discover it.

There is no personal relationship with Tian. As he does not speak to us, neither can we communicate with him. It would be an impertinence for human beings to suppose they had the right to address him. He may not be a supreme being, but he is far above us. If people insist on seeking supernatural assistance of some kind, they should seek it from some lesser god. The world is thought to abound with gods or "spiritual beings" of many kinds and ranks. They may be prayed to, but Tian is too exalted for that.

It might seem that all this is contradicted by the Mandate Theory we discussed earlier. There Tian is portrayed as having a hand in the rise and fall of dynasties. Does that not make him a dominating and involved God, like Allah? We have to remember two facts about Tian's intervention in such cases. First, he does not announce his decree to anyone. It is carried out in a very subtle and mysterious manner. No one can say, until the new dynasty is actually in place, that it truly has the Mandate. Secondly, Tian's intervention is always through the freely chosen actions of human beings. Men must exert themselves and put their lives at risk in the struggle against the old dynasty. They cannot passively wait for Tian to do this work.

There is no inconsistency between Tian's being the embodiment of energetic yang and his ruling in the passive manner of wu wei. We must understand that energy is expressed in other ways than just frenetic activity. The Chinese have a concept of de, "moral force." This is energy in its purest form, energy expressed through being rather than doing. It is by means of this moral force that both Tian and the earthly sovereign govern.

One might almost suppose from all this that Tian himself is more a natural force than a conscious person. This, you will recall, is a burning issue in Indian philosophy, whether God is a person (like Krishna) or a force (like Brahman). If we were to question Confucius (or Lao Zi or most of them) on this point, I suspect the answer would be that neither of these concepts from our worldly experience is applicable to Tian. He (along with Earth) is on a different level of existence. It is both presumptuous and futile to speculate about his nature.

We must note that Mo Zi's philosophy is out of sync with the above views on Tian. As discussed (page 130), Mo believed that the Tian was not such a remote and inaccessible figure but rather one whose will could be readily known (at least by Mo). As usual, the dissent to the prevailing idea comes from a marginal figure in the Chinese tradition.

WATER-FIRE. Water was a substance which held spiritual meaning for the Chinese. This is especially evident in the writing of Lao Zi who extolled its "humility": always flowing to the lowest place, taking on the shape of its container (Chapters 8 and 78, Dao De Jing). These characteristics, along with its coolness and nurturing power, insured that water would be associated with yin. Bright, burning, energetic fire was naturally classed with yang. These were just two of the five basic physical substances the Chinese believed to exist. The others were metal, wood and soil. Metal was the Lesser Yin in contrast to water, the Greater Yin; for metal was normally cold; but, when molten, it was obedient to the metalsmith's shaping. Wood was the Lesser Yang in contrast to fire, for it was the manifestation of vigorous growth. Soil stood exactly in the middle, with equal portions of yin and yang. All the substances together were known as the Five Agents.

The most interesting fact about the Five Agents was their mutual relationship. Water, for obvious reasons, controls fire. (The fact that it is yin does not prevent this, for in the cyclical course of things, yin must periodically assert itself.) Soil dominates water, damming it up or channeling its flow. Wood dominates soil by virtue of taking its own being and sustenance out of it. Metal, through cutting and carving, dominates wood. *And* fire, by the power of melting, dominates metal. Thus, there is a perfect balance among the five. None is all-controlling; each has its distinctive place.

WOMEN-MEN. No aspect of the yin-yang theory is more controversial than its extension to sexual difference. By the Chinese reckoning, yin and yang—*not* anatomical characteristics—defined the very natures of women and men. Thus, women were inherently destined to be submissive caretakers. A woman who asserted herself—except in her rightful domain of the household—was disturbing the natural order. This could not fail to have disastrous consequences for herself and all those around her.

Thus, the Chinese philosophers, especially the Confucians, demanded that women be excluded from public life. There is only one saying on the subject of women in the Analects, but that one speaks volumes:

> Women and servants are especially difficult to handle. Be friendly, and they take liberties; be distant, and they resent it. (XVII, 25)

Such disdain presupposed that women must keep to their lowly places, and that a wife could never be in a relationship of mutual respect with her husband. It was unthinkable that a woman should have any position of prominence. When women did sometimes acquire political power through being the wife or mother of a weak emperor, this met with severe censure. The history books (whose authors were invariably Confucians) would look back on these times as periods of unique corruption. In particular, it was believed that only a woman of monstrous cruelty could gain power. (Call it the Dragon-Lady Syndrome, if you like; it has by no means disappeared.) This was, to some extent, a self-fulfilling prophecy, given the obstacles that existed.

Be sure to understand that, in the perspective of the yin-yang theory, this was not oppression or degradation of women. They had their natural place, as did men. Their own true fulfillment, as well as the common good, required they remain in it. Yin and yang entail different roles; they must not be mixed up.

Daoism is somewhat of an exception in this particular matter. When the time comes, we will need to carefully discuss its views on the "feminine."

COMMONERS-GENTLEMEN. It is easy to see how this pair falls in with the yin-yang dualism. Gentlemen are the controlling yang, and commoners the submissive yin. But it goes beyond that. Remember Mencius' discussion of how the two groups complement each other, making essential contributions. (See page 134.) The commoners were not mere "dirt." They possessed (according to Mencius) an inherent goodness.

Thus, as with men and women, we are not supposed to see exploitation in the gentleman-commoner relationship. Instead, there is mutual dependence and harmony. This illustrates a profound general truth with regard to the yin and the yang. Each possesses what is lacking in the other. Their difference is a source, not of conflict, but of unity.

We can now see that Confucianism invoked the yin-yang theory as sanction for its own political doctrine. This invocation was not always explicit, certainly not with Confucius himself. But it was there nonetheless. The enormous and prolonged influence of Confucianism on China can only be understood against this background. The people of China accepted this philosophy because it seemed "right" in relation to the ideas of yin and yang which they had already known from ancient times.

SUPERSTITION-RATIONALISM. Chinese folklore is richly endowed with tales of the supernatural. I doubt whether there is any other culture in the world who has shown as much fascination for stories of ghosts, fairies, wizards and magical phenomena of every sort. Perhaps it is this very fact which led so many of the Chinese philosophers to adopt a vigorously skeptical stance. The Confucians and many others found the popular superstitions highly distasteful and unbecoming of a gentleman. Such beliefs incapacitated a person from dealing with problems in a practical, effective way.

There is a famous exchange (*Analects*, XI, 11) between Confucius and one of his students which brings out this attitude very nicely. The student had asked about serving the spiritual beings. These beings were the mysterious supernatural powers exerting influence on our world. Each household had its own little god, the kitchen god. Every lake, river and mountain had a god. Every phase of human concern (agriculture, business, etc.) had a controlling god. The student's question was really: how can we ingratiate ourselves with these spirits so as to receive their favors?

In the spirit of rationalism, Confucius rejected the student's question. "If we cannot yet serve man, how can we serve the spiritual beings?" His point was *not* to deny the very possibility that the spirits might exist. Rather, he was insisting that our knowledge of them is hopelessly limited. We have but an imperfect knowledge of our fellow humans, and what we know of the spirits is bound to be far less. It is truly a waste of our mental energies to speculate about who they are and how to deal with them. Far better to focus on what we, with our natural endowments, can accomplish than to seek supernatural aid.

This *humanistic* reliance on human abilities is characteristic of most of the Chinese philosophers. Their concern was for the enhancement of this present life, and they saw little benefit from delving into the mysteries of a spiritual world. This is even true of the Buddhist philosophers. Their co-religionists among the common folk embraced all manner of superstition, but this did not figure at all in the work of the philosophers. The only significant exception to this humanistic, rationalistic attitude in Chinese philosophy was (again) Mo Zi, with his heartfelt belief in avenging ghosts.

Rationalism in philosophy *coexisted* with the superstition of the common people. As always with the yin and yang, they had their respective places. The philosophers did not think possible or desirable to destroy superstition completely. We have already seen this stance in the quotation from Xun Zi (page 135).

Take the following story as an illustration.

> A Confucian official was appointed to serve as magistrate in a remote district situated on particularly wild and dangerous stretch of the Yellow River. On arriving to take up his new post, he was horrified to learn that the villagers had a barbaric custom of sacrificing young women. They called it the Festival of the River God's Marriage. Each spring, some unfortunate girl would be selected to become the river god's "bride." She would be bound up, put in a flimsy boat and launched into the river to be drowned.
>
> The villagers insisted to the magistrate that the festival must be held and that he must select, from all the marriageable girls in the village, the one to be sacrificed. So the girls were brought before him, trembling and wailing. Without a word, he coldly surveyed the entire group. Finally, he declared, "None of these girls is pretty enough to be the river god's bride."
>
> Then he turned to one of the village leaders. "You!" he said. "You must go into the boat instead. Convey to the river god our deep apologies for this regrettable situation." No one dared to object.
>
> Next year, it was exactly the same. Again, the magistrate found all the girls unsatisfactory; and again, he sent one of the village leaders to be drowned instead. In the third year, as the time for the festival approached, the villagers came to the magistrate and begged him not to hold it. Thus ended the sacrifices to the river god. [I have not been able to track down the source of this story and so cannot vouch for its accuracy. But such customs were definitely not unknown in ancient China.]

The story portrays for us the profound intellectual gap between leaders and common people, as the Confucians (and others) saw it. The magistrate embodied the virtues of a leader: utterly free of superstition in his own mind but at the same time resourceful and decisive in dealing with it. The villagers, by contrast, were hopelessly petty and ignorant. They could be governed but not enlightened. Undoubtedly, the magistrate would not have bothered with their custom at all, had it not been so brutal and hateful.

IV. THE MAIN ALTERNATIVES TO CONFUCIANISM

1. Legalism: The Manipulation of Human Nature

Of all the philosophies to emerge in the "Hundred Schools" Period, Legalism was by far the most successful at that time. Practically all the state governments in the late Zhou followed Legalism, though they might make a perfunctory bow to Confucianism. As we have seen, the state of Qin relied completely on Legalism in carrying out its conquest of all China. In this section we will discuss the Legalism of

Han Fei Zi, who in an especially persuasive way, brought together the various strands of Legalist thought.

The cornerstone of this philosophy was the teaching that humans are evil (i.e., selfish) by nature. This doctrine came from Xun Zi, but there was a vital difference between Han Fei and his Confucian teacher. Xun Zi believed that the original selfishness of our nature could be *corrected* through the disciple of li, poetry, music and all the other elements of Confucian education. To Han Fei, on the other hand, human nature could not be changed. The processes of maturing and being education would not eradicate a person's selfishness. They would merely cause it to be expressed in more subtle ways.

Han Fei Zi criticized the Confucians (including Xun Zi) for continually singing the praises of the great sages of the past, like the Duke of Zhou. Perhaps there were a few such noble figures embodying true goodness, but these examples were irrelevant to the general run of humanity.

> Every once in a while there is a stick which is perfectly straight for making an arrow, or a piece of wood which is naturally rounded to make a wheel. But the skilled workman attaches no importance to it. Why not? Because it is not just a single person who wishes to shoot a bow or ride in a carriage. Similarly, the enlightened ruler attaches no special value to the few who will naturally do good...Sound political practice requires a technique that will lead to the good behavior of all, not just of the exceptional few. (*Han Fei Zi*, Chapter 50)

From the natural, incurable selfishness of humans in general, Han Fei Zi derived his most famous doctrine: the Two Handles. These are reward and punishment. They are "handles" in that they provide the only means by which human behavior can be influenced or controlled. Reward, in a positive way, and punishment, in a negative way, invoke our self-interest. That is why they are effective. Any appeal that goes beyond self-interest is useless, say Han Fei. For example, it is completely pointless to urge someone to do something out of concern for the rights or needs of another person.

It is a sorry picture of human relations that is presented here, and Han Fei would not deny that. Each person is focused on a set of personal needs and desires. There can be no true common interest. All personal relationship is reduced to *manipulation*, each one seeking to use the other. The word *handle* aptly expresses this manipulative aspect.

What really interests Han Fei is how the general principle of human nature applies to the specific problem of governance. Here, one of the handles assumes far greater importance than the other. The ruler cannot possibly afford to reward his people for all that he wishes them to do. It is more practicable to control their actions by threat of punishment—the more severe, the better. This is where *law* comes in, for it is nothing more than the ruler's systematic application of the handle of punishment.

For most people the phrase *rule of law* has very positive connotation. Certainly this is one of the most cherished features of the American political system. But "rule of law" had a rather different meaning in ancient China. There are three features to take note of. First, law must be extremely simple, refusing to make allowance for special cases or subtle differences. It will not work unless ordinary citizens clearly understand it. One of the Legalists maintained that the legal code should be brief enough that all its provisions might be inscribed on a single slab of stone. Then, such an inscription could be set up in every village, so that each citizen would know exactly what was required.

Secondly, law must be supported by whatever degree of punishment is needed to make it effective. While Confucius wanted to minimize the use of the death penalty (page 121), the Legalists readily deployed it, even in cases where it would seem grossly excessive to us.

This leads immediately to the third point: Legalist law had nothing to do with justice. The concern was simply with the effectiveness of the punishment, not whether it fit the crime. As punishments were not regulated by any kind of moral principle, they quickly assumed ghastly proportions. This forever dishonored the name of Legalism in the eyes of the Chinese, as they bitterly recalled the excesses of the Qin dynasty which Legalism had sponsored.

Be that as it may, the Legalists themselves did not think of their philosophy as cruel or vicious. Rule of law (as they understood it) was absolutely necessary for the order of society. The greedy, turbulent nature of human beings would bring misery to all unless it was checked. And only harsh laws could do this.

In dealing with his own ministers, the Legalist ruler was obliged to be just as strict as when dealing with the people. The annals of the later Zhou were replete with stories of how rulers had been undone by the betrayal and rebellion of their subordinates. The Confucian idea that a ruler should respect and trust his ministers seemed preposterous to the Legalists. The operative principle is again the selfishness of human nature. Ministers will use for their own benefit whatever power they are entrusted with. Thus the wise ruler governs as a despot, jealously keeping all possible power in his own hands.

A final principle in the Legalist philosophy is what we may call *modernism*. The term has a strange ring to it as applied to a teaching more than two thousand years old. But Han Fei Zi and his colleagues did have a powerful sense that they were living in a new era, sharply different from what had gone before. Confucians, Daoists and Mohists vied with each other to find the most ancient precedents for their ideas, dwelling especially on the legendary pre-dynastic times. All this was very dubious, Han Fei pointed out, as we can have no assured knowledge of what happened so long ago.

> Confucius and Mo Zi transmitted the doctrines of the ancient rulers Yao and Shun. Although they differed in what they accepted or rejected, each claimed to represent the true teachings of Yao and Shun. Now Yao and Shun cannot come to life again. Who is going to determine the truth of Confucianism or Mohism? . . . If we are unable to determine the truth of Confucianism or Mohism and yet wish to determine the doctrines of Yao

and Shun some three thousand years ago, I believe it is impossible to be sure of anything. (from Chapter 50)

But even if the these tales of ancient times were true, they would provide no guidance for the "modern" era. Han Fei illustrated his point with the story "Waiting by the Tree Stump."

> A certain farmer had worked hard in his field all through the day. It was spring, and there was much plowing and planting to be done. Suddenly, a rabbit came racing through the field, running smack into a tree stump and breaking its neck. The farmer took the rabbit home and cooked it for dinner. Next morning, he returned to the field to resume his work. But then he thought to himself, "Why should I slave away like this? I will just sit down here and wait for another rabbit." (adapted from Chapter 49)

The Confucians and all the other worshippers of the past are just as stupid as that farmer, says Han Fei. They want to re-create the ancient, idyllic times, which are so glowingly portrayed in the folklore. But if these times ever did exist, they are gone for good. The new era requires an altogether different set of political practices.

One must admit a good deal of merit to Han Fei's point. China had changed drastically in the last centuries of the Zhou. Even amid political chaos, there had been considerable technological and economic progress. And the country had grown. At the beginning of the Zhou, China was not one-tenth its present size. By the time Han Fei wrote, it had expanded considerably and probably was already the world's most populous nation.

For better and for worse, the Legalists did create the first modern state in China or anywhere else. They devised the centralized bureaucracy which could govern a vast land. Clear laws and rigorous enforcement kept order, at least for a time. The economy was closely managed, with many enterprises under state ownership. These *impersonal* structures were held to be essential to the governance of so many people. As already noted, the Confucians, when they finally came to power, could not entirely dispense with these methods. They might well extol the ancient rulers' *de* (moral force), but in practice something more palpable was required. Confucianism would never have succeeded in China, had it not learned from the bureaucratic methods of the Legalists.

2. Daoism: Conforming to the Dao

The Daoist philosophy was, in the long run, the most significant alternative to Confucianism. Its political vision was nostalgic and impractical, so that it could never contend for power in the way that Confucians, Legalists and Mohists did. But Daoism offered a distinctive way of life, a path of tranquillity in place of the restless striving of Confucianism. Confucius himself had stressed how the gentleman must be acutely self-critical, always seeking to improve his character. Through the long ages of Confucian dominance, Daoism offered an inviting refuge for those who were weary of relentless moral exertion.

The two great Daoist philosophers, Zhuang Zi and Lao Zi, are of about equal importance, according to the general consensus. Neither is really the founder of Daoism, for its ideas had already been circulating previous to their time. Each gave expression to Daoism in a unique style: Lao, with brief, pithy poems; and Zhuang, with longer discourses abounding in humorous stories and examples. We will concentrate more on Lao, because he is more succinct and also more widely read. Lao Zi's entire output consists in a single book of eighty-one brief chapters. It is called the *Dao De Jing* ("Book of the Dao and its Power"), and you could read it all in less than half an hour.

The central concept is, of course, the Dao. This word originally meant "road", "path", or "way." Gradually, it came to be used with a more abstract meaning. There was said to be a characteristic *dao* that each kind of thing possessed; it was simply that thing's way of functioning. Thus, the dao of a knife is to cut; the dao of a pot is to contain. Daoism took the concept far beyond this by asserting that, along with the daos of individual things, there is a dao of the entire universe. This all-embracing, eternal Dao is what absorbs the interest of the Daoist philosophers. (Whenever I spell the word with the upper-case "D", realize that it is universal principle that is referred to. With the lower-case "d", it is just the principle of some particular thing that is designated.)

The descriptions of this Dao are rather mystifying:

There was something undifferentiated and yet complete,
Which existed before Tian and Earth.
Soundless and formless, it depends on nothing and does not change.
It operates everywhere and is free from danger.
It may be considered the mother of the universe.
I do not know its real name; I call it Dao. (*Dao De Jing*, Chapter 25)

Inasmuch as it is distinguished from Tian, Tao is clearly not God in any normal sense. It is simply a way or a flow of things which is in evidence everywhere. It is imperative for us to be in accord with it, for "Whatever is contrary to Dao will soon perish." (Lao makes this statement in two different chapters, 30 and 55.)

The most pertinent fact about the Dao is given as the very first sentence of Lao's book:

The dao that can be told of is not the Eternal Dao.

Lao is telling us that it is only the "little" daos which can be described and explained. The great, all-pervading Dao will always remain elusive. We cannot define it the way we defined the knife-dao and the pot-dao.

This certainly complicates the problem of bringing oneself into conformity with the Dao. Without clearly articulating it, we must somehow "feel" it and let ourselves be carried along in its flow.

A more technical way of expressing the point is to say knowledge of the Dao is *intuitive* rather than *intellectual*. This is a fundamental distinction, so we need to be

TRAVELERS AMONG VALLEYS AND PEAKS

"Travelers Among Valleys and Peaks," a painting by an anonymous Chinese artist, probably of the Tang dynasty. The travelers are tiny figures crossing the bridge. The painter was clearly imbued with the Daoist idea of the smallness of man within the immensity of nature. [Asian Art Museum Foundation of San Francisco]

very clear about it. Intellectual knowledge, contrary to what you might be tempted to suppose, is by far the more familiar of the two types. It definitely is not confined to scholars and their book learning. Any knowledge that can be clearly formulated and given some kind of justification is (in our present sense of the term) intellectual knowledge. If I know that today is Tuesday or that the sky is cloudy, this is intellectual knowledge. For I am able to *say* what I know and I have some basis for what I am saying.

Intuitive knowledge is that which cannot be articulated or justified. As an example, take someone's knowledge of what the color green looks like. Could this be communicated to another person who had never seen colors. Could one justify the claim that his own perception of green was "truer" than someone else's? Lao believes that knowledge of the Dao, if we ever get it at all, is like this. If one wants to acquire a knowledge of political conditions in the Zhou dynasty, one can get it out of a book. Gaining knowledge of the Dao is an incomparably more subtle and uncertain process.

Why, then, did Lao Zi write a book about the Dao, if he considered the task of explaining it to be impossible? There is a old legend which neatly explains the paradox. It is said that in his later years Lao became so disenchanted with the civilized life of China that he decided to go into the wilderness to lead a more natural existence. On reaching the border, he was stopped by the guard stationed there. This functionary, recognizing the great wisdom of the man before him, deemed it his duty to require Lao to write down his philosophy before leaving. Thus, the *Dao De Jing* is supposed to have to have come into being. We are given to understand that Lao, in his own free judgment, would not have considered it appropriate to put these matters into words. The story is obviously contrived; but it shows us that from early on, Daoists realized that the very existence of the book needed to be explained.

Ancient Daoism offered both a social philosophy and a personal philosophy. The latter is of more enduring importance, but it is useful and interesting to look at the social philosophy first. It shows us how the Daoists responded to those political problems which were vexing all the other philosophers, Recall that, with the exception of the Legalists, the Chinese philosophers sought political salvation in the models of the past. In the case of the Daoists, the past that was yearned for was the *actual* past, not some idealized version of it. The Daoists really wanted to abandon civilization and return to more primitive times.

Chapter 80 of the *Dao De Jing* gives the classic statement of this social vision:

> Let it be a small country, sparsely populated. Even if there were an abundance of tools, no use would be made of them. The people will abhor risk and stay close to home. Even if ships and carriages were available, there would be no travel. Even if there were weapons, they would not be brought out. Instead of writing, knotted cords are used. The people will enjoy their food, adorn their clothing, be content with their homes and delight in their customs. There may be a neighboring country so close that their barking dogs and crowing roosters can be heard. Yet the people grow old and die without ever visiting one another.

This vision is not Lao's own concoction. It is based on what he had seen of simple village life in China and what he knew of life among the barbarian folk on the borders of China. Other philosophers viewed the barbarians with scorn and contempt, but for the Daoists they represented a better way of life.

What made this barbaric society so appealing was its tranquillity and harmony. The people lived primitively, but they were content with what they had. They felt no need to produce more, and they had no burning curiosity to know of anything beyond their small world. They had simple pleasures and lived in blissful ignorance of "higher" culture. For a Chinese gentleman, writing was an essential attainment, the mark of one's superiority. Lao Zi was urging that it be cast aside as one more manifestation of artificiality.

The *most* important advantage of the simple society is its lack of class distinctions. The people are all on the same primitive level. No one has more, no one lords it over the others. Zhuang Zi's picture of the blissful primitive society brings this out even more clearly:

> In ancient times, all the people wove their own clothes and tilled the ground for their food. They formed one group, without distinction of class. They lived with the birds and beasts, forming one family with all creatures. How could there be distinction between gentlemen and commoners? The people had no "knowledge" and so kept to their natural virtue . . . (Chapter 9 of the *Zhuang Zi*, quoted from Needham, Vol II, page 106)

This society for which Lao and Zhuang yearned was hardly a realistic possibility. China had come too far on the path of civilization ever to go back. A very few Daoists might retreat from the world to live as hermits (including Lao himself, if we believe that legend). But most who read the Daoist literature could never bring themselves to abandon civilization. They needed another way by which to apply the lessons of the Dao, and that is what we now consider.

Lao and Zhuang offered a coherent idea of how to conduct one's personal life, an idea that could be practiced in any social setting. The heart of this Daoist lifestyle is the avoidance of whatever goes beyond our natural needs. "Make your desires few," say Lao (Ch. 19), for there is no happiness in chasing after one's desires:

> The five colors cause one's eyes to be blind.
> The five tones cause one's ears to be deaf.
> The five flavors cause one's palate to be spoiled.
> Racing and hunting drive one to madness.
> Goods that are hard to get injure one's activities.
> For this reason the sage is concerned with the belly and not the eyes.
> (Chapter 12)

Concern with the belly means concern for what is necessary to life. The Daoists have no wish to be liberated completely from this life, and so they are not, in the manner of the Indian philosophers, seeking to rid themselves of *all* desire. It is the excesses of sensual gratification which they consider dangerous.

Unchecked emotion can be just as destructive as sensuality. That is why Lao says:

> I treat those who are good with goodness,
> and I treat those who are not good with goodness.
> Thus is goodness attained. (Ch. 49)

The point is that one must show kindness to all, never giving way to feelings of anger and vengefulness. These only create stress and wear down one's own vital energy. This idea is in striking contrast to the Confucian way. Master Kong was once asked what he thought of the policy of being good to your enemies. He replied:

> In that case, how would you repay goodness? I would say rather: be good to those who have done you good, and be severe to your enemies. (*Analects*, XIV, 36)

To have strong feelings in the face of good or evil is very much a part of the Confucian gentleman's character. For a Daoist, on the other hand, calmness is essential; strong feelings of any kind are self-destructive.

This brings us to an even more basic difference between the Confucian and Daoist ways of life. With the Confucians, moral values are supremely important. We must always hold up to ourselves the ideals of filial piety, loyalty, moral righteousness and ren. To the Daoists these values are a sham:

> When the Great Dao declined,
> The doctrines of ren and righteousness arose . . .
> When the various family relationships fell into disharmony,
> Then began the preaching of filial piety and parental love.
> When a country's government is in disorder
> Then the praise of loyal ministers is heard. (*Dao De Jing*, ch. 18)

The talk of ren, filial piety, etc. is only a symptom of the deeply disordered times. If we truly desire to get back to a harmonious state, then we must "abandon ren and discard righteousness", as Lao says in the very next chapter. That is, we must avoid exhortation about these things. Striving for morality, like every other kind of striving, is just a disruption of our essential calmness and a destruction of our vitality.

The basic Daoist approach to life is one of *not* striving, *not* seeking, *not* asserting oneself. Lao likes to refer to it as "weakness." He uses a number of striking images to express it. In Chapter 55 he talks about a newborn baby who is utterly weak and helpless and yet possesses the maximum of vitality, "crying all day long without getting hoarse." As previously mentioned, he cites water as the perfection of weakness. But in that weakness is strength:

> There is nothing softer and weaker than water,
> And yet there is nothing better for attacking strong and hard things . . .

From this all the world knows that the weak overcomes the strong and the soft overcomes the hard. (Ch. 78)

Most interestingly, Lao Zi sees the Daoist way as embodied in femininity. In Chapter 6 he identifies the feminine with the undying "Spirit of the Valley." This spirit is humility and submission, but

> The abode of the mysterious feminine
> Is the root of Tian and Earth.
> It seems to endure forever.
> Use it and you will never wear it out.

Zhuang Zi would echo these principles for living which we have been illustrating out of Lao Zi's book. Nevertheless, there is a significant difference between the two Daoists. This is best revealed by considering their different attitudes to death. Lao sees the avoidance of death as a highly desirable objective. That is one of the primary reasons for practicing the lifestyle of tranquillity and simplicity. In Chapter 7, he compares the sage to Heaven and Earth. They live on and on because they do not live for themselves, asserting and grasping. Likewise, the sage can endure far beyond the normal span by practicing Daoism. Chinese folklore told of Daoist hermits who lived for hundreds of years.

By contrast, Zhuang Zi regards death, whenever it comes, as a natural process *not* to be dreaded. It is simply a *transformation* from one mode of existence to another. This vital energy which has been a human being may become a rat's liver or an insect's leg, suggests Zhuang. Whatever happens there is nothing to be upset about:

> The pure man of old knew neither to love life nor to hate death. He did not rejoice in birth, nor did he resist death. Without any concern he came, and without any concern he went. (*Zhuang Zi*, Ch. 6)

We find in Zhuang a casual, carefree attitude to everything—even to the point of flippancy. Nothing seems to matter to him. He asserts a doctrine of *relativism* to support this:

> If a man sleeps in a damp place, he will have a pain in his loins and will dry up and die. Is that true of fish? If a man lives up in a tree, he will be frightened and tremble. Is that true of monkeys? Which of the three knows the right place to live?
>
> Men eat vegetables and meat, and deer eat tender grass. Centipedes dine on the remains of snakes, while crows and owls like mice. Which of them knows the right taste?
>
> Monkeys mate with each other, and the buck mates with the doe. Fish mate with other fish. Now Mao Qiang and Li Ji were thought by men to be very beautiful. But at the sight of them, fish plunged deep in the water, birds flew away up high, and deer raced off. Which knows the true nature of beauty? (Ch. 2)

Zhuang is saying that none of the things we cherish possess value in any absolute sense. If we move away from our own partial standpoint and see in the perspective of the Dao, all things are the same. The matters we become excited about are really inconsequential, as shown in the story "Three in the Morning":

> A monkey keeper was once giving out nuts and said, "Three in the morning and four in the evening." The monkeys all chattered angrily. "Very well, then," he said, "it will be four in the morning and three in the evening." At this the monkeys were all pleased. (Chapter 2)

For Zhuang reality itself becomes something dubious, as expressed in his famous "butterfly" story:

> Once I, Zhuang Zhou, dreamed that I was a butterfly and was happy as a butterfly. I was conscious that I was quite pleased with myself, but I did not know that I was Zhou. Suddenly I awoke, and there I was, visibly Zhou. I do not know whether it was Zhou dreaming that he was a butterfly or the butterfly dreaming that it was Zhou. (Chapter 2)

From all this we can understand that Zhuang's calmness and contentedness are the expression of his belief that nothing is really important. This is not at all the situation with Lao. His is a *calculating* calmness. He adopts the attitudes of Daoism because he perceives that they will lead to certain goals. This calculating spirit is evident throughout the *Dao De Jing*. For example,

> A sage does not accumulate for himself.
> The more he uses for others, the more he has himself.
> The more he gives to others, the more he possesses of his own. (Ch. 81)

The great Neo-Confucian Zhu Xi expressed it very well when he said "Lao Zi still wanted to accomplish something, but Zhuang Zi didn't want to accomplish anything at all." (Quoted from Chan, *Sourcebook*, p. 178) That is, Lao still had goals, but Zhuang did not.

As a final note, it should be mentioned that there was an organized religion that associated itself with the Daoist philosophy. This religious movement especially venerated Lao Zi and made his *Dao De Jing* into a sacred text. But the real core of this religion was magic. It trafficked in spells, potions, talismans and superstitions of every kind. It was especially devoted to various magical techniques for indefinitely prolonging life. In this we see how far it strayed from the philosophical Daoism, where Lao wanted to prolong life by simple living and Zhuang didn't care to preserve life at all.

3. Buddhism: Hua-Yan's Universal Harmony

The Chinese Buddhists used to say "Hua-yan for theory, Chan for technique" so it is appropriate for us to discuss Hua-yan as probably the finest flower of speculative philosophy in Chinese Buddhism. It was based on an Indian Buddhist work, the *Avatamsakara Sutra*. However, Chinese thinkers gave this work a new dimension of meaning, so that the Hua-yan philosophy was something quite different from anything developed in India. The chief representative of Hua-yan is Fa-zang (643–712).

The Hua-yan philosophers were particularly moved by the *Avatamsaka Sutra's* depiction of the vastness of the world. In its scope the Sutra's cosmology went far beyond anything in the native Chinese traditions. Here is an example, where the Sutra is quoting the discourse of an enlightened bodhisattva:

> In the ten directions I see every place in all the worlds and universes pervading the vast expanse of space...Some worlds are made of pure light, suspended steadily in space...Some are shaped like flowers or like lamps adorned with jewels. Some are vast as the ocean...Some are slender, some small. They have countless forms and spin in various ways. Some are like a glowing wheel or a volcano or a lion or a seashell. (Quoted from Garma C.C. Chang, *The Buddhist Teaching of Totality*, p. xxi. This book is an indispensable source for navigating the difficult Hua-yan philosophy.)

We are shown here how indescribably large and diverse the world is. In other passages the Sutra speaks of how this vast world is just a bit of dust within a larger world. At the same time, every particle of dust in our world contains micro-worlds every bit as complex as what has already been described. And all this transpires over incomparably vast periods of time. Such a universe, in all its extent and detail, is given to the enlightened mind.

Along with this dramatic cosmology, the Hua-yan Buddhists imbibed the doctrine of Emptiness from Indian philosophy. They were particularly influenced by Nagarjuna, who had been extensively translated into Chinese. You should reread the section on him and especially the paragraphs dealing with the analysis of *svabhava* or own-being (page 100). This is an important point of departure for the Hua-yan Buddhists, though they are not in perfect agreement with him. Nagarjuna's limitation is to suppose that emptiness entails the illusoriness of the world. Fa-zang says

> Phenomena always exist but are at the same time empty, for Emptiness does not destroy existence. Phenomena are always empty but at the same time ever existent, for existence does not obstruct Emptiness. (Quoted from Chan, *Sourcebook*, p. 424)

In addition, Hua-yan cannot abide Nagarjuna's idea that the illusory phenomena will all be swept away leaving an undifferentiated unity of nirvana. Hua-yen agrees with him that all phenomena are lacking in independence, but it insists that they do have both reality and individuality.

There is an illustration which the Hua-yan philosophers loved to use as a clarification of their position. It is the analogy of Indra's Net. Indra was an ancient Indian war god who somehow made his way into Chinese folklore. He was said to possess an extraordinary net whose dimensions were in the thousands of miles. In each one of the interstices of the net, a precious jewel was affixed, so that the value of the whole was beyond calculation. The philosophical lesson of this derives from the fact the entire net was spread out in a gently curving manner, so that each jewel contained the reflection of every other. And not merely that: each jewel contained the reflection of the reflections of all the other jewels that were in each individual jewel. Ad infinitum. Fa-zang once set up an actual demonstration of this with ten carefully positioned mirrors. You could see much the same with just two mirrors directly facing each other.

The analogy expresses the fact that each entity perfectly reflects the rest of the universe. As the Buddhists like to say, the whole world might be comprehended in a single grain of sand, if we could just see it clearly enough. (Remember the dimensions of this world that Hua-yan has in mind!) The image of Indra's Net clearly shows the harmony and coordination of all things. As the Hua-yan like to phrase it, things do not obstruct one another in the slightest way.

There is a further lesson in the analogy which is somewhat less obvious. Each thing, while expressing and being conditioned by everything else, does so from its own unique perspective. This perspective is just as complete and perfect as any other. Thus, in all this vast universe, there is nothing which is special, nothing which constitutes the purpose for other things. Each thing has its own purpose; that is, each thing possess its own radiant enlightenment within.

These abstract ideas become more meaningful, if we realize the social significance of Buddhism in China. Buddhism was a religion of individualism and nonconformity. Its practices—especially the monastic life—defied Chinese norms. By these norms, an individual had no right to set aside duties to family and country for the sake of personal enlightenment. Hua-yan, with its emphasis on the unique and absolute value of each individual, was implicitly defending that right. As will be more evident later, the battle lines were drawn for a bitter controversy with Confucianism.

4. Buddhism: Chan's Sudden Enlightenment

Chan, which is better known by its Japanese name of *Zen*, is said to have originated in China with a certain Bodhidharma, who came from India as a missionary around 500 A.D. According to tradition, Bodhidharma was the twenty-eighth in a thousand-year succession of patriarchs going back to Buddha himself. In fact, Bodhidharma's existence cannot be verified, and the patriarchal succession that preceded him is still more dubious.

Thus, we set aside Chan's own account of its history and conclude that this movement started in China. The first figure in the history of Chan who can be positively identified is Hui Neng (about 638–713). He set the pattern for Chan by his emphasis on sudden enlightenment and by his rather iconoclastic way of dealing with issues.

This is shown in a famous story. Hui Neng had recently become a Buddhist monk and was working in a very humble capacity in the monastery kitchen. At this time the head monk, having become quite old, decided that he must choose his

successor. He announced to all the monks that whoever considered himself qualified should post in the main hall a brief verse displaying his understanding. The
Master's star pupil was quick to respond with these lines:

> The body is the vehicle of perfect wisdom.
> In the mind is fixed a bright mirror.
> Always diligently wipe this mirror.
> Do not allow it to become dusty. (*Platform sutra*, Section 6)

In the dead of night, Hui Neng slipped into the hall and posted this verse in
response:

> In reality there is no vehicle for perfect wisdom.
> The bright mirror is not fixed anywhere.
> Buddha-nature is forever pure and clear.
> Where is there any dust? (*Platform Sutra*, Section 8)

Hui Neng was confirmed by the Master as his successor.

What did this signify? The other monk's quatrain expressed a conventional
understanding of the quest for enlightenment. Through steady adherence to spiritual discipline, the mind will gradually be purified and wisdom won. Hui Neng
rejected this idea, because he believed that perfection was already present. To see
this perfection, we need a drastic and immediate reversal of our habitual ways of
thinking, not a gradual purification. Thus, the principle of *sudden enlightenment*
emerged.

In the third line of his little verse, Hui Neng alludes to Buddha-nature, and
this is a point that requires considerable elaboration. In the Buddhist perspective,
Buddha-nature is synonymous with perfection, since Buddha's attainments were
the maximum that could be achieved. The Chinese Buddhists had, in general,
adopted the principle "Buddha-nature in all things", by which they meant that all
things were as good as they could possibly be. Buddha-nature was the harmony
and beauty underlying all the apparent trouble in the world.

Hui Neng was making the point that this Buddha-nature is already clear in us;
it does not need to be fashioned or refined. But he certainly recognizes that this
truth is *not* evident to our normal, intellectual mode of thinking. Remember that
distinction we made earlier (p. 151) between intellect and intuition. It will be just as
relevant for Chan as for Daoism. To say that Buddha-nature is in all is to say
something hopelessly repugnant and incomprehensible to the intellect. Looking at
the world intellectually (that is, rationally, analytically, objectively) one cannot help
seeing the many imperfections. Indeed, *imperfection* is far too mild a term when you
consider the disasters and tragedies in life. How can it be Buddha-nature when so
many die of disease, famine, floods, earthquakes, etc.?

An instructive example as to the magnitude of this problem is provided by the
thought of the eminent German philosopher and mathematician, G.W. Leibniz. He
formulated and defended the principle that "we live in the best of all possible

worlds." This is actually a pretty close equivalent to saying that the Buddha-nature is in all things. In each case there is an assertion of the perfection of our existing world. Though individual things may appear "wrong", they are "right" when seen in the larger perspective.

Now Leibniz arrived at this idea by strict logical deduction. God, he noted, possesses unlimited wisdom, goodness and power. By His wisdom, He knows what is the best of all possible worlds; in His goodness, He wills to create it; and through His power, He is able to accomplish what He wills. Other philosophers (e.g., Voltaire) ridiculed him for holding this view in the face of so many problems. Leibniz valiantly tried to explain how various misfortunes might ultimately be "for the good." In the end, he convinced practically no one.

Chan Buddhists would not have been surprised at this outcome. It simply testifies to intellect's inability to resolve these deep matters. The Chan would have put their own coreligionists, the Hua-yan, in the same boat with Leibniz. Their reasoning was very different than his, but it was intellectual all the same. It was an attempt to show the perfection of the world by a vast and glorious *theory*.

Like the Daoists, the Chan are convinced that an intuitive understanding is needed to clarify these matters. But how can one develop this subtle and elusive power of intuitive thinking? We all possess it, but it remains, for the most part, on the periphery of the mind, which is dominated by intellect. In keeping with the long monastic tradition of Buddhism, the Chan see the discipline of the monastery as the key to this attainment. Above all, they emphasize the role of the spiritual master (in Japanese: roshi) in bringing this about.

Chan believes that the master often needs to use a certain harshness in order to "jolt" his pupils into the sudden enlightenment that is sought. The Chan literature contains many stories of masters grabbing, shoving or beating their pupils. A good example is provided by this incident involving Master Lin-ji (died 867), who is one of the most influential and revered of all the Chan masters:

> One day, Master Lin-ji came before his students and asked whether any of them could give him a beating. Now this came as a great surprise, for it was a complete reversal of the usual situation. The Master was in the habit of administering harsh beatings to the students. Whenever one would ask him what he thought to be a stupid question, he would respond with a whack of his staff rather than an explanation.
>
> In fact, the students understood well enough the meaning of Lin-chi's request. He wished to see whether any of the students was enlightened. Under normal circumstances, it would be unthinkable for a student to strike his master, even a harsh master like Lin-ji. But in enlightenment, one would no longer need the master and would be free of all such inhibition.
>
> As it happened, one of the young monks did respond to the request. "Yes, Master," he said, "I can do it." Lin-ji beamed with pleasure and beckoned his student to come forward. As he approached, Lin-ji held out his staff for the student to take. But then, at the last moment, the Master pulled it back and struck the unfortunate monk. (adapted from Chan, *Sourcebook*, p. 446)

It is not really a case of arbitrary cruelty, though it was definitely a "mind-game" the Master was playing with his students. There must have been a moment of hesitation on the young monk's part, a wavering that showed he still had some inhibitions. The beating was Lin-ji's very direct way of showing the monk that he was not yet enlightened. Most masters had somewhat less violent methods, but they would have agreed with Lin-chi that verbal explanations are generally not appropriate—they are too *intellectual*.

Such exchanges as these took place in the context of an exacting daily routine required for the monastic life. Chan monks had to spend many hours each day in meditation and many more hours in hard physical labor. The latter is a particular feature of Chan, not found in many other kinds of Buddhist monasticism. It is especially noteworthy in the Chinese context, for Confucians made a point of their disdain for manual labor. This was a distinguishing feature between gentlemen and commoners, as Mencius had noted (p. 134). A Confucian gentlemen was reluctant to perform even the most trifling physical work; and the Chan monks, in their way of life, were quite deliberately dissociating themselves from that attitude.

Chan's rigorous methods of discipline have been ably carried on by the modern followers of the tradition in Japan. Chan (or *Zen*, as we may now call it) has flourished in Japan and become an integral part of Japanese culture. It has certainly taken on features there which it did not have in China. But the spirit of Chan has been preserved, and the teachings of the great Chinese masters such as Lin-ji (known as Rinzai to the Japanese) are reverently studied.

The Zen monasteries in Japan are well known for their severe discipline. They stand apart from other Buddhist monasteries in this respect. Zen's method of practicing meditation is a good illustration. Several long sessions of meditation (approximately two hours each) are held each day. Interestingly, the monks are gathered together for this purpose. Other meditative traditions emphasize the need to isolate oneself and eliminate distraction, but Zen considers the group environment to be beneficial in that it provides a certain mutual reinforcement. In these sessions each monk will have a particular topic of meditation which has been assigned by the roshi (master).

The monks are usually seated in a semicircular arrangement. Walking quietly behind them is one of the senior monks, who carefully observes the posture and concentration of each meditator. If there is any lapse, he will deliver a sharp slap on the errant monk's shoulder with his staff. This is a valuable stimulus which should be appreciated by the one who receives it. Bear in mind the length of these meditation periods. It is extraordinarily difficult to sit up straight, eyes directly ahead, mind alert and focused, for such a time. The topic of meditation is often something very monotonous, such as the contemplation of one's own breathing. The Zen monk is, nevertheless, expected to adhere to the practices with the utmost intensity.

The image of these proceedings in the meditation hall gives us a clear idea of the energy—even fanaticism—which Zen believes necessary in the quest for enlightenment. It is important to keep this in mind, for one sometimes gets the impression that Zen is something simple and effortless. The notorious Lin-ji (Rinzai) is quoted as saying:

> In Buddhism no effort is necessary. Just do nothing, except move your bowels, urinate, get dressed, eat your meals and lie down when tired. (Chan, *Sourcebook*, p. 446)

The point to understand is that this "letting go" occurs *after* enlightenment. Once attained, it is something very simple and obvious. But getting to that point is another matter entirely.

Many of the Japanese Zen monasteries employ a technique known as the koan, and this shows just how paradoxical "sudden enlightenment" can be. A koan is essentially a riddle, a problem that has no logical answer. The most famous of the koans was devised by the great Japanese master, Hakuin (1685–1768). He asked, "What is the sound of one hand clapping?" The logical way to deal with this question is to point out that the act of clapping, by definition, requires two hands. One hand cannot, by itself, clap, any more than one person alone can get married. Needless to say, the logical answer is not what Hakuin was looking for. The enlightened response to this question requires some different kind of response which our minds, initially, cannot even begin to fathom.

Here are some other well known koans. Like Hakuin's, they have a certain craziness about them. They all seem either pointless to ask or impossible to answer.

> Why is Buddha the same as three pounds of flax?
> How do you take a mountain out of a teapot?
> A girl is crossing the street. Is she the younger or the older sister?
> A cow is passing through the window frame. The head, the horns, the four
> legs have all passed through. Why can't the tail pass through?

Having mastered various preliminary meditations, a Zen monk will be given some koan as the final test of enlightenment. A desperate struggle ensues, as the monk tries to make sense of the senseless question. It is the object of his meditation during those many hours each day that are devoted to this purpose. The monk will continually sift through the few words of the question, trying to see some previously overlooked meaning. There are daily conferences with the roshi, where the monk can propose any solution he may have come up with. But these tend to be exercises in humiliation, as the monk's ideas meet with harsh rebuke.

Over many months the frustration gradually builds. Finally, the monk reaches (or should reach) a breaking point of complete disgust with the whole process. He stops trying to "figure out" the koan, and that is precisely the point of it all. *Figuring out* is an intellectual endeavor, an attempt to formulate an explicit, rational solution. The monk has been unwittingly engaged in a kind of aversion therapy in which he strained the intellect to its limits in probing the koan. Now the incapacity of the intellect is completely evident, and intuition can take over. The presupposition in this is that we all have a power of intuitive thinking but that it is normally pushed into the background by the domineering intellect.

There are many ways in which the monk might express to the roshi this new understanding. The Zen literature suggests a simple waving of the hand as an "answer" to the koan about one hand clapping. This response would express the reality of the one hand without going into useless explanations. If one said, "The meaning of the koan is that the truth must be found by intuition, not intellect", that would be correct in a way; but totally unsatisfactory from Zen's standpoint. It is still an intellectual response, even though it talks about the limits of intellect.

In general, the solution to a koan must be spontaneous, giving direct expression to our deepest feelings. There are various ways this might be done for any given koan, but any answer that is contrived or calculated is definitely wrong. This enables us to get a better understanding of that story of Master Lin-ji. The Master had, in effect, posed a koan for his students when he asked whether anyone could give him a beating. The young monk was claiming to have "solved" it by coming forward to take Lin-ji's staff. His hesitation showed that his actions were not spontaneous. He was preparing to beat the Master because he calculated that this was the "enlightened" thing to do; but he couldn't quite carry it through without showing a flicker of doubt.

Now that we have seen a little of the Chan-Zen methods of enlightenment, we can begin to delve into the purpose of it all. How exactly is a person's life transformed by enlightenment? The power of intuitive thinking, released by the koan exercise, is obviously the key; but what exactly does that accomplish? The answer is that intuition enables us to see what intellect never could: the Buddha-nature in all things. To see Buddha-nature everywhere is to see a world without true problems and conflicts. It is to be able to relax and approach life in a completely carefree spirit.

This attitude is actually quite similar to what we found in Zhuang Zi, and there is no doubt that he—and Daoism generally—was an important formative influence on Chan. The Daoists shared with the Buddhists a belief in an underlying order of the universe and a resulting harmony of all life. And with Chan in particular they shared a belief in the need for intuition to grasp this order. Daoism differed in that it neither had nor sought a *method* for realizing intuition. At least in its philosophical form, it had nothing like the Buddhists' monastic discipline. To the Daoists, intuition was something that must just come naturally; it couldn't be controlled.

One useful way to characterize the Chan-Zen attitude to life is to say that it is non-judgmental. What I mean to say is that the enlightened mind finds no need to classify or to judge things as good/bad, right/wrong, beautiful/ugly, etc. The normal mentality is continually engaged in making these distinctions; once made, they create concerns and desires. But in the Buddha-nature perspective, there is no basis for all these judgments. All things are good, right and beautiful.

From this it is evident how profoundly different Chan Buddhism is from its Indian antecedents. Indian Buddhists saw this life as miserable and (in the case of the Mahayanists) illusory. Their aim was, through enlightenment, to be liberated from this world. With Chan, on the other hand, enlightenment was a means of enhancing life by manifesting the inherent beauty and harmony of our world. By the way, Hua-yan's position in this is exactly the same as Chan's. They have very different methods but a common aim: to live life in a carefree and accepting manner.

Such an attitude, in the two most developed forms of Chinese Buddhism, show how successfully that religion acclimated itself to China. The "native" Chinese philosophies were, in their various ways, quite worldly; and Buddhism eventually absorbed this spirit. The accommodations that Buddhism made were not nearly enough to satisfy the Confucians, however. That Confucian reaction to Buddhism is the subject of our next and final section.

V. NEO-CONFUCIANISM: REVISION AND REAFFIRMATION

The influence of Buddhism during the Tang dynasty deeply concerned the Confucians. They saw Buddhism as a philosophy challenging the most fundamental moral values. It was not just that the monastic life drew young men away from their families. Buddhism challenged all morality whatsoever with its relativistic, non-judgmental way of thinking. If Buddha-nature is indeed in all things, then one person's life is just as good as another's. Each one should just spontaneously follow personal inclinations without regard to any general principles of morality.

To Confucians, the distinction between right and wrong was an absolute and all-important one. True, they advocated flexibility in applying the principles of morality. Each case needed to considered carefully and in its own right. But once the individual case was focused on, a definite moral truth in that situation could be discerned. For Confucianism there could not be a principle of letting each one do as the inner Buddha-nature might dictate.

The problem for Confucians was that Buddhism claimed to have proof for its relativism in the state of enlightenment. The essential thing about enlightenment is that it illuminates *everything*. Chan and Hua-yan might disagree as to how this enlightenment was gained, but they shared the conviction that one could somehow reach this all-encompassing understanding. In this understanding each thing's inherent perfection and right to self-expression would be vindicated.

There was nothing comparable to enlightenment in Confucianism. That is, it offered no general understanding of reality. This was precisely as Confucius himself had wanted. That prudent and practical man had quite deliberately set aside questions about God, the universe and man's destiny in the life to come. He thought there were far more urgent matters in our present experience that we should attend to.

Sensible as this stance was, it did not meet the need of those later Confucians who were seeking a basis for refuting Buddhism. Their need was for a theory whose scope could rival what was given to the mind in Buddhist enlightenment.

This theory would vindicate moral judgment rather than dismiss it. Accordingly, they set about revising the original Confucian philosophy so that its basic moral principles could be reaffirmed. Bear in mind that they did not and could not explicitly state that there was some deficiency in Confucius' thought. The Master's prestige was far too great to allow for even the most limited criticism of his work. What these later Confucians did was to develop their own new theories and then insist that they were *implied* in Confucius' words.

The movement in Confucianism that I have been describing is called *Neo-Confucianism*. It got under way early in the Song dynasty (960–1267) and culminated with Zhu Xi (1130–1200). In the Ming dynasty (1368–1644) a new form of Neo-Confucianism came to prominence in the thought of Wang Yang-ming (1472–1529). In one form or another, Neo-Confucianism continued to dominate Chinese thought up until the twentieth century. It succeeded extremely well in its objective of diminishing the influence of Buddhism.

Zhu Xi's Neo-Confucianism has, in the long run, been most influential, and we will now examine it in detail. Zhu sought something which could be a universal moral standard. He referred to this as the *Tai Ji* (roughly, "ultimate principle"—the phrase is still used to designate a popular form of physical training in China). He defined the Tai Ji as a tendency to give or to create, and he elaborated a grand theory which displayed this Tai Ji in every phase of the universe's activity.

Zhu Xi presented an account of a five-tiered universe, based on a diagram used by previous Neo-Confucian thinkers. The five levels are:

I.   Tai Ji in itself
II.   Yin and Yang
III.   The Five Agents
IV.   Tian and Earth
V.   Living Creatures

Tai Ji perpetually creates the yin and yang by producing subtle, invisible matter which displays either the calmness of yin or the energy of yang. Zhu actually likens the process to flour being produced in a grinding mill. In great clouds the flour rises from the mill, and so the subtle, ethereal material of yin and yang are continually produced. These two, combining in various proportions, give rise to the Five agents. (See page 144.) The Five Agents, along with yin and yang, condense and solidify to produce Tian and Earth. These last two, by their quasi-sexual interaction, engender all the creatures of our world, including humans. Living creatures do not create a new level, but they do unceasingly reproduce themselves.

There is a simple moral point behind this complicated scheme. The essential nature of every being in this universe, from top to bottom, is to exist for something beyond itself. It is of the utmost importance to mark this point, for there is a very common tendency to believe the opposite: that what all things strive for is survival and self-gratification. Legalism and Buddhism are, in very different ways, instances of this position in China. Zhu Xi maintains that by the simple "investigation of things" (an old Confucian phrase) we can see the error of this view.

We see, for example, that yin and yang exist for each other and for those things which they produce. Likewise for all the other cosmic entities (Levels I–IV). Living creatures cannot exemplify this spirit of generosity on such a vast scale, but still they express it. Most of all, it is shown in the fact that reproduction and care of the young are such powerful drives in living things. If we existed only for ourselves, why would there be any desire to reproduce?

Aside from reproduction, creatures show the Tai Ji in many other ways. Consider a tree, for example. It gives shade to those underneath and a nesting place for birds. It may provide fruit to feed us and eventually lumber that we may build with. Now it might seem absurd to speak of the tree as "generous." How can something devoid of all consciousness possess moral characteristics? Zhu understands the objection perfectly well. He is not supposing that trees have feelings of any sort. He *is* insisting that trees and everything else possess the characteristic of being useful. He is convinced that we must see a moral significance in the universality of this property. It means that selfishness is not just morally wrong; it is against nature.

We must appreciate just what this means in the case of human beings. The Tai Ji in man, say Zhu, is *ren*, that instinct of kindness which Mencius had seen when people rushed to help the boy in the well. All human goodness and, ultimately, all human action come from ren, though its most perfect expression is in the deep filial love and respect which children show their parents. In the various expressions of ren, we can see that some are much clearer and truer than others. Thus, there is a basis for moral judgment (which is all that Zhu ever really wanted from his theory).

To illustrate, here is Zhu's own favorite example: Confucian filial piety versus Buddhist monasticism. The Buddhist position is that each of these is legitimate. Note that well—Buddhists would never condemn a Confucian for remaining with his parents. It is not their way to condemn (i.e., to judge) anyone. The Buddhist view is that each should follow his own heart. It goes back to the analogy of Indra's Net and the idea that each individual thing has its own uniquely precious perspective.

Zhu Xi rejects the notion that the Buddhist who leaves home and the Confucian who stays may be put on the same level. He does see ren in each case, but it is pure in one instance and distorted in the other. He invites us to consider what happens when the young Buddhist monk takes up his monastic life. He will, with the utmost devotion, submit himself to a spiritual master. He will obediently apply this master's instructions to his religious quest. It is actually a distorted filial piety. The monk has abandoned his real father and bestowed this devotion on a stranger. Thus, we may pass our moral judgment, holding that the natural expression of filial piety is superior to the debased mimicry of it which Buddhism has propagated.

Zhu Xi's moral philosophy is a form of what Western ethical theory calls *naturalism*. It is a view that some natural, verifiable quality (in this case, giving) is the standard by which all moral questions may be judged. As he acknowledges, it is essential to the success of this theory that said natural quality be present in all things. Because things are fundamentally trying to achieve the same objective, we may judge them on the basis of how well or how badly they do so.

From the Buddhists' perspective, the fundamental tendencies of things are different. They would say that making moral judgments is like asking whether a dust mop is better than an alarm clock. How can we compare the two when they serve such different purposes? In the spirit of Indra's Net, Buddhism teaches that each thing has its own unique value. It cannot be judged from any external standpoint and hence it cannot really be judged at all.

One way of bringing the whole issue between Zhu Xi and the Buddhists into better focus is to address the issue of man's place in this world. The Buddhist (and Daoist) view was that humans were of no greater significance than chickens or ants or oak trees. Each form of life had its own inherent purpose and thus its own right to exist. Confucians, on the other hand, thought that man was the most exalted of living creatures and that other forms of life were here for our use. So they felt no compunction about eating chickens, stepping on ants and chopping down oak trees. Human beings possess a far greater capacity to express the Tai Ji than any of these other creatures, and so they have a right of dominion over this world.

Thus, the whole vast theory of Tai Ji on the five levels is Zhu Xi's attempt to validate the Confucian approach to life. He believed himself to have found a universally applicable moral standard. In so doing, he also transformed Confucianism from a rather narrow and practical philosophy of human life to an all-encompassing vision of reality. This certainly did enhance the power and appeal of Confucianism, and Zhu's influence was enormous. For centuries, those who studied Confucianism in China saw it in his Neo-Confucian perspective.

Zhu Xi was not without his critics, however. Wang Yang-ming was the most prominent of these. His philosophy is summed up in two teachings: mind as the basis of principle, and unity of knowledge and action. To understand the first, we need to remember that Zhu Xi had insisted on a thorough—almost a scientific—investigation of the phenomena of the material world in order to identify the principle that would govern morality. Wang totally rejected this approach, saying that Zhu was looking in the wrong place. His view is that the human mind contains all moral principles. This means that human beings naturally possess sound moral instincts. To judge the rightness of something, they need only look inward and observe the mind's natural reaction.

Thus, for Wang Yang-ming, trees bearing fruit have absolutely nothing to do with ren or filial piety. The validation for filial piety is in the mind's own natural feelings of filial love and its abhorrence of disobedience and disrespect to the parents. Wang even goes so far as to derive non-moral principles from the mind. When a student once asked him what flowers blooming high on a mountain have to do with the mind, he replied that the color and fragrance of the flower became a reality only when they were "activated" by the mind's perception of them.

Closely related to this is Wang's second main teaching, the unity of knowledge and action. Where there is true knowledge, there is no gap between theory and practice. Knowledge will lead immediately to the action it deems appropriate. The deficiency in Zhu's moral philosophy is shown precisely in the fact that it does not entail a direct connection with action. It is too theoretical. Real moral knowledge is immediately and convincingly felt.

Wang compares moral knowledge to our perception of a bad odor. To perceive that the smell is bad instantaneously involves hating the smell. Perceiving is a matter of knowledge and hating pertains to action; and yet they are completely bound up with each other. In the same way, true moral knowledge would consist in the mind's instinctive reaction, leading necessarily to action.

Do you notice a certain resemblance between Wang Yang-ming and the Chan Buddhists? Each opposed a sister-philosophy which featured a grandiose account of the nature of whole universe. Each considered this theoretical approach to yield, in the end, only a feeble, unconvincing knowledge of what really mattered. Each upheld a direct, intuitive knowledge as our proper goal. This is certainly not to say that Wang had any real sympathy with Chan's outlook and way of life. Just as vigorously as any other Confucian, he taught that there is an absolute distinction between right and wrong and that we must act on this distinction rather than retire into a monastery. But the parallel exists all the same. Just as Chinese Buddhism had done, Neo-Confucianism offered these two distinct approaches to knowledge.

REVIEW QUESTIONS ON CHINESE PHILOSOPHY

1. Describe Chinese political and social conditions in the time of Confucius.

2. What did Confucius see as the solution to China's problems? What idea did he derive from the Duke of Zhou?

3. Describe the various subjects that Confucius taught. Discuss his style of teaching.

4. Explain what filial love requires and why it is so important in Confucianism.

5. With examples, explain the *flexibility* of Confucian morality.

6. What are the *li* and why are they so important? How do they produce their effects?

7. Discuss the many ways Mo Zi differed from Confucius.

8. Explain what is meant in saying that the Legalists saw the solution to political problems in methods rather than men. Contrast with Confucianism.

9. Discuss what the incident with Confucius and the two Daoist farmers shows about the difference between the two philosophies.

10. Contrast Mencius and Xun Zi on human nature. How does each support his view?

11. How does Mencius view the relation between a ruler and his ministers?

12. Discuss Xun Zi's view on the value of the li.

13. How did the Qin dynasty come into being, and how did it fall?

14. Why did Confucianism come to power at the beginning of the Han? How did the Han Confucians differ from what Confucius himself taught?

15. What features of Buddhism were disliked by most Chinese?

16. Describe the Buddha-Tooth Incident. What two characteristics of Confucianism are shown in this incident?

17. What is the basic relationship of the yin and the yang? Illustrate with various examples.

18. Explain Tian's relationship with Earth. Why is it said that Tian does not speak? How does Tian enforce the Mandate?

19. What did the yin-yang theory prescribe as the place of women in society, and how was this justified?

20. How is yin-yang thinking expressed in the Confucian theory of gentlemen and commoners?

21. Explain the position which Confucius expressed when asked about serving spiritual beings.

22. How do Han Fei Zi and Xun Zi differ in their view of human selfishness?

23. What are the features of the rule of law in the Legalist theory? How are they justified?

24. How did Han Fei Zi criticize other philosophers' veneration of the past?

25. What is the Dao and why is it so important for us to know it? How can it be known?

26. What kind of ideal society did the Daoists visualize?

27. What principles do the Daoists advocate in the conduct of one's personal life?

28. How does Zhuang Zi's Daoism differ from Lao Zi's?

29. How did the Hua-yan Buddhists use the analogy of Indra's Net to express their view of life?

30. How does Chan differ from Hua-yan in its approach to enlightenment?

31. What is meant in saying that Buddha-nature is in all things? Why is this so difficult to grasp?

32. Give examples of koans. Describe the process of solving a koan. What is solving it supposed to accomplish?

33. In what way did both Hua-yan and Chan differ from Indian Buddhism in their approach to life?

34. Why did Confucians feel such moral outrage at the Chinese Buddhist philosophies? Why was there a need for them to adapt Confucianism to meet the Buddhist challenge?

35. Explain the various manifestations of the Tai Ji in Zhu Xi's Neo-Confucianism. How did he use it to justify his belief in the Confucian morality?

36. How is the difference between Wang Yang-ming and Zhu Xi similar to that between Chan and Hua-yan?

A NOTE ON SOURCES FOR THE QUOTATIONS IN THIS BOOK

The following are the translations which have been consulted for the major works cited in the text. However, I have often made changes to the translations in the interest of clarity or fluency.

Koran: *The Meaning of the Holy Koran*, translated by Abdullah Yusuf Ali. This is available in many editions and is the most widely used by Muslims themselves in the English-speaking world.

Upanishads: *The Principal Upanisads*, translated by S. Radhakrishnan

Bhagavad Gita: translation by S. Radhakrishnan, as given in his and Moore's *Sourcebook In Indian Philosophy*

Analects: I have relied most on two translations, by Arthur Waley and Simon Leys. Many others exist. For this and other Chinese works, the task of translation is truly daunting. There will be radically different renderings of the same sentence. It is advisable to consult as many as possible.

Dao De Jing: Again, I have relied primarily on two translators: R.B. Blakney and Victor H. Mair. Note that the latter (but not the former) uses a new system of numbering the eighty-one chapters based on recent discoveries. I have stayed with the old numbering in this book.

Mencius, Zhuang Zi: The quotations are based on the translations in Chan, *Sourcebook in Chinese Philosophy*

Mo Zi, Xun Zi, Han Fei Zi: The primary sources are Burton Watson's translations of these authors.

SUGGESTIONS FOR FURTHER READING

Islam

Of course, the best place to begin is the Koran, preferably the Abdullah Yusuf Ali translation already mentioned.

There are many biographies of Muhammad, and you should read several, in order to get a balanced picture. Some good possibilities are:

The Life and Times of Muhammad, by J.B. Glubb

Muhammad: The Man and His Message, by Tor Andrae

Muhammad, by Maxime Rodinson

Twenty-three Years, by Ali Dashti

The last is particularly interesting, giving an account of the time from Muhammad's calling to his death from a "liberal" but still devoutly Muslim perspective.

I would recommend two general accounts of Muslim philosophy:

A History of Islamic Philosophy, by Majid Fakhry

A History of Muslim Philosophy (two volumes), by M.M.Sharif

In general, there is a dearth of translations of the great Muslim philosophers' writings into English. A significant exception is

Al-Farabi on the Perfect State, by Richard Walzer

This gives a translation of one of the philosopher's major works, covering the whole range of his thought, from the angelic intellects to political theory.

For ibn-Rushd, there is:

Averroes on the Harmony of Religion and Philosophy, by G.F. Hourani

Averroes' Tahafut al-Tahafut (two volumes), by S. van den Bergh

The first translates the work referred to in this book as the *Decisive Treatise*. The second includes not only ibn-Rushd's famous reply to al-Ghazali, but also practically all of Ghazali's original objections, as given in the *Tahafut al-Falasifah*. An illuminating book about Ghazali is:

Muslim Intellectual, by W. Montgomery Watt

There are an abundance of books on Sufism. As a start, I would recommend:

Mystical Islam, by Julian Baldick

Ibn-Khaldun's masterwork has been translated into English in three volumes:

The Muqaddimah: An Introduction to History, by Franz Rosenthal

An excellent study of the complex issues involving Active Intellect is: *Al-Farabo Avicenna, and Averroes, on Intellect*, by Herbert Davidson

India

An invaluable compilation of excerpts from the writings of practically every school of Indian philosophy is:

Sourcebook in Indian Philosophy, by Radhakrishnan and Moore

The selections are accompanied by useful introductions. Here are some excellent general histories or surveys of Indian philosophy:

A History of Indian Philosophy (five volumes), by S. Dasgupta

History of Indian Philosophy (two volumes), by S. Radhakrishnan

Philosophies of India, by Heinrich Zimmer

Asian Philosophies, 3rd Edition, by J.M. and P.J. Koller

The last also covers Chinese philosophy and (to some extent) Islamic thought. It is an excellent introduction to the whole range of Asian philosophies.

A general study of Indian civilization that gives very useful background to the philosophies is:

The Wonder That Was India, by A.L. Basham

On the two great Hindu philosophies of ancient India (Upanishads and Bhagavad Gita), the two translations by Radhakrishnan mentioned in the previous Note can be used. There are many others available, and the widely available

Bhagavad Gita As It Is, by Bhaktivedanta Swami

will serve very nicely.

On Buddha's life you can get a realistic and interesting account in:

The Buddha, by Trevor Ling

A very useful historical survey of Indian Buddhist philosophy is:

Buddhist Thought in India, by E. Conze

The writings of the great Russian scholar, F.I. Stcherbatsky, are also extremely informative on the subject of Buddhism. Among other works of his, there are

Buddhist Logic (two volumes)

The Conception of Buddhist Nirvana

The latter provides excellent material on Nagarjuna.

The definitive presentation of Shankara's philosophy is in his commentary on a work known as the Vedanta Sutras. It is published as:

The Vedanta Sutras with the Commentary by Sankarakarya, by George Thibault

The other Hindu scholastic philosophies are best approached through the general works already cited. On yoga there are innumerable how-to books and many translations of Patanjali's Yoga Sutras. For example,

Dreams of the Soul: the Yoga Sutras of Patanjali, by Daniel R. Condron

China

The ideal starting point would be the classic philosophers: Confucius, Lao Zi, Mencius, Zhuang Zi, Mo Zi, Xun Zi, Han Fei Zi. For the first two, see the previous Note on translations. For Mencius there is the James Legge translation. For Zhuang there is a complete translation by Burton Watson. For the last three there is a combined volume of "Basic Writings" by Watson. Keep in mind that these names occur in different forms. You will often encounter "Chuang" instead of "Zhuang", "Tzu" instead of "Zi", etc.

A more wide-ranging compilation of philosophical writings is:

A Sourcebook in Chinese Philosophy, by Wing-tsit Chan

This gives substantial selections from all the major Chinese philosophers. The major history is:

History of Chinese Philosophy (two volumes), by Fung Yu-lan

There is also a useful one-volume abridgement of Fung's work. Other general treatments of Chinese philosophy are:

Chinese thought from Confucius to Mao Tse-tung, by H.G. Creel

Three Ways of Thought in Ancient China, by Arthur Waley

Disputers of the Tao, by A.C. Graham

Waley's "Three Ways" are Confucianism, Legalism and Daoism. Graham's book is not just about Daoism; it covers all the intellectual movements of the Zhou. Creel also has a very helpful book devoted entirely to Confucius:

Confucius and the Chinese Way

An extremely interesting and distinctive survey is contained in:

Science and Civilization in China, Volume 2, by Joseph Needham
This is part of a extraordinary multi-volume study of Chinese science, the second volume providing the philosophical background.

There is a vast literature on Chan/Zen. The latter name is what one almost always encounters in the book titles. The most useful for me, by virtue of its description of actual monastic practices in Japan, is;

Three Pillars of Zen, by Philip Kapleau

Also useful are:

The Way of Zen, by Alan Watts

History of Zen Buddhism, by Heinrich Dumoulin

A fascinating book on Zen is:

The Sound of One Hand: 281 Zen Koans With Answers, translated by Yoel Hoffmann

The book was originally published by a renegade Zen monk who wanted to give away the koan answers. However, the Zen community is not any longer distressed at its publication, and some Zen masters recommend it.

As mentioned earlier in the text, a valuable resource on Hua-yan is:

The Buddhist Teaching of Totality, by Garma C.C. Chang

There is also the fascinating and influential:

The Tao of Modern Physics, by Fritjof Capra

which argues that basic concepts in modern physics are paralleled in ancient Eastern philosophy.

INDEX